Invisible and Voiceless

The Struggle of Mexican Americans
for Recognition, Justice, and Equality

Martha Caso

iUniverse, Inc.
Bloomington

Invisible and Voiceless

Portions reprinted or cited from North From Mexico: The Spanish-Speaking People of the United States, *(Carey McWilliams, Praeger Press, Updated material copyright © 1990 by Matt S. Meier), were reproduced with permission of ABC-CLIO, LLC.*

iUniverse books may be ordered through booksellers or by contacting:

iUniverse
1663 Liberty Drive
Bloomington, IN 47403
www.iuniverse.com
1-800-Authors (1-800-288-4677)

ISBN: 978-1-4502-9499-7 (sc)
ISBN: 978-1-4502-9501-7 (dj)
ISBN: 978-1-4502-9500-0 (ebook)

Library of Congress Control Number: 2011901979

Printed in the United States of America

iUniverse rev. date: 02/22/2011

Contents

Preface

After the end of World War II, when I was a child, I remember going to a segregated Mexican American school. It was a large white building in the shape of a box with a bare schoolyard and two outhouses. The school consisted of only three classrooms: first low, first middle, and first high. We attended first low when we were six; if we did not fail, we attended first middle at age seven, and we would finally finish first grade by the time we were eight. Many stayed until they were nine or ten because they could not speak English well. By the time I reached second grade, they had transferred me to a bigger school built of brick. The children in that school were older, and they soon warned me I was going to hell because I was Protestant. I attended a very small segregated Protestant church, which had about three families, mostly old people.

When I was about eight, my mother cleaned the Anglo church of the same denomination as ours, and I used to help her; I think she took me because she wanted to keep an eye on me. I spent most of the time playing with the minister's daughter. The kind, good-hearted pastor invited me to attend Sunday school at their church. He did not realize his terrible sin, and a week later, he was terminated. How dared he invite a "Mexican" to integrate their church? The minister left the church, but the deed had been done. As an eight-year-old, I did not realize the sacrifice that minister had made. I personally liked the Anglo church because the children did not mock me for being Protestant.

At the time, I did not realize the gravity of being Mexican American. For the congregation, it was a question of having the church invaded by Mexican Americans. I did not understand the issue of segregation, so I remained in church. My mother would say that the Anglos were afraid Mexicans would overrun the white church. I knew that my young Mexican American friends, who told me that I was going to hell for being Protestant, would not come and join me. I assumed there were not any Catholics dying to go to a Protestant church if all Protestants were going to hell. Catholics showed no interest in becoming Protestant, and for a long time I remained the only Mexican American in that church.

Years later, when I was finishing high school, after two new ministers who had no racial prejudice had been pastors of our church, I decided to ask our minister to help me get into college. He was very kind and generous and did not hesitate; he immediately set out to fill out my college application. The congregation agreed they would pay the tuition and buy me the clothes I needed to attend college; they even gave me a home permanent.

The moral to the story is that one learns to hate that which one fears. The church learned that accepting a young Mexican American child gave them an opportunity to learn, to love, to nurture, and to cherish that which they had feared. Fear of the unknown causes aggression and anxiety and leads to hate.

At present the United States is suffering an anxiety about immigrants, especially Mexican immigrants; thus the aggression toward anything that looks Mexican and the attitude of "show me your papers."

Introduction

And those who knew the most important facts [history] were the idol's priests and the sons of Nezahualpiltzintli, the King of this city and its providence, they are now dead and their paintings on which their history was written are gone. Hernan Cortes and the rest of the conquerors ... when they first arrived there, burned them. They burned them in the royal palaces of Nezahualpiltzintli, in a room where they kept the archives, where they kept their manuscripts ... where all the paintings of everything ancient [history] were kept. Today their descendants weep with a heavy heart after being left in darkness without knowledge and memory of their ancestor's deeds ...

—Juan Bautista de Pomar,
Relación de Tezcoco
(Mexico, ed. García Icazbalceta, 1891)

In order to understand the historical, social, and psychological culture of Mexicans and Mexican Americans, we must return to Spain's conquest of the Americas. Its invasion of Mexico led by Hernan Cortes in the year 1521 resulted in an indigenous holocaust and the clash of two cultures: the old Mexican Aztec culture and the Western European Spanish culture; the new Mexican culture was forged out of violence and bloodshed. Without understanding the traumatic events that occurred during the Mexican conquest, we cannot understand the nature of our historical past.

Every culture—even those with no written language—preserves an oral history in the form of religion, myths, and legends. The destruction of Mexico's history by the Spaniards left the inhabitants of the area with an obscured and blurry understanding of their past. Today in the United States, most young Mexican Americans know very little about

1

their ancient history. During the 1960s and 1970s, there was a renewed interest in ancient Mesoamerican culture, which taught our people about Mexico's past. Today some Mexican Americans feel that young people no longer have to be as concerned about the past; therefore, many of our children are no longer searching for our historical roots, our *raíces*.

Historically, the United States also had many moments that were very anti-Mexican and violent. After the Mexican-American War and the signing of the Treaty of Guadalupe Hidalgo of 1848, Mexico lost vast amounts of territory. Mexicans who stayed in the new United States territories struggled to keep their lands from the advances of Anglo Americans who invaded Texas, California, New Mexico, Arizona, Colorado, Nevada, and parts of Utah, taking over ranches and large Mexican land grants. In the treaty, the United States had promised full citizenship and equal rights to Mexicans who wished to remain on their lands, but a large number of Anglo Americans did not honor that treaty. The invading Anglos coming to the Southwest viewed Mexicans as non-Americans, just another group of Indians, non-whites with no right to own property. Anglo Americans soon raced to make claims on the newly acquired lands and water rights that legally belonged to Mexicans already occupying those territories, who had become United States citizens as a result of the treaty. Anglo Americans established tax laws that Mexicans could not afford. The Anglo Americans took lands for extremely low prices, leaving Mexican Americans destitute and poor.

According to professor and sociologist David Montejano, the Laredo newspaper *La Cronica* on April 9, 1910 wrote, "The Mexicans have sold the great share of their landholdings, and some work as day laborers on what once belonged to them."[1]

As Mexican Americans lost their lands, they were also segregated. They had to live in segregated neighborhoods and attend segregated schools, and they were kept out of certain stores, hotels, and restaurants.

It would take generations before Mexican Americans could regain equal rights in the United States; being racially different and poor made them the object of extreme prejudice, segregation, and persecution. This historical reality continues to interfere with their acceptance in society, where they are still seen as foreigners and outcasts.

As long as Mexican Americans are closely tied to their Mexican heritage by race, they need to be aware of their past no matter how many generations they have lived in the United States. As a whole, Mexican Americans have a strong allegiance to the United States, yet many of their fellow Americans still associate them with Mexico; they consider them outsiders. This is why modern Mexican Americans must remember their history—to understand why they are still not considered real American citizens in the United States.

Today in Texas there are some conservative politicians in the State Capitol who are trying to erase what little Mexican American history exists in school textbooks. A panel of "experts" working for the State Board of Education in Texas recommended removing Cesar Chavez (the farm worker organizer and civil rights champion) from textbooks, claiming that he is irrelevant and not a good example for our youth. Mexican Americans should understand that racism is not a thing of the past but a serious and present danger.

Today our problems are aggravated by the drug war going on in Mexico; because of it, it has become commonplace to identify Mexican Americans with crime. Either we find a way out of poverty, or it will be increasingly easy for Mexican drug lords to recruit Mexican American youth to sell their drugs in the United States. In turn, this will increase racial bias and send Mexican Americans on another downward spiral. More of our youth will be destined to serve their lives in prison. We must not fall into that trap of racism again. Instead we must find ways to assert our rights as citizens and be included in professions that will allow Mexican Americans to have their rightful place in the United States. One way to accomplish those goals is to demand better education for our children. Education is the key to the survival of our race.

Our past will influence our future. The fact that we are descendants of indigenous American people will forever distinguish us as racially different from European American citizens. The prejudices used to justify Spanish aggression toward Mexicans and other Native Americans were similar to the justifications used by the British, the French, or the Dutch to subjugate Indians. Basically, those Europeans claimed that the indigenous people of the Americas were savages, less than human, as expressed by the well-known saying, "The only good Indian is a dead Indian." This idea was applied to our brothers and sisters on the reservations and to all of us as well. This sentiment will continue to haunt Mexican Americans living among European Americans, some of whom still think of us as savages.

For instance, Barbara Coe, the leader of the California Coalition for Immigration Reform and a member of the Council of Conservative Citizens, refers to Mexicans as savages. She criticized Home Depot for allowing day laborers looking for work to gather in front of their stores. According to the Southern Poverty Law Center, she repeatedly refers to poor Mexican and Central Americans as savages.[2]

Another example comes from cyberspace where, encouraged by the anonymity of blogs and opinion forums, some people freely insult Mexican Americans and so-called Hispanic immigrants, referring to them as subhuman and savages. In 2006, some Mexican citizens set up a website to initiate a dialogue between Mexico and the United States; they called it MATT (Mexicans and Americans Thinking Together). The result was that United States conservatives immediately started to insult and rave against Mexicans. They claimed Mexicans should be grateful that the United States had started the dialogue, which could not take place in Mexico. In reality, the dialogue had been started in Mexico by people who were trying to create better relationships with the United States.

Today in the United States, there are strong prejudices against anything south of the border; by association, Mexican Americans are also subject to those prejudices. Mexican Americans still live and work secluded in their barrios. Their children often attend inferior schools, dropping out before graduation due to the high incidence of poverty.

Very often in the workplace, Mexican American men and women receive smaller salaries and fewer promotions than their Anglo American counterparts. In the field of entertainment, our presence is almost nonexistent, despite the fact that we are supposed to be one of the largest minorities. Madison avenue discriminates in commercials; often we see ads where other minorities are included, but Mexican Americans are left out. In the few cases where our presence is visible, we are often portrayed as menial workers, maids, or garbage collectors or featured in public service advertisements dealing with drug abuse or teenage pregnancy. These are all negative portrayals that affect our image, especially among our youth, and we must seek to stop them. We are not an untouchable society destined to be the slaves.

We must also be aware that commercials and films not only influence

American society but also take money out of their pockets. Consumers pay for advertising, and the advertising agencies and television programs discriminate against Mexican American consumers by not hiring them as actors. Hollywood hires very few Mexican Americans, and this makes media the most segregated industry in the United States. We are aware of how many people from India and China live in the United States because we see them as comedians, doctors, and newscasters, but the television screens keep Mexican Americans out. This increases the myth that we are not truly American. I personally know there are many aspiring young people in Hollywood who never get a chance to act except in negative roles. This leaves Mexican Americans invisible and voiceless in the United States.

With the passing of Arizona's controversial racial profiling law, which requires legal immigrants to carry proof of United States citizenship at all times and gives police broad power to detain anyone even suspected of being in the country illegally, we must be aware of our Mexican American heritage and its close links to Mexico. Historically and racially, Mexican Americans and Mexicans are brothers and sisters; there is no way to distinguish between legal and illegal Mexicans living in the United States. Laws like SB1070 in Arizona can spread to other states and damage our communities. We may find ourselves victims of blatant discrimination.

In the past, many Mexicans and Mexican Americans were treated as illegal immigrants and sent to Mexico. Many Mexican Americans who were not aware of their rights as American citizens remained in Mexico. Today we are aware of our rights, but there are still many Anglo Americans who refuse to recognize them. To recognize who we are as Americans (some of us have lived in the United States longer than other citizens of European descent have), we must learn our history and learn about the lives of our ancestors. We must refuse to be treated as second-class citizens.

In this book, I will attempt to show that the tragedy and suffering in Mexico was no different than the tragedy that the rest of North, Central, and South America and the Caribbean islands suffered when the Europeans invaded these continents. The genocide affected native people from every corner of the Americas.

Today the fires of racism are burning and blowing anew. This time it is against Mexicans and Central and South Americans, brown-skinned immigrants whom Anglo Americans often cannot tell apart.

The Mexican American community, because of racial and historical ties to Mexicans, is very much affected by this anti-immigrant sentiment. The escalation of verbal abuse is not limited to the traditional racist groups of the United States but is prevalent among politicians who promote the buildup of troops and fences along the southern borders. Examples of this rhetoric include aggressive innuendo from Washington politicians like Steve King from Iowa, who implies that Mexico is trying to take over parts of the United States, and the book *Who Are We? The Challenges to America's National Identity* by professor Samuel Huntington of Harvard, which also serves to inflame racism toward Mexicans and other Spanish-speaking immigrants.

It is my hope that this book will provide a small window of knowledge about Mexican Americans and where we should proceed as Americans who helped built this nation. We deserve respect and equal treatment, just like other citizens.

We Are Americans!

We built America! We cleared the brush with axes and sweat!
We built the roads with burning tar, with the burning sun on our backs!
We built the city streets with heavy gravel and with anguish in our bones.

We built the railroads with mallets and picks and thirst!
We farmed, we harvested, we cultivated the land during wars and peacetime!
We kept America's food basket full for the entire nation!
Only our bellies were empty. Our children cried for food.

We kept America free; we have shed our blood for America!
We have given our souls for democracy!
Our mothers are always in mourning for their sons who lie buried in the cold American soil.

Yet we remained America's unsung heroes.

*Mocked for our poverty, despised for our culture and
skin color!*
Always striving for our birthright as Americans.
Never given the right to be treated as Americans!

Racism

*"But I do believe in God. So much, you know, that I can't imagine
He put us on earth to be no one."*

—Carlos Fuentes,
Diana, the Goddess Who Hunts Alone

America has suffered over five hundred years of racial violence. In
the United States, the first time the American continent experienced
European violence was against the Indians. The Europeans had never
encountered the American people who populated these continents.
Many of the conceptions Europeans had about Native Americans came
from explorers who reached the Americas earlier. Some of the stories
about the Indians were true, but others were myths, often promoted
by Indians who wanted the Europeans to leave their territory and
take their explorations elsewhere. Such was the case of the search for
El Dorado, which lead the Spaniards in a long trek throughout the
Americas searching for the legendary city of gold. They had already
encountered cities in Mexico and in Peru, which were actually exploited
to enrich the Spanish crown.

Lewis Hanke wrote that the "Spanish captains went forth to their
conquest expecting to encounter many kinds of mythical beings and
monsters depicted in medieval literature: giants, pygmies, dragons,
griffins, white-haired boys, bearded ladies, human beings adorned with
tails, headless creatures with eyes in their stomachs or breasts, and other
fabulous folk."[3]

The people of the Americas spoke languages that Europeans did not
understand. To them, the indigenous languages sounded unnatural and
strange. In many films, Indians speak in short, one-syllable sentences.
The truth is that Indians used rich vocabularies in their languages but
probably had to communicate with short words and signs with the

Europeans, who could not understand them and made no effort to do so. In Massachusetts, the native language was difficult; today all that is left is the name of the state and some cities named in the Massachusett language. In Mexico, the Nahuatl language was also difficult, with complex words like *cacahuacuauhuitl* (cacao tree). This language was hard for the Spaniards to decipher and understand.

The languages of the American indigenous people made communication between Europeans and natives very difficult. The diversity of languages became one of the principal barriers between the Europeans and the Indians.

Indians also looked physically different; they were not blond, their skin was bronze, and their hair was dark and straight. They did not have hair on their bodies, and this amazed the Europeans.

Their culture, their clothing, their homes, and their lifestyles were different. Some indigenous groups were nomadic, creating the impression among Europeans that they owned no property; and finally, they were not Christians.

The communication problems with those strange cultures made it hard for Europeans to accept Native Americans as humans. Not being Christian implied they could not have souls, and not having souls made the Indians inferior and thus less than human. According to Europeans, the Indians had no concept of ownership of property; thus, they owned no land, and their territories were available for the taking. It was what Europeans considered a vast territorial gift from their Christian God.

Sarah Vowell explains with her humorous tone that when the Puritan leader John Cotton preached to the immigrants coming to America, he spoke to them about being like the Old Testament Jews who had journeyed to the Promised Land. They were God's new chosen people: "And, like the Old Testament Jews, God has printed eviction notices for them to tack up on homes of the nothing-special, just-folks who are squatting there."[4]

This notion was not limited to the Puritans but was similar to the general Spanish and English concepts of what it meant to be white, European, and Christian. It gave them the notion of superiority. God ordained it: white man should occupy and take possession of the land.

Thus began the holocaust of the American natives. The Spaniards did whatever was necessary to get rid of the "savage" natives in the Caribbean, in Mexico, and down to the tip of South America. They burned them, they killed them, they enslaved them, and they infected them with diseases to which the Indians did not have any immunity.[5]

To quell indigenous resistance, the Spanish concluded that for every Spaniard killed by an Indian, they should in turn murder a hundred natives. [6]

When the Europeans went to Africa to obtain slaves, they had the same experience with the African natives. Africans looked different, spoke different languages, had different cultures, and were not Christian. Those reasons made Africans also less than human. They too were savages and were treated as subhuman. They were imprisoned and shackled and their families separated. On the trip to the Americas, many got sick and died.

Thus, since the arrival of the Europeans on the American continents, racism has existed. This racism was based partially on religion; only European Christians had souls and were therefore racially superior.

Europeans considered Indians an inferior race. In addition, Indians did not own land. Thus when Europeans came seeking economic prosperity, they would enslave and own Indians. When the first Puritans came to America, they claimed to have come over to help the Indians. What they really did was to help themselves to what the Indians possessed.

Indians and Africans were destined to serve and work for the benefit of the European race. They fitted the classical definition of slavery according to Aristotelian philosophy, an old philosophy that existed five hundred years before the time of Jesus Christ. Aristotle used this argument to justify the enslavement of warriors during the Greek wars. Europeans used the same theory to justify the enslavement of Indians and Africans. Europeans rationalized that since Indians and Africans did not have souls, it was acceptable to exploit them, murder them, deny their rights to the land, and break up their families.

When the Europeans came to America, they also engaged in wars with the Indians. During those battles, they had to defend their families and the lands they had taken from the Indians. However, when they ended the wars, they were the only ones who had the power to write their own history.

Later the British realized that if they converted the Indians and the African slaves to the Christian faith, it would be easier to subject them and manage them, but they would have to worship in their own churches. Thus, a given Christian denomination could become segregated into two or three separate churches. This practice carried on when the United States became independent from England. During that period, churches became racially divided into White churches, African American churches, and Native American churches.

In New England, John Elliot really wanted to convert the Indians and did what no other British person had done before; he actually translated the Bible and other Protestant tracts into the Massachusett language. He did not work alone; he got help from his friend Sassamon, an Indian translator.[7]

Nevertheless, in England no one took the ethics and morality of slavery very seriously. During colonial times, the Church of England never took a strong stance against slavery.

On the other hand, possibly because of the enactment of the Law of the Indies, the Spanish crown and the Spanish Catholic church accepted that Indians actually did have souls and were part of God's family, so the Spaniards never totally segregated the Catholic Church.

This did not mean that the Spaniards were more benevolent than the British were; the violent and cruel treatment of the Indians in the lands the Spaniards conquered was no different than the treatment of American Natives in North America.

If we start from these premises, we need to admit that racism in North, Central, and South America was buried deep in the souls of many pious European Christians. It is a tradition so deeply ingrained in their minds that it has never completely abandoned their souls and hearts.

Jill Lepore writes that while some Indians were awed by the looks of Europeans when they first arrived, "the reverse was not true; Europeans usually regarded the Indians with pity or disgust rather than admiration."[8]

White men have for generations believed that America belongs to the white race; it is there for them to own and govern. That is why today in the United States many Americans cry out, "Give us back our country." Having a partially African American president is too challenging for them, so they try to bring him down. Yes, it is racial; we cannot pretend the age of racism is dead. Americans can struggle to eliminate racism, but it is still there, looking for poor and powerless people to persecute.

Today we have seen a revolution in racial equality for many in the African American community. Yet a large number have been left behind, and they live in dire poverty. This rise in political power in the Black community has left many Anglo Americans fearful that they might lose their political and social power in the United States. They feel they are losing control of their old traditions and family values, so they seek to re-assert their political power by turning on what they consider the second soulless racial group, the so-called Hispanics and the old indigenous American groups from Mexico and Central and South America.

This antagonism started during the 1990s with a campaign to promote fear that the Spanish language was taking over the English language. Another demonstration of fear was the building of a wall to prevent Mexicans and Central and South American people from coming into the United States. All of this racism is often justified by the premise that many of the people come through our borders illegally. Some Anglo Americans feel these people are coming over to claim American territory in much the same way Europeans came and obtained Mexican territories in the 1800s. The third fear is the fear of terrorism and drugs coming over the border. It is the sum of all these fears that some Americans still carry deep in their minds, but the fear of drug trafficking is the only fear with any basis in reality.

The traffic of drugs comes into our country thanks to the free trade of weapons from the United States to Mexican drug dealers. It is mostly border states, such as Arizona, New Mexico, California, and Texas, that provide Mexican drug dealers with weapons. Guns fuel the increase of drug violence in Mexico.

As American prejudices against Mexicans continue to grow, Mexican Americans and other Spanish-speaking Americans can easily become victims of the growing anti-Hispanic sentiment. That is why we must understand who we are and where we need to go—in order not to fall into the claws of racism.

Is this simply paranoia, or does it have some real factual basis? One only has to point out some of the racist indoctrination going on in the United States. One good example is academics who publish books and articles in which they teach students and the public to shape their minds against Mexican Americans. Those pseudointellectuals' influence will continue to ignite the flames of prejudice against Mexican Americans and other Spanish-speaking people not only in the United States but anywhere else their works are published.

Some of these academics allege that when Mexican American schoolchildren are asked how they identify themselves, only a small percentage claim to be Americans. They imply that Mexican Americans are not truly American. The fact is that every Mexican American has been taught in schools to call him- or herself every hyphenated name but American. Our children have been taught that they are Mexican Americans, Hispanic, Latinos and People of Color. Mexican American children will respond that they are Americans when their schools teach them they are Americans and call them Americans. In other words, when they are accepted as Americans!

Another voice of American racism has consistently come from CNN, where Lou Dobbs used racial innuendos when speaking of Mexican Americans and promoted racial distrust and hate against Mexicans and other Spanish-speaking workers. He claimed that immigrants were responsible for illnesses (such as leprosy), crimes, and joblessness. The kind, smiling image hid a true racist, and CNN supported all his wild accusations against immigrants, because they hired him to do that kind of programming. The organization Democracia Ahora (Democracy Now) confronted CNN and Lou Dobbs. Fortunately, CNN agreed with some of its sponsors and Democracia Ahora that Lou Dobbs had to tone down. Lou Dobbs probably felt it would be best just to leave CNN, so he did.

Hitler started out as a mildly patriotic German but turned into a monster; the same thing can occur in our country if the voices of racism and intolerance are left unchecked. History has shown they can destroy and annihilate minorities and entire ethnic groups.

After World War II in Germany, Martin Niemoller, a Protestant Lutheran minister who was imprisoned during the Nazi regime, wrote:

> *First they came for the communists and I did not speak out because I was not a communist.*
> *Then they came for the socialists and I did not speak out because I was not a socialist.*

Then they came for the trade unionists and I did not speak out because I was not a trade unionist.
Then they came for the Jews and I did not speak out because I was not a Jew.
Then they came for me and there was no one left to speak for me.

Today it is time for Mexican Americans to speak out; paraphrasing Rev. Niemoller, we could add the following lines:

First, they came for the Ecuadorian undocumented immigrants, and I did not protest, because I am not Ecuadorian.
Then they came for the Guatemalan undocumented workers, and I did not protest, because I am not Guatemalan.
Then they came for the Mexican undocumented immigrants, and I did not protest, because I am not Mexican.
Next they will come for me, and there will be no one left to speak for me.

In reality, if we do not speak out for our civil rights, we can become victims of racism and intolerance, which are alive and well in the United States.

History can also be a tool to express racism. Every day, new evidence shows that there were thriving civilizations in the Americas as far back as the time when Egypt was developing its ancient culture. Archeologists might someday discover that people from the Americas traveled across the Bearing Strait and populated Asia. Why not? we could ask. Native Americans are just as intelligent as the people from any other continent. We often hear how savage American aboriginal people were and how travelers from other continents imported civilization. Today, some people try to minimize the cultural wealth of American natives by attributing their wisdom to foreigners who came from other continents and instructed them on civilization, astronomy, and social issues. Some say American natives got their knowledge from Egypt, others claim that people from Japan or China came over, and still others go so far as to declare that Vikings came to America and influenced American culture.

The knowledge of civilization in the Americas is still in its early stages; conquerors usually write history, and it changes frequently. The true nature of early American civilization may still not be up to date.

The most common misconception was and still is that this is a new continent—the "New World"—and that all the people who were here traveled from other areas of the planet. There are many theories as to the origin of the indigenous American people, some outlandish like the one involving extraterrestrials and some more "reasonable," such as the idea that they came from Egypt, China, Japan, or Vikings from Europe. The most respected and accepted theory is that they came through the Bering Strait from Asia.

All of the above theories are used to justify making aliens out of the original dwellers of the Americas, who can then be viewed as immigrants who just beat Columbus to this paradise. Columbus himself described this continent as a paradise: And now, as the news arrives … about these lands which again I have discovered, my heart is fixed on claiming that this is the Earthly Paradise … so that Your Majesty will be served and find pleasure. Thank God.[9]

Unlike the early church of colonial times, if we take our Judeo-Christian tradition seriously, we have to admit that God did not create inferior races, and that even the wisdom of Aristotle was wrong when he talked about a specific group of people doomed to be slaves because of their inborn nature.

In the sixteenth century, during the conquest of the Americas, Europe was experiencing a proliferation of new concepts and ideas. Many Spaniards and other Europeans went back to the old theories of the Greeks, especially Aristotle's ideas about slavery. He had proposed that some men were by their very nature meant to be slaves in the service of masters born for the life of virtue and free from manual labor.[10]

Europeans have never fully accepted the fact that American indigenous people were not simply savages but intelligent people like themselves. Today the notion that somehow American Indians are not as intelligent as Europeans is still kept alive by archaeologists who still believe in the transoceanic diffusion. This theory claims that Native Americans got their culture from other continents. Those theories reflect cultural bias and racism by assuming that "native Americans were backward savages, incapable of devising sophisticated cultures without the benevolent assistance of more advanced white-skinned tutors."[11]

In the United States, a democracy, inferior and superior races should not exist. Likewise, there should be no one created to serve others as a slave. In reality, there are still people who live in quasi-slavery, working people who labor on a daily basis and still cannot afford decent housing, adequate food, appropriate education, and health care for their families. In America, that includes many Mexican and Mexican American farm workers who are still treated like slaves: poor pay, poor housing, poor education, and the inability to participate in politics are all signs of slavery. As Americans, we still insist on keeping some people as slaves. We see other minority groups gain respect and participate in politics and economic growth while Mexican Americans remain as farm workers, feeding the nation and doing menial work. European and Asian immigrants who actually come to take jobs from Americans often hold jobs that pay respectable wages.

Europeans portrayed Indians in the Americas as inhuman savages so they could make them slaves. In the Spanish conquered lands, this was true until Spanish courts enacted the Law of the Indies. The king of Spain formed an official group of men to debate the human nature of the Indians. The argument was that if the natives were pagan savages, they could be enslaved due to their nature. If they were mere savages, there would be no need to convert them to Christianity. Therefore, the Spanish missionaries' efforts would have been in vain. Hence, it was in the interest of the Catholic Church to treat the Indians as humans. Some of the missionaries who went to Central America, South America, and Mexico to convert Indians to the Christian faith became defenders of the Indians. They claimed the Indians had souls, so they were ready for Christianity.

From the royal family's perspective, if Indians were deemed humans, they could be royal subjects answering to no one but the monarchs of Spain; therefore, the Spanish crown would have dominion over their souls and material gains. The Catholic Church and the royal family agreed on the humanity of the Indians.

For the Spaniards, the question was not really whether the Indians had souls but their own economic status. According to the Aristotelian argument for slavery, people of inferior mental capacities or people from a conquered or defeated nation are by their very nature slaves. In either case, the enslaved "being" was destined to benefit his master. In the Spanish colonies, that meant Indians could be possessions of the *encomiendas*.

For Mexicans and other natives of the Americas, being subjects of the Spanish crown meant that they would no longer be treated as animals, beaten and worked to death. Nevertheless, the Aristotelian definition remained the practice; the idea that someone else should do the manual labor appealed to the Spaniards, who did not like to do hard labor.[12]

Thus, the argument in Spain about stopping mistreatment and slavery of Indians was not really taken very seriously. Spain was too far from the colonies to carry out its edict. The Spaniards continued the abuse and exploitation of the Indians in the Americas.

Other Europeans in North America also labeled and treated the Indians as savages. The British took Indian slaves and sold them in what is now Jamaica and on other Caribbean islands. For Europeans, slavery was universal; in America, no one escaped being traded as a slave.

Those who wanted to keep slaves would often refer to Saint Augustine, the great Catholic theologian, who believed in slavery and claimed it was good because it provided slaves with "certain virtues, such as humility, forgiveness, modesty, obedience, and patience."[13] Saint Augustine might have gotten the idea that slavery is good from the Bible. Saint Paul talks about slaves being faithful to their masters. For example, in the book of Ephesians, Paul writes, "Slaves, obey your earthly masters with fear and trembling single-mindedly, as serving Christ." (Ephesians 6:5)

Thus Spanish Catholics and Protestant Puritans could justify slavery by turning to the teachings of their churches. This still follows the old concept that conquerors have a right to make slaves who labor in the fields and reap the crops. Today some United States congressional representatives and senators encourage agricultural businesses to bring immigrants from Mexico and South and Central America to work in the fields and do back-breaking work for very low wages, jobs that other people do not wish to perform because they are essentially slave labor.

Racism against indigenous and mestizo people in America not only exists in the United States but has been the subject of literary works all over Mexico, Central America, and South America.

Gabriel Garcia Marquez in Colombia, Miguel Angel Asturias in Guatemala, Carlos Fuentes in Mexico, and others have dealt with the problem of racism in a realistic and charitable manner. Jose Vasconcelos dealt with it in a more romantic and optimistic manner, but most authors dealing with this topic never deny there is a great deal of prejudice in Latin America against indigenous people. The exploitation of the indigenous and mestizos in Mexico, Central America, and South America is seen in the poverty and lack of education among the poor. Keeping indigenous people poor and often homeless or living in slums maintains a large pool of cheap labor for the upper classes. Low wages increase profits, which in turn increase the wealth of the rich. Capitalism is based on greed, not patriotism.

In Mexico, racism against mestizo and indigenous people has increased. This is most evident on the television screen, where people with European features always have the lead parts and dark-skinned indigenous actors always have the menial jobs. Those indigenous-looking actors assume subservient roles and are usually portrayed as ignorant and devious. One never sees educated, intelligent mestizo Mexican women. Poor Mexicans are usually dressed as clowns and are extremely stupid on the television screen. From soap operas to the news, the emphasis seems to be on white actors and newscasters, unless the actors are maids or servants. If someone from outer space came to this planet and watched Mexican television, he or she would assume that Mexico was a white European nation instead of a nation made up of millions of indigenous and mestizo people.

In Mexico and in South America, generations of mestizos were brainwashed by their Spanish conquerors into believing that being "Indio" was equal to being inferior. They taught them that only the Europeans had intelligence and beauty and that it was a disgrace to acknowledge indigenous roots. Therefore, mestizos looked down on their own children because they looked like their indigenous ancestors. They looked down on their dark children as inferior to their white children. Many years ago, one of my sons went to Mexico to attend a Boy Scout gathering. The American Boy Scouts were given a tour of a museum featuring indigenous artifacts; my son, as a young boy, was shocked to see young Mexican Boy Scouts mocking the indigenous culture and people, calling them ugly and ignorant. The worst part was that those young boys were actually very indigenous looking themselves; somewhere they had learned that being indigenous was bad. Possibly, their parents or friends consciously or unconsciously taught them to reject their own heritage. My son was surprised to hear those boys talking so negatively about Indians. In the United States, this poor self-image is also prevalent among some Mexican Americans who do not want to acknowledge their Indian roots.

In Mexico, people use names like Blanca to denote that they are white. Also, the nickname Güero, or blonde-haired, is used with pride. A person may never use his or her birth name because there is so much pride in being blonde. This is even more evident among wealthy families.

In a conversation with Bishop Samuel Ruiz of Chiapas many years ago, I learned that in Mexico some establishments, such as restaurants or hotels, deny entry to Indians. The fact seems to be that Mexico is a nation run like the South Africa of yesterday where a minority of people descended from European immigrants make up the upper echelons of government and society. We could call them Mexican European immigrants, because their ancestors have been in the Americas less than five hundred years, and many have been here as little as half a century; some people went to Mexico after the Spanish Civil War to escape Franco's regime. Frenchmen went to Mexico during the short-lived reign of Maximilian I, the Emperor sent by Napoleon III to set up a French dynasty. A handful went from Ireland and Germany. All these foreigners left Europe for different motives, but once in Mexico they united with the old Spanish settlers to form a powerful upper class that has been exploiting the indigenous and mestizo people of Mexico ever since.

Unfortunately today, much like in the 1940s when Miguel Angel Asturias of Guatemala wrote *El Señor Presidente*, many Mestizos still identify with the Spanish conquistadors instead of with their own indigenous ancestors.

Years ago, I took a course in Nahuatl, the Aztec language, at the University of Texas in Austin. That summer I met a young Anglo American woman who studied in Mexico City under Dr. Miguel Leon-Portilla. She claimed that while living in Mexico, she had met people who invited her to their home, and after accepting their invitation, she had learned that this particular group of people were Nazi sympathizers meeting in secret. They wanted her to join them, since she was an Anglo blonde woman.

Those Nazi people may be the extreme, but racism in Mexico displays its ugly face in other ways. One only has to look at the Mexican military that burned homes and abused the people of Chiapas in the 1990s; the majority of those soldiers were mestizos but suffered under the illusion that they were white because they had been given an insignificant rank by the ruling class. Most of the upper class in Mexico consists of the old European families. This was the reason there was no compassion or outcry in Mexico from the upper classes for the Mayan people of Chiapas when they were suffering mass extermination by starvation, disease, and homelessness. Ironically, their suffering came at the hands of their own brothers, who admired the ideal wealthy class so much they were willing to persecute their own people for a fistful of pesos.

This kind to racism drives capitalists to move their sweatshops to Mexico. Thus, they avoid having to pay livable wages and comply with labor laws, laws that protect workers from job violations, child labor, and unhealthy conditions. Those mighty corporations exert so much power over the indigenous and mestizos that those people are in virtual slavery. Those people often try to escape this harsh slavery. They attempt to immigrate to the United States, hoping to shed the chains of oppression. Once here, these semiskilled and unskilled workers compete for jobs with Mexican American workers. Eventually they all suffer from the lack of jobs, and poverty remains rampant in the barrio and in the agricultural fields.

Finally, our own families have been brainwashed to believe that they belong to an inferior race. Here in the United States, many of our people also have problems accepting their indigenous roots. As a child, my own aunt used to call me "India" to show she disapproved of my unkempt braids and dirty face. She would scold me when I went to the neighborhood baseball games, because I was out in the sun all afternoon, and that meant my skin became even darker. She would say that I looked like an Indian. When I grew up, I finally decided that I did look like an Indian, because I was one—a mestiza. And by the way, she too looked like an Indian, because she was also a mestiza who shared the same indigenous roots.

After the Civil Rights movement of the '60s and '70s, many people accepted the fact that our indigenous roots were something we should take pride in. Fortunately today a large number of us who were born in the United States have taught our children to take pride in their indigenous roots. Yet many still cling to the illusion that we are racially white, even when our skin tone and our features tell otherwise. Unfortunately, until we accept our roots and examine our past, we will continue to believe that being bronze is a genetic flaw. We must come to the realization that we are genetically adapted to the American continents where our ancestors lived for thousands of years. That is, our physical appearance is a product of our environment. In that sense, we are no different from people who originated on other continents and reflect the environments in which their ancestors lived. Mexican Americans are a noble people, as smart as any other people, and we demand to be recognized as a race of intelligent beings worthy of equal education and equal respect. We are not untouchables doing only jobs no one else wants to do. We do not belong to an inferior caste. Mexican Americans in the United States have experienced many racial prejudices, and some European Americans still consider us to belong to an inferior society.

The indigenous people of the Americas built great civilizations and developed highly sophisticated languages, arts, poetry, sciences, and agriculture independently of Europe or any other continent. Why should we allow ourselves to accept the big lie that somehow we are an inferior race doomed to failure? Why should we allow ourselves to accept that we are not capable of grasping intellectual concepts? We must insist in raising children who are astronauts, architects, scientists, political leaders, pilots, doctors, and professors. Any profession they choose should be available to them, not just the ones selected by our European American teachers.

Since the Europeans first set foot in the Americas, they have had one mission: to conquer, enslave, and deprive the children of America of their heritage as indigenous people. In order to take possession, they have systematically set out to prove that we are lesser beings. The truth is that when the Europeans first traveled to the Americas, they had gunpowder. If they had not gained the knowledge of gunpowder from China, their spears and arrows would not have made them any superior to our spears and arrows. They could move quickly because they had horses. It was their weapons and horses and not their presumptuous divine right that gave them the power to cause so much destruction among the American indigenous people.

If, as devout Christians, the majority of the people of the Americas accept the doctrine that somehow God favors Europeans over indigenous Americans, then we have to either find another God or distrust our Christian faith, because it would mean that we live under a capricious God who favored first the Jews as the chosen people and then the Europeans. We would come at the bottom of the list as an afterthought. Thus, we must be the stepchildren of God. If this sounds like a heresy, I can say that this concept is alive and well in the United States of America today. The most obvious example is the cruel neglect that Native Americans suffer in extreme poverty and hunger, living in the worst concentration camps. In Mexico it can also be seen in the cold-blooded murder of the indigenous people of Chiapas, who suffered starvation, genocide, and extermination. Yet the voices of the powerful nations remained silent because of the economic boom that stealing those lands will bring them. The capitalist motto seems to be, "For God loves petroleum so much, that he allows his Mayan children to suffer mass destruction." If this were true, God would have to be either very cruel or a White man's myth.

Paul Tillich, a German theologian exiled in the United States after the rise of the Nazi regime, stated that all that man has to reach God are signposts pointing toward Him, but when we stop at any signpost and confuse it with God, we end up worshipping the symbol and not the real God. This resembles what is happening to many American Christian leaders; they cannot go beyond the symbols they interpret as their God. Corporations attain more capital by oppressing more people. Because of globalization, these enterprises are able to move to places where they pay lower wages, leaving people jobless here in our country. In turn, the people with the least power are blamed for this loss of American jobs: the undocumented immigrants. Politicians like to exploit resentment against Mexican and Central American immigrants when in reality the high-paying jobs in fields like manufacturing and information technology have gone mostly to Asia. Yet Christian leaders and politicians, stuck at a signpost, tell their audience that the real moral issues are the teaching of human evolution, Islam, homosexuality, and undocumented immigrants. Tillich stated, "Politicians, dictators, and other people who wish to use rhetoric to make an impression on their audience like to use the word God in this sense. It produces the feeling in their listeners that the speaker is serious and morally trustworthy."[14]

The truth remains that the indigenous people of these continents are racially one people. Indigenous people from North America and South America in some cases may have European blood in their family trees—it could be French, English, Dutch or Spanish. They may also have some African blood. Nevertheless, as a whole, people living in reservations and barrios have one thing in common, and that is race. It was our race that has kept us from acquiring equal rights. The reason we have not assimilated into the so-called European American society is not our inability to assimilate culturally or to speak English. Race is the reason. In the United States, we stand out because of our physical features. We are Americans by birth, by citizenship, by tradition, and by service to this country, but as long as our skin remains dark and our features remain Indian, this nation will never acknowledge our citizenship and our rights as Americans. The issue is purely and simply racism, systematically promulgated by European immigrants who invaded our lands and savagely and brutally attacked our people while accusing us of being savages.

In Spain, church and government leaders held big debates in the sixteenth century on the question of our humanity. In North America, the British, French, Irish, and German colonizers found the answer by eradicating the original nations and pushing them from one reservation to another until thousands upon thousands were exterminated.

This story of extermination today continues in Mexico with low-intensity warfare. There the Mayan people of Chiapas are systematically dying. The government continues to buy military weapons to keep them oppressed and allows them to die of starvation. While those Mayan brothers and sisters were having their homes burned to the ground, we remained silent. When the rain forest in Chiapas caught fire, no one claimed the fires were man-made. This was part of Mexico's plan to displace the people from their lands. That way they could seize those lands and cede them to greedy European and American businesses. Foreign corporations covet the oil lying underneath the ground and the opportunity to build hydropower electric plants on Mayan territory without benefiting the Indians at all. This warfare amounts to nothing but herding the Mayas into concentration camps, but not many in our country protested, because they are indigenous people and therefore do not deserve the same consideration as the white race. This blatant execution by Mexico's elite continues even more than fifteen years after the Zapatistas first rebelled. Race is the issue here, not culture or language or religion.

Slavery in America

"Hoy decimos Basta! Today we say enough is enough! To the people of Mexico: Mexican brothers and sisters: We are a product of 500 years of struggle: first against slavery, then during the War of Independence against Spain led by insurgents, then to promulgate our constitution and expel the French empire from our soil, and later [when] the dictatorship of Porfirio Diaz denied us the just application of the Reform laws and the people rebelled and leaders like Villa and Zapata emerged, poor men just like us. We have been denied the most elemental education so that others can use us as cannon fodder and pillage the wealth of our country. They don't care that we have nothing, absolutely nothing, not even a roof over our heads, no land, no work, no health care, no food, and no education. Nor are we able freely and democratically to elect our political representatives, nor is there independence from foreigners, nor is there peace nor justice for ourselves and our children."

—Declaración de la Selva Lacandona, EZLN, Chiapas,
México, December 31,1993
George Collier and Elizabeth Lowery Quaratiello,
Basta! Land and the Zapatista Rebellion in Chiapas

The American continents have a long history of slavery, starting with the earliest European invader, Christopher Columbus. He was a pious man who, upon landing on Hispaniola, knelt down, praised the Holy Trinity, and proceeded to take America's natives captive. Christopher Columbus wrote in his journal, "It appears to me, that the people are ingenious, and would be good servants; and I am of the opinion that they would very readily become Christians, as they appear to have no religion." Then he proceeded to say: "If it pleases our Lord, I intend at my return to carry home six of them to your Highness ..." [15]

Afterward Columbus made three more trips to the Americas, trading and selling Indian captives. On his first return trip to Spain, Columbus took six Taino Indians, whom he sold as slaves; he claimed he needed the money to pay the king for his expeditions. The Spaniards were responsible for the cruel treatment, enslavement, and extermination of entire native populations; the account of their crimes came to us thanks to some Spanish missionaries who recorded those stories.

Anton Montesino, often called Antonio Montesinos, was a Dominican priest who became appalled by the mistreatment of Indians; he was probably one of the first friars to come out in the defense of the indigenous people. As a priest of the church in Santo Domingo, during the fourth Sunday of Advent of 1511 he delivered a sermon to an audience that included civil officials. Preaching from biblical text, he proclaimed: *"Ego vox clamantis in deserto"* (I am a voice crying in the wilderness) ... I have come up on this pulpit to make your sins known to you, I am a voice of Christ crying in the wilderness of this island, and therefore listen with all your hearts and all your senses ... all of you are in mortal sin, and in it you live and die, because of the cruelty and tyranny with which you treat these innocent people.[16]

Pedro de Las Casas was a Spanish nobleman who accompanied Christopher Columbus on his second voyage to the Americas. Upon their return to Europe, Don Pedro brought his son Bartolomé an Indian youth to be his personal servant while he was a student at the University of Salamanca.[17] Eventually Bartolomé de Las Casas traveled to the Caribbean and became an *encomendero*; as such, he participated in the injustice his fellow Spaniards were committing against the Indians. While in the Caribbean islands, he joined the priesthood as a Dominican, and he probably heard the preaching of Montesinos and his fellow friars. Later in life he would experience an epiphany of what it meant to defend the Indians in the name of God and spent the rest of his days defending the rights of Indians to be called humans and not be enslaved. He was probably influenced by Montesinos's sermon to such an extent that he also became one of the greatest defenders of Indians in the so-called New World. He traveled through the Caribbean and Central and South America recording what he witnessed, exposing and speaking against the horrendous crimes committed by the conquistadors. He is the man who first used the term Black Legend to describe the atrocities perpetrated by the Spaniards, describing how they committed so many evil deeds, great sins, robberies, and abominations that it was incredible. He claimed they had nearly wiped the Indians from their land, and he wrote about the large number of Mexican slaves the Spaniards took in their boats to sell in neighboring islands, such as Cuba and Hispaniola. He wrote that in Mexico the Spaniards could trade a horse for eighty Indians. [18]

In the Caribbean islands, entire tribes were wiped out by the Spanish sword and by disease. During 1518–1519, smallpox killed Tainos by the thousands in what is now Puerto Rico and Santo Domingo.[19]

Bartolomé de Las Casas related how an encomendero took eight thousand Indians to build a wall around his land, working the men without rest, without food, and without pay. Eventually a great number of those Indian slaves died.[20] He also spoke about how the Spaniards rounded up a large number of Indians to carry the soldiers' cargo during their exploration and conquest of Mexico. In one instance fifteen or twenty thousand of them were tied up and taken on the conquistador's expedition, but only about two hundred Indians returned home.[21]

Bartolomé de Las Casas made the following claims of what he saw in Peru: I swear that I personally saw with my very own eyes the Spanish cut off hands, noses and ears of female and male Indians, without any purpose just because they desired to do it … I saw the Spaniards throwing dogs on the Indians so that the dogs could tear them to pieces, and I saw them stone a large number of Indians.[22] He also relates how in Jalisco, Mexico, a woman had her daughter wrestled from her arms by a Spaniard, and when she resisted, her hand was cut off with a sword as she tried to hold on to her young girl; the daughter was stabbed to death for resisting rape.[23]

Bartolomé de Las Casas also claimed that between 1518 and 1542, … the Christians who went to settle in Mexico committed many horrible atrocities. That they had lost all respect and fear of God and King … because there were so many cruelties, killings, destructions wiping out of towns, robberies, violence and tyranny.[24]

Today there are people who try to discredit Bartolomé de Las Casas, claiming he exaggerated and that he made up the stories, but de Las Casas traveled with other priests who also witnessed those crimes. Fray Juan de Umbrage, a Franciscan bishop in Mexico, also wrote about the atrocities the Spaniards committed. Early Catholic missionaries, such as Bernardino de Sahagún, Fray Diego Durán, and Toribio Benavente (Motolinia) devoted their lives to recording the subhuman treatment of the indigenous people and sometimes to defending them against those atrocities.

Native Americans did not share the European Christian faith or did not understand immortality in the same way as Europeans, and this made the American natives savages in the minds of the Europeans.

The fact that indigenous people in the Americas did not own private property meant that anyone could come and claim property. The land was there for the taking! For over a century, Europeans denied that there were people in the Americas. According to many Europeans, the story about *"Los Indios"* was "a lie invented by Columbus".[25]

In reality, there were many nations and tribes in America at the time the Europeans landed. Just in North America, there were the Aztecs and the Mayas, who had magnificent high cultures. In South America, the Incas had a great civilization. In the rest of North America, there were many organized tribes, such as the Massachusetts, with highly developed languages that the Pilgrims did not understand. The Indians learned English more quickly than the Europeans learned the native Massachusett language—or any other Native American languages. Nevertheless, it was the Indians who were considered the savages!

John Sassamon learned to speak and write English and his native language. With his knowledge of both languages, he was able to help John Eliot, a Puritan minister, translate the Bible into the Massachusett language. The Puritans believed the only authority that came from God was in the Bible and that the Indians needed to learn to interpret the Bible so they could serve God.[26]

Nevertheless, among the Protestant clergy, there was no one who served as advocates for the Indians' souls in Europe or in America as the noted Catholic priests did in Spain. The English were more interested in gaining wealth in America by acquiring territory and selling American and African slaves.

In Mexico, missionaries like Sahagún helped the Chichimec record their history in Spanish by learning their language. As a result, much of the indigenous history was recorded by those missionaries in cooperation with Indians who became writers of their history in a European language. Those Indians converted to the Catholic faith and learned not only Spanish but also Latin. They helped the priests write their Indian history before and during the conquest.

Bernardino Sahagún was one of the first Catholic missionaries to arrive in Mexico and the first to record the history of the fall of the Aztec empire. He got information from many indigenous people who had lived during the fall of Mexico.

Sahagún narrates the following: It seems that the Aztecs would go to the temple to worship their gods. There they would perform their religious ceremonies. The temple was sacred, so they would not take their weapons into the temple. Pedro de Alvarado, one of Cortes' soldiers, prepared a trap for the worshippers; he placed his soldiers at the temple gates and prepared his soldiers for war. They attacked the temple and rushed in with their swords, lances, and guns. The soldiers attacked, beheading the Aztec warriors and cutting off their arms and legs to get to the golden jewelry and any valuable articles the Indians were wearing. The result was that Indian body parts were scattered all over the temple, and blood ran in rivers down the temple floor. The walls of the temple were also covered with blood, and the doors were blocked so the Indians could not escape, so that most of the Indians died that day. The Aztecs lost not only their material wealth in the attack but also their military leadership and strong soldiers.[27]

The valuable work of priests continues to this day. In modern times, Angel Garibay, a Catholic priest, was the first twentieth-century Mexican scholar to study literature left during the conquest. Today, Miguel Leon-Portilla, a university professor in Mexico City, continues to study and translate Aztec literature and history.

Today we also learn the wisdom and culture of ancient indigenous cultures from anthropologists like Sophie D. Coe and Michael D. Coe, who for many years studied and documented Mayan and Aztec civilization. She states, "Aztec royalty and nobility were devoted to music, song, dance, and poetry. Great poems—and many have survived from Aztec times ..." According to Mrs. Coe, the poems were usually performed in the courtyards and to the beat of drums by poets and members of the royalty, such as King Nezahualcoyotl.[28]

The following ancient poem, composed by an Indian poet who lived during the conquest of Mexico, is testimony to the cruelty of the Spaniards. This poet appeared to be a witness of the terrible pain the Indians suffered under the Spanish conquest.

I carry you
all Christians, everyone.
You kick me. You sit on me.
You throw nixtamal water* on me ...[29]

*nixtamal water: lime water left after curing corn.

The poem goes on to describe the degrading abuses committed by the conquistadors, such as defecating and urinating on the Indians, crying out that the Spaniards only want to keep going to different places. It also tells about not receiving food or water and suffering pain from being overworked. The final lament is that Indians were made unclean every day.[30]

The poem is one of hundreds of literary works left by the Indian natives and translated by modern day Mexican scholars into Spanish (and eventually into English). Some of the indigenous pre-Columbian and conquest era literary works were saved by sympathetic Spanish priests, but other documents were unfortunately destroyed by religious zealots and conquerors as works of the Devil.

Fray Diego Durán, the Spanish missionary who witnessed many of the crimes committed against the Indians, wrote, " ... the Spaniards went from conquest to conquest, subjecting the land." Once a city was taken and secured, a Spaniard would request that Cortes give him an *encomienda*—the right to land and property—and then once the conqueror received the encomienda, he would make the Indians on this land his property; he would take men, women, and children and brand them on their faces and sell them as slaves.[31]

Fray Durán wrote, "... and they were marked in the face with the name of the man who had sold them"; and added, " ... even though I did not actually see slaves being branded on the face with hot irons, just like horses in a corral ... I did see those men who had been branded"
[32]

Fray Bartolomé de Las Casas also documented the branding of Mexican slaves; he stated that in the year 1525 in the province of Panuco, a tyrant committed many cruel acts, among them the branding of Indian slaves and sending them in ships to Cuba and Hispaniola to be sold.[33]

The arrival of the Spaniards brought cattle; one of the ways of displacing the indigenous people from their lands was to allow the cattle to graze on the cornfields to destroy the crops, forcing the people to abandon the land.

History also records that in Mexico the natives lost their lands through fraud: the Spaniards would occupy the land and then get another native to sign a paper giving them possession to those lands. They would pay the false owner an insignificant amount of money and dispose of the real owners by killing or enslaving them.

Bartolomé de Las Casas recorded that in New Spain (Mexico), the Spanish captured about a hundred Indian noblemen and tied them up and then put a piece of wood between their arms and made them kneel and set them afire. One of the noblemen escaped to the Cuu (ceremonial meeting place) in the temple and gathered with some of the Aztec men to discuss what was happening with the Spaniards. The Spaniards found them, set the temple afire, and burned them alive. Tradition claims that while the Aztecs burned, the Spaniards sang, just as Nero fiddled while Rome burned.[34]

Diego Durán echoes this idea:

> *From the Tarpeian Rock*
> *Nero watched Rome on fire.*
> *Not even the tears of the women*
> *His pity did inspire …*[35]

Durán wrote that on one occasion after many Indian warriors had died, the Spaniards discovered that many of the new warriors were female.[36] The women felt they needed to defend their country to avoid becoming enslaved. Hence, the women had decided to take up their families' weapons and fight against the invaders.

Juan Troyano documented an event that took place in what is today the southwestern United States: Don Garcia Lopez, who was *maestre de campo*, ordered that some posts be set on the ground. He then ordered that some Pecos Indians who had come to meet with the Spanish in peace be rounded up and tied to the post two-by–two, and then he ordered them burned alive. The number of Indians burned alive was fifty. The rest of the Pecos Indians tried to defend themselves using tent poles and stakes. They were also killed with lances and knives.[37]

In the Pecos territory (the southwestern United States), the Spanish searched for gold. There they saw a man they called "Bigotes" because he had a mustache. Bigotes was wearing a gold bracelet. The Spaniards asked him to show them where the gold came from. The Indian claimed he did not know, so the Spaniards had him attacked by their dogs and badly injured. He eventually told them where to find his meager possessions.[38]

In Peru, Bartolomé de Las Casas claimed that the Spaniards rounded up a large number of Indians and locked them up in three large houses and set fire to them and burned them alive.[39]

Burning Indians alive was a common practice among the Spaniards, a custom they probably brought from Spain, where the church often burned heretics during the Inquisition.

In Cuba the Indians were also branded and sold as slaves during the time of Columbus. According to John Kessell: "They fought Taino resisters, branding and enslaving those taken as prisoners of war."[40]

Those testimonies show that there is no question that the Spanish branded Indian slaves. This occurred from the time Spain took possession of the Americas. Columbus was a slave trader and probably used the same techniques to mark his slaves.

In the Americas, Spaniards and Portuguese became slave traders. Some of the slave traders were Spanish Jews who had fled to Portugal to avoid the Inquisition. Some of the new slave traders came from the Netherlands and tried to take over the Portuguese trade. Those traders brought slaves from Africa to the Americas. They also conquered and made slaves out of the indigenous people of North, Central, and South America. In Brazil, Portuguese slave traders raided Jesuit missions and took Guarani and other Indians to sell to the European settlers in their colonies. Those Portuguese slave traders were the *Bandeirantes*, a colonial guard that launched expeditions from Sao Paulo to enslave indigenous people and to look for precious stones. The first *Bandeirantes* raids started in 1628, led by Antonio Raposo Tavares. They captured 2,500 natives from Jesuit villages. The original estimated indigenous population of Brazil was over 2.5 million. By the middle of the eighteenth century, their numbers had dwindled to just one million or at most 1.5 million.

There were several Jesuit missions in the area that is now the border between Argentina, Brazil, and Paraguay, the site of the beautiful

Iguassu Falls. It was in this beautiful sanctuary that the *Bandeirantes* captured many Indians whom they then sold into slavery.

Besides Bartolomé de Las Casas and Fray Diego Durán, there were other Spaniards who acted as early witnesses who recorded the bloody and violent history of the conquest of the Americas: Franciscan Jacobo de Testera and Dominicans Juan de Torres, Pedro de Angulo, Luis de Morales, Rodrigo Calderon, Licenciado Loaysa, Bishop Diego Aleman, Pedro de Aguilar, and others. All these people had similar arguments against the cruel treatment of the Indians; some even went to Spain to present their defense in favor of the indigenous people.[41] An outstanding theologian speaking on the rights of Indians was Francisco de Victoria. Many complaints regarding the ill treatment of Indians filled the Spanish courts. The court in Valladolid petitioned the king to "remedy the cruelties which are committed in the Indies against the Indians to the end that God can be served and the Indies preserved and not depopulated as is now the case."[42]

Other Europeans who came to North America committed similar atrocities, but their histories were not as closely documented. In North America, slavery took place mostly in the form of African slaves brought in by the British and other early European settlers. Those African slaves' pasts have been well documented.

The Europeans also took Native Americans as slaves in North America, selling the Indians outside their native lands. Nevertheless, neither the British colonists nor the United States have ever fully accounted for the number of Indian slaves they captured. History textbooks in our schools do not document the history of this slavery. We know how those people suffered from their own oral accounts, but they did not have Catholic priests or Protestant ministers documenting their tragic history as precisely as it was documented by the Catholic priests that arrived in Mexico with the conquistadors.

With the English settlers, the fate of the Native Americans was no different. The English Puritans were appalled by the cruel acts of the Spanish, but as their war against the Indians continued, they too became embroiled in cruel and bloody deeds. An Indian asked the European invaders, "Are not women and children more timid than men? The Cheyenne warriors are not afraid, but have you never heard of Sand Creek? Your soldiers look just like those who butchered the women and children there."[43]

Some of the Pilgrims did try to convert the Indians. John Eliot, "the Apostle to the Indians," did religious translations into the Massachusett language. He also taught some Indians the English language.[44]

Jill Lepore states that people like Sarah Savage urged European settlers to allow Indians to be "civilized" and Christianized and ultimately assimilated into European society.[45] This did not happen, as most Europeans never assimilated the Indians into their cultures outside of trading with them. Most Native American history is oral history preserved by people who related it to their children. This is valid history, but one cannot but wonder how much more precise this history would have been if it had been documented in writing. The history could have been written down as it was in Central and South America by the priests who came to convert the Indians.

There is no question that some of the Europeans did make an effort to bring Christianity to the Americas. Divine destiny determined that Indians should die and Europeans should inherit the earth on these American continents. According to the Puritans and other early settlers, Europeans came to America as part of God's plan. The theory of divine destiny developed very early in American history.

Puritans justified their journey to America by claiming the Indians were glad they had come. The Puritans drew a banner of an Indian with the caption that read, "Come over and help us." This became the great seal of the Massachusetts Bay colony, which is still in use in that region. In reality they were coming over as illegal immigrants; the Indians had not invited them to come over and steal their lands. Maybe those immigrants from Mexico and South America should come over with a banner that claims they are coming over to help save the European Americans from themselves.

The harsh reality is that most Europeans came with two main goals: to take land and to take resources.

French conquerors and colonizers burnt Iroquois villages in the late seventeenth century. Later they formed campaigns of genocide against the Fox, Natchez, and Chickasaw in the early eighteenth century.[46]

The French brought missionaries to convert the Indians, but the French also brought over European diseases, and out of fear, many Indians converted to Christianity, hoping the wrath of the Christian God would not fall upon them.

The British in Virginia and South Carolina traded guns with the

Westo Indians, who used those weapons to fight other tribes, such as the Yamassee, Creek, Cherokee, Catawba, and Casabo. The Westo would capture their enemies and trade them for British guns. Those captive Indians were sold as slaves by the English in North America and exported to other colonies and to Europe.

Most European nations participated in the enslavement of Indians when they arrived in America.[47] This enslavement was as horrific as the enslavement of Africans; however, the slavery of the Indians has never been recognized as a crime against humanity. No American government has ever paid any serious restitution for the crimes committed against the Indians.

Regardless of what nation the European conquerors came from, they plundered and killed the indigenous people. They murdered so many natives of these Americas that more than half of the original population was exterminated.

These invaders from Spain, England, Portugal, Holland, France, and other European countries massacred the indigenous people without mercy; most of the First Nations were decimated, killed by weapons, starvation, and imported diseases. In the United States, many of the buffalo were deliberately killed in order to deprive Native American tribes of their main food source. "The buffalow and Bare are gone, and there are but a few Deer, not sufficient to justify an Indian to depend upon for support, more particularly those that have familys."[48]

Not only did the warriors die in battles; often Europeans would raid villages to kill women and children. This was a systematic and deliberate extermination. This massive killing of indigenous Americans was perpetrated in order to take possession of their lands. Europeans did not stop the murder until they left them completely powerless, without land and without children to defend their land.

United States history books rarely speak about the enslavement of Indians, although they explain how so many Indians had to abandon their lands and their families and why there are so few Indians left in North America. When Native Americans were killed in war or enslaved and lost their lands, Europeans were ready to take over those territories.

Today those original Americans usually live in rural ghettos called reservations in places like New Mexico, Oklahoma, and Arizona, where the land is usually arid and not very productive. In general, the indigenous people in Mexico, Central America, and South America are not better off than their indigenous brothers and sisters in the United States. They do not participate in the wealth of their respective countries. They often lack jobs, housing, schools, and hospitals. Many times their communities are tourist attractions where visitors take their children to be entertained.

In modern times Indians have been isolated in reservations. Approximately 51 percent of Native Americans live in reservations and often lack water and electricity. Those who live outside the reservation often do not fare much better; they too get lost in the poverty and poor economic conditions of large cities. They are much like the mestizos coming from Mexico and Central America, poor and jobless.

Indians have the highest unemployment rate of any Americans, and those that do have jobs often are unable to earn more than $2,600 a year. Many Mexican American migrant workers have a similar income working in the fields. I have actually seen some of their income tax returns, so I know it is true. In the United States, the richest nation in the world, the indigenous people have the lowest incomes.

Slavery of the indigenous people was definitely a problem in what is today the United States. British colonists would capture Indians and sell them in Europe or in the Caribbean islands. Nevertheless, their policy was the eradication of the people to facilitate the taking of their lands. For cheap labor, they found it easier to capture their slaves in Africa. Thus, they wiped out the native North Americans; they killed men, women, and children. They burned their villages and purposely starved them into submission and extinction, and finally they profited from the selling of Indian slaves.

The British acted as savagely as the Spaniards did in the lands they conquered; the difference was in the manner they wrote their history. Jill Lepore writes, "fighting like savages: wage the war, and win it, by whatever means necessary, and then write about it, to win it again. The first would be a victory of wounds, the second a victory of words."[49]

In other words, the British justified their savage treatment of the Indians by rewriting history and providing their version of how they had conquered America in a civil manner when in reality they were just as savage and cruel as the Spaniards.

The British Puritans justified their murdering of Indians by claiming they were acting on God's ordinance. John Richardson preached that war "is an ordinance appoynted by God for subduing and destroying the Churches Enemies here upon Earth."[50]

All European nations that came to America participated in one way or another in the destruction of Indian families from North, Central, and South America. Indian blood spread like a flood all over the Americas. The natives defended themselves but were no match for the Europeans, who had been fighting long wars with each other, and who also had superior weapons; they had steel swords, guns, and cannons as opposed to bows, arrows, and lances. The Europeans also had horses that allowed them to move swiftly through the territories they invaded. Later the Indians would also acquire guns and horses, but it was too little, too late.

After American independence from Britain, the Native American fate did not improve but got worse; some tribes were fought to extinction, and others were offered peace treaties. The Cherokee, Chickasaw, Choctaw, Muscogee-Creek, and the Seminole were asked to assimilate into European culture by converting to Christianity, dressing in European clothes, and speaking English. These nations adopted the European lifestyle; they settled down, kept private farms, and became prosperous. Their original territories were in what are now Alabama, Tennessee, and Georgia. They lived peacefully until the European Americans and European immigrants reached their borders, coveted their lands, and demanded that the Indians leave their homes. Also, the discovery of gold in Georgia precipitated the incursion of miners into that region. Since the Indians had signed a treaty, they took their grievances all the way to Washington DC, where the Supreme Court ruled in the Cherokee's favor. However, President Andrew Jackson went against the Supreme Court decision and demanded that the Indians leave their homes and start their journey immediately. That was the first and only time in history a president disobeyed a Supreme Court ruling. It took the European Americans from 1831 to 1838 to remove most of the Indians. The Choctaws stated that the European Americans "have had our habitations torn down and burned; our fences destroyed, cattle turned into our fields & we ourselves have been scourged, manacled, fettered and otherwise personally abused, until by such treatment some of our best men have died."[51]

This tragic journey to a different land would become the famous Trail of Tears. This was one instance of the many horrendous and tragic crimes against Native Americans. This journey foreshadowed what the Nazis would do to Jews, Roma, and other ethnic minorities one hundred years later by sending them to concentration camps. The Indians were ordered to leave right before the winter started, without sufficient food and without protection against the elements, a form of genocide. They suffered hunger and slept in torrential rains and on the bare ground. Eventually they reached the frozen territory where many fell ill. Others just continued walking barefoot in the snow and blistering cold. Only a fraction of them survived. American settlers and European immigrants were able to buy lottery tickets and bid for the Indian Territory. They took the Cherokee farms and kept the Cherokee lands.[52]

Native American people have many stories to recount of cruel bloodshed, of savage treatment, and of treason. One such story, which happened in 1890, is told by the Lakota people, who now live in the Pine Ridge Reservation in South Dakota.

Thomas Shortbull, President of the Oglala Lakota College in South Dakota, recalls a story told by his grandfather about a journey his ancestors took after a battle with the United States military that left them with many dead in a place that lacked food and hunting resources. In their search to find a place to rest and feed their families, they reached Porcupine Bluff and asked the United States military stationed there for a place to camp; they were directed to the west side of Wounded Knee Creek. Once there, they offered a service of worship and healing for family members. Many women, children, and elderly people had died in the last battle with the United States. The religious ceremony was a spirit of medicine dance, viewed with suspicion by the white man. Newspapers called these dances "ghost dances" and claimed they were war dances.

Thousands of American soldiers converged on the Pine Ridge area. On the morning of December 29,1890, soldiers of the US Seventh Cavalry (George Armstrong Custer's old regiment) went to disarm the Lakota. In the confusion, a shot was heard, and the soldiers ordered their troops to open fire on the Lakota families; mostly women, children, and old men died. The soldiers took Lakota clothing and baby moccasins from the deceased and auctioned them off as souvenirs. This story of horror and slaughter was the Wounded Knee Massacre.

The United States reaffirmed slavery in March 6, 1857; Chief Justice

Roger B. Taney in his decision for the Court in Dred Scott v. Sandford declared that "the federal government had no power to restrict the spread of slavery within the United States and its territories."[53]

It was not until after the Civil War, with the victory of the Union, that President Lincoln declared all slaves free with the Emancipation Proclamation of January 1, 1863.[54]

On the other hand, Spain did not find the issue of slavery to be that difficult. In the Americas they settled mostly for native slaves except in places where Africans were introduced after indigenous populations had been wiped out. In the Spanish courts, the issue of slavery was discussed for many years. In a famous mid-sixteenth century debate, church leaders such as Juan Ginés de Sepulveda argued against Fray Bartolomé de Las Casas that the people of the Americas were by nature slaves as described by Aristotle.[55] Objecting to that premise, Las Casas claimed that Aristotle was a "gentile burning in Hell" and he had no jurisdiction over the Catholic Church when his philosophy contradicted church doctrine.[56]

Sepulveda argued that indigenous people of the Americas lacked intelligence and culture; therefore, because of their subhuman nature, they were not entitled to basic human rights and could be treated as slaves. On the other hand, Bartolomé de Las Casas argued that they were completely human even if they had different cultures and languages; he defended the rational humanity of the Indians. He added that Indians were being conquered by unjust wars and that the Spaniards butchered them in such a sadistic fashion that they were treated as inanimate things, very much like cattle in the meat market. Las Casas proposed that the Council of the Indies should make the necessary laws to stop the crimes against the Indians; he won the argument in that round.[57]

In the book *The Spanish Struggle for Justice in the Conquest of Americas*, Lewis Hanke devotes the whole volume to the argument between Las Casas and Sepulveda. Most importantly, Hanke documents how many other Dominican and Franciscan friars went before the Spanish Courts in defense of the Indians.

Some writers claim that it was to the benefit of the Spanish crown to make the Indians royal subjects instead of slaves: as subjects, they would be under the control of the king and not of the encomienda masters, who then had to share their wealth with the Crown.

Bartolomé de Las Casas had at one time suggested bringing people from Africa to perform labor, but after witnessing the treatment of African slaves, he eventually argued for the equality of all races in the Americas. Las Casas felt that his purpose in life was to convert the Indians to Christianity and save their souls. Therefore, he continued his struggle to treat the Indians as equals with European society.[58]

Imperialism swept the Americas. Europeans came and took land, gold, and other precious possessions. From Peru and Mexico, they took gold, but they also took the most precious treasure: they took away the freedom of the people. The enslavement of the American natives was cruel and ferocious. The crimes committed by all the European invaders were horrendous.

The fate of the indigenous people of North America was no better than the fate of the African slaves. They rebelled, they fought for their lands, and they were executed. The Europeans continued the onslaught against the indigenous people. They took their lands and rivers, and they killed the buffalo, one of the main food sources. Without buffalo and rivers to catch fish, many tribes starved. The invaders enslaved, burned, and murdered men, women, and children until only a handful of Native Americans survived.

"At an early day white settlers from the East coveting this beautiful country begun pushing their settlements into it." Treaties were made, and the whites kept taking larger and larger portions of Indian territory.[59]

On the other hand, Spain continued to gain cheap labor by intimidation, enslavement, horrendous and cruel punishments, religious conversions, and wars. The Spaniards obtained their victory thanks to the might of their weapons and the speed of their horses.

The invaders from England and the invaders from Spain both proclaimed that their victory came from God. God had awarded Europeans the northern and southern continents because it was a "new world," empty of human beings and full of savages who, according to them, had no culture, religion, or notion of property. Slavery and cruel inhuman treatment engulfed both continents in the name of the respective churches and God. The imperialistic trail left no part of North, Central, or South America untouched.

This was a gigantic genocide, a holocaust never repeated in history in which entire continents with all their nations decimated, their lands taken as war booty and their survivors used as slaves for centuries.

In order to understand North, Central, and South American Indigenous peoples' dilemma, we must first understand the meaning of imperialism. Imperialism is extending a nation's dominance by territorial acquisition.

Mexico has never been free from imperialism since its conquest by Spain around 1519–1521. To read the history of the conquest is to learn about the horrible holocaust that took place. The pain and bloodshed that covered the Americas was disastrous to the indigenous people.

Mexicans were to experience the claws of imperialism several times. A second invasion of the Mexican territory came after Spain lost its colonies. Mexicans continued to live in their homes in what is now the southwestern United States. After their independence, Mexico occupied the territory that Spain had claimed before.

When the Spaniards came to explore California, Texas, Arizona, New Mexico, and other territories in North America, they brought their Mexican slaves, peons, and soldiers. Some of these people were Indians who had been subjugated in Mexico; others were mestizos of mixed descent. Some women came as wives, others as servants to the Spanish families. They were brought by the Spanish in their territorial conquest. As they incorporated those lands into their empire, some of the native people living in those lands also became assimilated into Mexican society.

By this period of history, the Spanish coexisted with the Mexican natives and often fathered children with their women, so they allowed those people to claim territory in North America. The king of Spain even extended some of those land grants. Because of this, a large number of Mexicans had valuable lands in what is now the southwestern United States. They lived there for several generations. As small farmers, they grew crops and tended their animals. The United States was aware that these families were legal citizens of Mexico and were settled in a land that was legitimately owned by Mexico after its independence from Spain.

In 1786, Thomas Jefferson feared that Spain would be able to hold onto its territories until the United States became sufficiently populated and powerful to conquer the rest of the continent piece by piece. Henry Clay's dream since 1811 was to expand the United States over the American continent from the Arctic to South America.

In Texas, Sam Houston claimed that the Anglo-Saxon race should have dominion over the southern extreme of this vast continent, that Mexicans were no better than Indians, and that there was no reason to keep whites from taking their land.[60]

The idea of conquering more territory was not the idea of a small number of people who came to form the Texas Republic; it was the sentiment of most Americans.[61]

As the United States drew closer to Mexico, many European immigrants and Anglo Americans asked Mexico for permission to come and settle in the Mexican territory of Texas. The Mexican government agreed on condition that the new settlers would become Mexican citizens, Roman Catholic, and would not allow slavery.

The settlers agreed to Mexico's terms, but it turned out that many of the immigrants who populated Texas came from the southern United States and had found slavery to be very profitable. Later, when they broke away as the Republic of Texas, they saw fit to reintroduce slavery.

According to David Montejano, "The Anglo-Saxon nation was bound to glory; the inferior, decadent Indian race and the half-breed Mexicans were to succumb before the inexorable march of the superior Anglo-Saxon people."[62]

For most of the history of the southwestern United States and up to today, the descendants of American Indian and mestizo slaves mostly perform cheap labor. They work on farms, at construction sites, and in sweaty kitchens and clothing sweatshops. In modern times, these people are not in forced slavery; they just receive meager wages. They take low-paying jobs because they have no other option. It is serving or starving. Insufficient wages deprive them of adequate housing, medical care, food, and education. Because of their poverty, their children are often born with serious medical problems, such as asthma, deformed bones, and many other ailments mainly caused by malnutrition or environmental hazards.

The indigenous, the mestizos, and the African Americans have not been able to break the cycle of slavery in any part of the Americas. They continue to be poor and perform menial labor. The descendants of the European invaders and some of new immigrants continue the exploitation, be it in New York, in Peru, or anywhere else. The term slavery has been dropped, but the tradition is alive; slave owners do not exist as such. Slavery has taken a new face; people have a similar status to slaves, or worse. They work for inadequate wages, and the slave owners do not have to provide housing, medical service, or food. In the past, the loss of a slave was a monetary loss; nowadays, people are expendable. If they die, they are simply replaced by new slaves; the people who exploit the workers do not provide aid to the families of the departed. They do not even bury the victims. Those workers are doing jobs no one else wants to perform because they are degrading jobs. For example, Mexicans and other immigrant laborers from Central America are cleaning up the horrible mess left by Hurricane Katrina in New Orleans, Louisiana. Those jobs are hazardous and dirty. People who perform those jobs work as slaves, and they are paid low wages and have no health protection.

Other immigrants coming from Central and South America take on dangerous military jobs in the United States. America's policy is that if those men and women die in war, they will get posthumous American citizenship, which is not extended to their families. What honor there is in American citizenship if you are dead has never been explained in a satisfactory manner.

Workers are often exposed without protection to very hazardous environments, such as exposure to pesticides. The United States brought over Mexican workers during World War II (Braceros). Before they entered the fields, they were sprayed on their heads and bodies with DDT, a strong, dangerous pesticide.

Cesar Chavez, the great Mexican American leader who fought for farm workers' right to a union, denounced the perils of spraying pesticides on migrant workers while working in the fields. When I was young, there were no child labor laws in the agricultural occupations. I have not heard of any law that protects farm worker children. As a twelve-year-old farm worker, I labored in the cotton fields weeding out cotton plants. I vividly remember looking up at the crop dusters spraying the fields with toxic chemicals and touching the cotton plants and feeling the sticky residue of the spray on my hands. I vividly remember the smell of DDT. I know that to be a migrant farm worker, you do not have to be an immigrant, just someone like Cesar Chavez or myself, poor American citizens.

Farm workers are disposable slave workers; if one gets sick or is not needed, he or she is told he or she no longer has a job. This disposable society keeps the upper classes wealthy and many cities prosperous;

without inexpensive food, America would not prosper the way it does with cheap labor in its agricultural fields.

Peons in Central and South America are still held by wealthy landowners, who punish them if they try to abandon their haciendas. Some extremely large plantations are owned by American corporations, such as the United Fruit Company (Chiquita Banana). This company has been exploiting Guatemala and other Central American countries for ages. When Guatemalans elected a president who promised reform, he was accused of being a communist and ousted. President Eisenhower aided the United Fruit Company overthrow of Guatemala's Jacobo Arbenz Guzman. Thus grew America's wealth, amassed by powerful imperialists. Money is made from the extreme low wages paid to the slave worker. Racism is born from this slave society's need to sustain itself; those in power justify their actions by claiming that the people they exploit are inferior, that they lack a will to work, that they have no ambition to be educated, that they prefer being poor, and that they lack the motivation to improve their social condition. They claim poor workers are violent by nature, that they are criminals, and that they depreciate the community. "The conqueror sees himself as virtuous, industrious, highly motivated, and God-fearing, and the colonized people as lazy by nature, morally degenerate, unintelligent, and inherently inferior." Thus the colonized become the "White man's burden."[63]

Today, keeping undocumented aliens from Mexico and Central and South America out of the United States has cost the nation millions of dollars, yet the poor keep coming in hopes of getting jobs. Immigrants crossing into the United States are often exploited before they get here by Mexican and Central American criminals, but they face other obstacles in our country. Coming over the high fences our government has built can have dangerous results. Hospitals in border states where the fence has been erected have seen an increase of injuries among immigrants who have climbed the wall only to hurt themselves as they descended to the United States side. A friend of mine, a doctor in Arizona, told me some of those immigrants are suffering from broken legs and arms. Others have spinal injuries and are paralyzed for life, while others have serious internal injuries. In the hospitals, their rooms can be easily identified, because they are guarded by police officers waiting to take them back to prison once they get well.

In another story, the chief medical examiner for Pima County in Arizona, Dr. Bruce Parks, stated that their morgue was running out of space, and the county had to bring in a refrigerated truck to store more bodies. Since the beginning of the year, more than 150 corpses have been found in the desert.[64]

People in Mexico and Central America continue to view the United States as their only place for refuge from poverty, which is so extreme that they risk traveling through the smoldering heat of the Sonora desert to escape it; they are literally willing to walk through hell to reach the United States. The southwestern deserts are littered with the dead bodies of immigrants.

The question is why so many immigrants risk their souls and bodies to come to our country. Why is Mexico so poor that it constantly keeps people on the sharp blade of distress?

Judging from the large amounts of vegetables and fruits that arrive in the United States, there is no question that Mexico is rich in agriculture. Why are so many Mexicans starving and dying in their own country?

The wealthy in Mexico can afford to buy luxury yachts that cost millions; why aren't they able to provide jobs? As long as they refuse to open their nation to new industry and begin building their infrastructure, the most impoverished will continue to seek our country as their only refuge and continue to risk their lives coming to the United States, a nation that is increasingly despising, maligning, and persecuting immigrants from Spanish speaking nations.

Only Mexico can save its people from dire poverty by using its capital to create jobs. They have sufficient human resources willing to work hard, as they do when they immigrate to our country. Mexico also needs to educate its people, to create a strong nation. Today we have seen Mexico fall to the point where it has lost some of its airlines. The economic instability that has devastated its poor is now affecting the upper classes. The growth in drug trafficking is affecting the poor, who become members of the drug cartels in order to get jobs.

In reality the majority of those Mexican workers are not criminals; they are hard–working, decent people. They are building our communities with their cheap labor. Immigrants from Mexico and Mexican American workers are making billions of dollars for the United States by providing cheap labor in agriculture and construction.

Most Americans usually refuse these jobs because of the low wages; laboring in a cotton field or in a potato patch is backbreaking, and the wages are meager. Many live under very poor conditions. They sleep in cardboard boxes while doing seasonal work, and they often work from sunrise to sundown seven days a week. The United Farm Workers Union has documented and filmed these deplorable conditions in California's fields.

At the present time, the wealthy of the world are trying to obtain more oil for their cars and factories; the industrial powers, which today include China, are desperately seeking petroleum. As nations in the Middle East become unreachable, powerful corporations are going to Ecuador and other South American countries looking for oil without regard for the environment. The indigenous people of those countries are protesting the destruction of their ancestral forests; they claim that the pollution will destroy the ecological system that provides for their livelihood and health.

In Bolivia, water is a precious commodity. Several years ago, a water company, in conjunction with the government, tried to outlaw collecting rainwater. Their plans were thwarted after the indigenous people protested this injustice. Today, Bolivia has elected Evo Morales, an indigenous president; this new administration is trying to undo five hundred years of slavery.

What we do not wish to acknowledge is that when we hurt and destroy the environment —be it in the United States, in Brazil, in Mexico, or in Ecuador—we are actually destroying ourselves. When we destroy the environment in other parts of the Americas, we destroy our own environment. We all depend on one ecosystem around the world, and we all need the rain forests in Central America and Brazil. This is not a new world; it is part of our only planet. We cannot exploit our neighbors without exploiting ourselves.

Many people in the United States are still living in poverty, even working two or three jobs to survive. The maid who works all day at a hotel often has to clean private homes during her time off in order to make enough to feed her children. The man who works all week as a mason, standing on a scaffold and catching bricks with his bare hands to help build multimillion-dollar mansions is still not able to afford decent housing for his own family. He often does yard work on his time off. These workers are relegated to living in substandard conditions with no hope of ever earning wages that will allow them to provide the necessary financial tools to break out of the poverty cycle. Many of them have been seriously hurt in accidents at their places of employment and have become disabled; now they have to depend on private charities for food and clothing. For those families, access to higher education is out of the question. Even state or community colleges are out of their reach.

Hence, the cycle perpetuates itself. Workers continue to work for low wages without hope of breaking out of their poverty and illiteracy. They do not have proper nutrition or health care; their poor diets cause ailments such as diabetes and obesity. Yet they are America's workers who do the hard labor that no one else does. They are the migrant workers who feed the nation with inexpensive food. They are America's untouchable caste.

When the economy falls and work becomes scarce, these workers are the first to see their jobs turn into part-time jobs or no jobs at all. Part-time jobs mean never being able to work enough hours to get full benefits and often being passed over for promotions. When things go wrong, these workers become the scapegoats. Since not all part-time workers are college or high school students, McDonald's and some other big corporations are planning on setting up insurance for these workers. However, other companies—like Walmart—intentionally design jobs in which people only work part-time so they get away with not providing retirement plans and medical benefits. Instead, those workers have to look for government health care and welfare assistance. Thus, the poor and middle-class taxpayers pay so that the wealthy corporations can save money.

In California, racism reared its ugly head during the 1990s when Governor Pete Wilson promoted Proposition 187. This proposition, once approved by the voters, created a state-administered citizenship screening system to prevent illegal immigrants from obtaining health care, education, and even access to public libraries. It also required that all state and local government employees report suspected illegal immigrants. Doctors and nurses working in California hospitals did not like the idea of playing the role of immigration agents and objected, as did federal government agencies, who felt the state should not take over immigration enforcement duties. Many Mexican American organizations protested in California, and federal judges discussed the proposition and decided it was unconstitutional. Proposition 187 was never enforced except in California state colleges.

A person with neo-Nazi tendencies from California promoted similar movements in other states. In the Texas legislature, a Republican state senator attempted to enact such an immigration law and organized hearings to rally support. I happened to attend one of those hearings in the San Antonio courthouse, where I raised questions about the rumors that the promoter was a neo-Nazi. His response was "affirmative". After that point, the senator disassociated herself from him, and that day the issue of Texas adopting measures like California's Proposition 187 faded away. These anti-immigrant sentiments awakened dormant racism against Mexican Americans.

The cruel irony is that California cannot survive without the labor of immigrants. Everywhere from sweatshops to agriculture to the hotel industry relies on cheap labor. These new slaves are disposable; it does not matter if the workers poison their bodies with deadly pesticides in the strawberry fields or wear out their bodies with hard labor. Once those women, men, and children lose their health, they are simply replaced by healthy workers, and nothing is lost; the profits continue coming in, and the growers increase their wealth.

Our Historical Heritage

Mexico is a producer of food. Corn and tomatoes are two of the few food staples that depend on human beings for their existence; they never existed as wild food staples. Intercultural exchange of agricultural techniques as well as ideologies was happening long before the Europeans arrived on these continents.

For generations, students have been taught the theory that Asiatic tribes crossed the Bering Strait around eleven thousand years ago. The theory is that there was once a land bridge between Siberia and Alaska and that it later disappeared.[65]

The claim is that that those people were our American ancestors, the first to arrive on these continents. Those tribes generally have been referred to as the Clovis tribes. They are supposed to be the ancestors of all the indigenous people in the Americas. This notion makes us seem alien; sometimes, invoking this idea, people would say, "after all, we are all immigrants." If this theory is correct, that would mean there has been an indigenous presence in the Americas for over eleven thousand years. That occurred a lot earlier than when the Germanic tribes invaded Europe or the Israelites took over ancient Palestine, yet no one says they are immigrants. Who knows? Maybe we just came from a different Adam and Eve!

Thus, Euro-centrism and cultural bias might be the reason for the implication that American indigenous people were incapable of developing their own cultures, that somehow they lacked the intellect to discover and invent. Some scholars claim that Amerindians would not have been able to survive and develop civilizations without the guidance of outside intervention. They study the American indigenous people with unconscious prejudice. In reality, no current theory of the origin of indigenous Americans may be valid; perhaps as new evidence is unearthed, theories will continue to evolve or change in the future.

Some archaeologists dismiss the claim that trade between North and South America existed. Some people go out of their ways to prove that outsiders visited the Americas and sparked native civilizations. They claim people from Egypt, Japan, or Denmark or even beings from outer space came here. They cannot accept that indigenous people from this vast continent could have traveled from one part of the continent to another. This theory is mostly because Europeans have never fully accepted the reality that people on this continent were as intelligent as people living on any other continent were. Some say that, geographically, it would have been an impossible feat. Yet today poor immigrants from all parts of the Americas travel on foot to reach the United States border. There is no question that even today there are great obstacles; every year, a large number of undocumented immigrants die of heat exhaustion while traveling on foot across the deserts into the United States, but some make it.

Before the coming of Europeans, indigenous people from both American continents traveled freely without borders. The national borders that exist today between Mexico and the United States—or between any other American nations—are all superficial borders made just a few centuries ago by the invading Europeans.

The different European settlers have influenced the lives of indigenous people differently so that their modern day cultures are different. Indigenous people in the Americas were forced to attend schools where their children were deprived of their native languages and customs and where they were forced to accept the religion and ideology of the Europeans.

The Spanish and Portuguese conquered most of Mexico, Central America, and South America, while the Spanish, British, French, and Dutch conquered North America. These patterns of conquest affected the indigenous peoples' languages and customs differently.

Although all the different nations in the Americas before 1492 had different cultures, languages, histories, and religions—much like every nation in Europe had different cultures and traditions—the fact remains that we are one race in the same way that all Europeans are one race even though some may be darker than others.

Hollywood films like to portray Mexicans as enemies of the Native American people, perhaps to divide and conquer, but our oral history reveals just the opposite. The stories our ancestors told us have never been recorded in the history books. These stories tell of Indian families fleeing from the United States army, hiding by day and seeking asylum by night among Mexican families. They also relate how those Mexican families provided for the fleeing Native Americans out of their food pantries. The fact that my great grandfather's family was poor did not keep him from sharing food with Apaches who came in the dark of night to ask for food because they were running from the United States army.

My mother and my aunt always showed concern about the great pain and suffering of those Native Americans. They told of how the old men spoke of the agony of knowing there was no future for their children, no young men to wed their daughters. Many died in battle.

As a child, listening to my mother and aunt retell the stories they heard from their grandparents made me angry, because I felt a great injustice had been done to those Indians. When my relatives told those stories, it was always with a great deal of sympathy for the Apaches. It never occurred to me that our families living in poverty were probably no better off. When I went to the movies, I learned to suspect the European Americans who portrayed the indigenous Americans as evil. I remember identifying with the Indians and not the cowboys.

Nevertheless, maybe the reason I identified with the Native Americans was that my aunt, who looked like a poster child for indigenous people, always accused me of being wild as an Indian or dark skinned as an Indian or dirty as an Indian. Any time she wanted to reprimand me or say something negative, she would accuse me of being an Indian. So finally I accepted my true roots very young in life. On the other hand, my aunt had grown up all her life with an illusion that she was not an Indian. She was typical of many Mexicans and Mexican Americans. It is sad that some families in our community still cannot accept their indigenous roots. In the United States, the acceptance of our indigenous roots is becoming more commonplace, but in Mexico the denial still exists, and the myth originally promoted by the Spaniards that somehow one is inferior if one has indigenous roots continues. Racism in Mexico and the rest of the Americas is sometimes more prevalent than here in the United States. In South America the upper class prides itself on speaking of "our Indians" (*nuestros indios*) as if they were property to be used and manipulated. Mexico likes to keep its indigenous people in poverty. They are allowed in the museums for the amusement of tourists, but they are never to be part of the household except as servants.

Many years ago, after I started living in San Antonio, Texas, a woman who saw blond women and children coming from Mexico and speaking Spanish decided that there must have been a white slave market there. She imagined blond children kidnapped in the United States and sold to Mexicans. She even got a day care center to place posters warning parents to keep an eye on their children. What this poor woman did not know is that in Mexico, the majority of Mexican families who are wealthy come from European stock, and they never allow their children to marry outside of their caste. This European descended minority owns and runs the country, while the majority of Mexicans are mestizos or indigenous and for the most part poor. Thus the white elite who come shopping in the American malls are not kidnapped children from the United States but the upper layer of the Mexican nation.

In the United States, our identity has always depended on the political ruling class. We have been denied the right of self-determination and have been assigned many names, with the exception of the term *Chicano*. Perhaps we need to reassess ourselves, to come up with a new term that identifies us as legitimate United States citizens without cutting us off from the indigenous roots to which we are eternally bound. I personally like the term "indigenous mestizos of Mexican descent," because it makes no bones about who we are and in no way hides the fact that we are mestizos. We belong to indigenous people, heirs to the soil of this nation, who lived on this continent for thousands of years before Europe was even aware of the existence of this land. The indigenous people cultivated the land, built cities, created nations, and managed the land from Alaska to Tierra del Fuego.

There were different tribes, different nations, and different cultures but only one race. From the Incas to the Mayas to the Mohawks, we are all one race with countless tribes and nations all living and striving on these wondrous continents, because these continents belong to us by birthright. This land had a different race than Europe, different languages and different societies. But they were societies who governed themselves, lived with families, and worked to provide for the needs of their communities. We were a noble race made up of diverse cultures. We were never savages. One has only to study Mesoamerica to see the large variety of languages spoken in just the region of Mexico. When studying a language like Nahuatl, one can find definite grammatical patterns, and while this Mesoamerican language is completely different from European languages, it was capable of expressing sophisticated ideas. Poetry, politics, religion, business, and government were all conducted efficiently and precisely in this language. This language developed in such a way that the aristocracy and the lower classes did not speak in the same manner. As for cultures, there is no doubt that in the Americas there was many, each of which had adapted to its environment and knew how to survive and flourish. Indigenous people did not know dire poverty in this abundant land unless there was a natural disaster; until the coming of the Europeans, who stripped them of all their lands and resources and even of their rights as human beings.

For Europeans, racism has always been a way of justifying slavery, whether in the case of Africans or in the case of Indians. In England and France, there was no one like Fray Bartolomé de Las Casas to argue the indigenous case; thus their humanity and rights as human beings never became a question. They were considered savages and subhumans, so the Protestant churches never questioned the mass extermination of indigenous people in the North American continent and sometimes even provided a theological justification for the massacre of Indians.

One could argue that perhaps Bartolomé de Las Casas and other friars like him might be responsible for the greater indigenous populations in Latin America or that the Spanish spared the lives of indigenous people by keeping them as slaves. However, we should never pretend that the Spaniards showed any more mercy or respect for the indigenous of these continents.

While some of the Catholic missionaries sent over to the "New World" as young priests took their mission of evangelism very seriously, the Spanish military and adventurers came to exploit the people and lost no time in enslaving them. The conquerors branded indigenous women and sold them as slaves. Some women had multiple brands, showing how many times they had changed masters. The mestizo race was not born within Catholic matrimony; it was born in plunder and violent rape. Malintzin (la Malinche) is the Mexican symbol of those unions. She was a daughter of an Aztec royal family. When her father died, her stepfather gave her away to a Mayan royal family. A prince from this family presented Malintzin and other young women as a gift to Hernan Cortes, who took the women, baptized them, and handed them out to his captains. Malintzin was baptized Marina. When Cortes realized how intelligent she was, he took her as a concubine to help interpret for him. At the time she was approximately seventeen years old. Later they had a son named Martin. She also learned to speak Spanish, her third language. She proved a valuable asset for Cortes; she was immortalized and vilified as the mistress of conquerors. Once she had fulfilled her usefulness as a translator, Cortes gave her to another captain, Juan Jaramillo.[66] Later, when Cortes returned to Spain, he married a Spanish woman in the Catholic Church, which probably started the tradition of Spaniards abandoning their indigenous brides. In Mexico, Spanish soldiers would often take young brides and claim them as slaves. When they got tired of them they would just abandon them and sell them to someone else.

Although it is romantic to believe that Spaniards treated those indigenous women well, in reality, they called them "horse-hair savages." Many of the Spanish families in the Americas were not aristocratic families from Europe. They were the descendants of soldiers of fortune who got their wealth with the edges of their swords. Upon gaining riches and respectability, they would return to Spain and marry Spanish women. Later, they would return and keep enslaved indigenous women as their servants and concubines. Spanish fathers rarely recognized the mestizos who were born from those unions. The offspring became servants and were taught to respect the Spanish women of the wealthy homes, but often they were also taught to disrespect their own mothers and sisters in the same way their fathers mistreated the Indian women.

Our race cannot take pride in this conquest; the Spanish conquest was not a romantic conquest. Mexican literature about the first century of Spain in Mexico tells us that Indian women were routinely raped by the Spaniards who used them as slaves. Families were broken up and their lands plundered. The people of Mexico were left landless and without wealth.

Today the extermination continues. In the United States, many indigenous people continue to live in subhuman conditions on reservations. Without sufficient fertile land, they try to eke out a living from some of the most arid lands in the nation, often with little water and without electrical power. Segregated and ignored, they lack resources to raise their standard of living. They live in desperation.

Many reservations have high suicide rates and high rates of drug and alcohol abuse. Their children suffer from malnutrition and lack of education. They are the silent Americans, the forgotten Americans. The United States has parceled out and divided reservations until the inhabitants barely have sufficient land to distribute among themselves. Thus, the extermination of the American Natives in Mexico and the United States has been universal.

On the other side of the Rio Grande and the Sonora desert sits the United States' largest indigenous reservation. While it may be called Mexico, there is no question that the intent for this land was that it should remain as a reservation for Mexicans. After all the best lands were taken over, after the United States took over California, New Mexico, Arizona, Texas, and other parts of the southwest; it decided that it would draw its borders. Between Mexico and the United States there are no real natural borders, just imaginary borders; that is why it is so hard to control immigration. The United States could have invaded Mexico and continued its land grab, but it did not want the land south of the border; for some reason it did not appeal. Perhaps it was because the land appeared infertile and most of the gold had already been pilfered by the Spaniards. The United States of America today feels it made a mistake, so today there is another land grab. This time it is in Chiapas. Now that the United States and other Europeans countries realize the value of the vast oil reserves buried underneath Chiapas, they make sure Mexico gets the weapons necessary to obliterate the Mayan people.

The Mayan Zapatista rebellion of 1994 tried to change the scenario, but the Mexican Army soon invaded Mayan territory, taking military tanks and weapons into the Lacandon jungle. While this silent war is one of America's most cruel wars, it is at the same time the best-kept secret. Only occasionally, when documents such as the Chase Manhattan memo make their way to the public, do we know just how much the United States has to do with the manipulation of Mexican politicians. Riordan Roett, a professor who specializes in Latin American Studies at John Hopkins University and an expert in Mexican and South American affairs, worked as a consultant with Chase Manhattan Bank. It seems that Mr. Roett wrote a memo claiming that while the Zapatistas (the Mayan rebels) were not a threat to Mexico's political stability, many in the investment community of the United States perceived it to be so. On January 13, 1995, Roett claimed that it was essential from the investors' point of view to resolve the Chiapas issue as quickly as possible by eliminating the Zapatistas.

Chase Manhattan released the memo internally. Immediately after that, the president of Mexico, Ernesto Zedillo, ordered a military crackdown on the Zapatistas. The Mexican military surrounded Mayan communities who defended their territory. While modern genocide took place and Mayan people were burned out of their homes, foreign corporations searched their lands for oil and sought to build hydroelectric plants on their soil. In America, very little was heard about the burning of Mayan homes, the destruction of their *milpas* or farms, and the scattering of the people into the hills without food and water. Their meager possessions, such as grinding mills and sewing machines, were broken or stolen. At the time, some people protested outside the Chase Manhattan Bank, which denied it had approved the Roett proposal.

The Mexican government suppressed citizen protests in Mexico. Protests also happened in the United States and around the world. Defying the military operations, some brave Mexicans went to Chiapas to record and interview the Mayan people in their struggle. They claimed the military was laying siege to their communities and keeping them encircled in concentration camps. They produced videos that showed Mayan people, including women and children, standing in front of army tanks telling the soldiers to leave their territory.

For the most part, the media ignored these events. The United States government did not issue any of its sanctimonious pronouncements about violations of human rights. Dr. Riordan Roett went back to teaching his Latin American courses at John Hopkins. These kinds of practices totally disenfranchise the rightful owners of Mexico and allow for their exploitation with the blessing of all the powerful nations of the world, who have yet to accept the indigenous Americans as human beings.

If Mexico and other Latin American countries have politicians that are sordid and corrupt, they are our sordid, corrupt politicians, because we keep them in power. We provide the secret operations and the weapons to keep the people of Mexico and Central and South America indentured to corruption. If we do not approve their politics, we tell them how to run their countries and pay them to be dictators.

When the poor, who are literally starving, come to this nation, they are persecuted like criminals. Poor people who emigrate from Mexico and other so-called third world nations in the Americas often come here because they are displaced in their own countries. If someone who wants justice for those people speaks up, he or she is branded a communist. The rulers of the People's Republic of China are real communists; they profess it. But the United States treats them with kid gloves because our capitalists have sold our nation to them. They have conquered us without having to raise a hand or fire a shot. Mao Tse Tung used to say that the United States was a paper tiger; time has proven him right. Today our government sees communist threats only in those nations that are trying to free themselves from imperialism.

As the European and Asian populations grew, many have immigrated to North and South America. But there is also a population of people here that has also continued to grow. This population has not had an outlet for its growth. Since the invasion of the Americas, our indigenous and mestizo populations have never emigrated in large numbers from the American continents. There has never been a massive emigration of indigenous Americans or mestizos to Europe, Asia, Africa, or Australia. American indigenous people have the right to move within their own lands. They just want a better life within their own continents. It is only natural that they want to do as the Europeans did by coming over here for the past five centuries. They are immigrants but not illegal; human beings who have committed no crime should not be illegal. They are, as Supreme Court Justice Sonia Sotomayor stated, undocumented. They are seeking economic refuge in the United States just like the millions of immigrants who have come from Europe, Asia, and other continents.

Archaeologists like to talk about the Bering Strait, claiming that our people also immigrated to this continent. Europeans like this theory, because it eases their guilt about their invasion of the Americas; but just as valid is the idea that perhaps our people have existed on these continents for as long as human beings have existed on other continents. After all, these lands contain all the living elements that human beings need to survive; these continents are not a planet in a far away galaxy. It is just as easy to say that the indigenous Americans immigrated to Asia as it is to say that Asians immigrated to this continent. The difference is that sometimes scientists seek not the truth but facts that will satisfy their hypotheses. At the present time, what we know for sure is that our indigenous roots and the physical characteristics that bind us together on these two continents distinguish us from the European Americans and others who have come to our shores during the past five hundred years. There is only one issue preventing our acceptance as United States citizens, and it is race. It is not culture, or religion, or language, or national origin.

Many Europeans who come to the United States are considered Americans in one generation; if they come from England, Canada, or Australia, the assimilation is even quicker. Bob Hope came to the United States as a young man, and by the time he reached middle age, European Americans wanted to elect him president even though he was not even born here. It was not because of his experience with government but because he volunteered to entertain the troops overseas and acted American so well. As the old adage says, it's not what you know but who you know, and he knew many politicians. In recent times, when California elected Arnold Schwarzenegger as governor, there were some rumblings about his prospects for the presidency of the United States and the possibility of changing the Constitution to allow him to run. He used to have more access to the White House than any fourth- or fifth-generation American of mestizo Mexican descent. Why? Because he is Austrian and wealthy.

In this country, race defines who you are and to what caste you belong. The myth that the caste system does not exist is simply a myth; the caste system is alive and well, and race is the determining factor. If you look indigenous, you belong in the lower caste no matter what side of the border you were born on or how many generations you have lived here or how well you speak English or know the so-called American culture. If America would stop propagating the notion that this is an open society where everyone can be successful, it would at least be honest; instead, it blames us for our unwillingness to merge with mainstream society, propagating the idea that somehow our poverty is due to this unwillingness.

At the same time, our intellect is always being questioned. There is an idea that somehow our lack of progress in this nation is due to our inability to compete at an intellectual level. The idea that somehow we are mentally inferior is constantly being reinforced by those who insist that any advanced civilization that existed on our continents before the arrival of the Europeans had to come from either another planet or another continent, such as Asia or Europe. Some anthropologists are constantly trying to prove that it was the Egyptians who build our pyramids or the Japanese who developed the advanced pottery found in America. But agriculture, mathematics, art, politics, and language were just as advanced in this continent as they were elsewhere. In Mexico, there existed a large and rich variety of languages. Many of the people at that time spoke several languages and conducted business along a long trade route. These routes brought them in touch with a variety of cultures not only their own region but also far beyond. They went all the way into Central America to the south and into what is now the United States to the north. Utah, California, New Mexico, and Colorado bear archeological testimony to the cultural exchange between all the indigenous tribes in the north.

Merchants from ancient Mexico came north to trade gold for turquoise. Relics of ancient Native American ceremonial vestments adorned with gold bells show evidence of this trade. The technique for processing gold and silver shown on those bells existed only in Mexico at the time, although the art developed much later in the southwestern United States.

The social relations among neighbors in the Americas can be demonstrated by how they shared their cultures. Corn can only spread through human interactions. The fact that the earliest corn plants were developed in central Mexico but that corn was found all over the northern and southern continents shows that there was trade between all the American nations. The Uto-Aztecan family of languages encompassed peoples and cultures ranging from Oregon, Utah, the United States southwest, Texas, Mexico, Guatemala, El Salvador and Honduras. The fact that some Native Americans speak similar languages to indigenous Mexicans is another hint of relationships between ancient Mexicans and ancient Native Americans. Finally, there are some close religious connections, such as the jaguar cult, which spanned from Mexico to Peru. Who worshipped the jaguar first is not clear. Nevertheless, there is no question that many early American nations communicated with each other.

The art of poetry was not a new art; it had a long and scholarly tradition. Some Native American groups preserved their histories and literatures in a pictorial manner, and this practice was developing into a more sophisticated phonetic alphabet when the Europeans arrived.

It is claimed that the Aztec Empire was in decline when the Europeans arrived, but there is no question that there were other tribes or nations in Mexico who very well could have taken their place and continued the flourishing of a Mexican culture. We will never know, because the conquest destroyed all of Mexico's advanced culture in less than a century. While remains of the ancient culture still exist, Mexico has never been able to recover the splendor and grandeur of what once was, because the key word in any civilization is education. In the ancient Mexican culture, education played a very important role, and while the system may have been elitist, a vast number of children attended school and prepared for leadership roles in the government.

Our ancestors were able to develop great civilizations on these continents without outside influences; the art was unique, the culture was unique, the sciences were unique, and the ancient Mesoamerican calendars were not imitations of Asian or Egyptian calendars. It is obvious that our ancestors possessed great intellects, so why don't European Americans get it? Why can't they conceive that we might be as intelligent as they are? Do they fear that if we find out we might rebel against being treated as inferior?

It has been said that during the Nazi regime in Germany, the propaganda machine repeated lies until they appeared to be facts. In our society, we experience similar tactics; white supremacists propagate the big lie that Mexican Americans and other minorities score lower on college entrance exams because of their intellectual inferiority and that because of Affirmative Action, superior European American students are kept from attending college. This is a belief that is widely held, but the truth is that there is not a single college who keeps any low-performing student enrolled, regardless of race. If a minority student fails, he or she is out, if not by the first semester then by the second semester. That is as it should be, but the fact is that many mestizo students who attend college work hard and often surpasses students of other races. At the University of Texas in San Antonio, people of all races graduate, yet many times top students are young Mexican Americans. Even when our students surpass all expectations, they are not always recognized, because being mestizo and intelligent is a concept so alien to most

European Americans that they are suspicious of any successful mestizo students and refuse to recognize them.

Why is this hate so prevalent? Is it because every European who arrived in America came to claim territory that previously belonged to indigenous Americans? The indigenous people were different; they were not white, and they spoke different languages and had different religions and different cultures than Europeans. To Europeans in the United States, Mexican Americans looked identical and were no different than other American Indians. The invasion by Europeans began with violence against the native people of the United States and continues in racial hatred today. There is still racial violence against Native Americans; most of them live in dire poverty and are powerless to protest. Some Native Americans leaders go to Washington seeking equal rights and equal medical and educational protection, but those issues are not a priority for our politicians. Mexican Americans also go to Washington seeking rights and immigration reform, but those issues are not a priority for Congress either; it plans to get to them by and by.

An American Tragedy: The Enslavement of a Continent and Its People

For thousands of years, indigenous American people coexisted with their neighbors and never engaged in any great wars that annihilated entire populations. There is no question that tribes in America often battled one another over territorial rights, but in general they had established boundaries that determined their territories and knew one another's migration patterns and habits. The land was rich and vast so they respected their neighbors' territories. Their conflicts were never large enough to eradicate entire tribes completely in the manner the Europeans would later rampage and ravage the land. It was not until the Europeans arrived and started to take large portions of land and rivers that belonged to the indigenous people that the American Indians started to war among themselves and the European invaders for territorial rights.

Europeans took wild animal herds that served as sources of food for Indians. They took over waterways that provided fish and other resources. The competition for resources and territory started when Indians participated in serious wars with the illegal European immigrants and other Indian tribes. Native Americans lost men in battling the European invaders and in wars with their native neighbors.

Mexico and Central and South America saw a decrease in indigenous populations. People often died in wars, working in gold mines, or carrying heavy burdens for the conquerors in the territories they explored. Spanish or Portuguese soldiers violently murdered others for their sheer entertainment.

The distinguished Mexican historian Miguel Leon Portilla, a scholar of Aztec history and literature, states that there are presently more than forty million native people in the Americas. He also reported that in central Mexico, the original Mexica population had decreased by 1620; today there are only 1.5 million Nahuas (descendants of Mexicas). Those Indians are still struggling to preserve their cultural identity and their lives.[67]

When the European illegal immigrants arrived, they had a thirst for the wealth they could gain by stealing territories and possessions from native peoples. Spanish, Portuguese, British, Dutch, French, and Russian conquerors stole land in North, Central, and South America.

Europeans have never acknowledged our true identity. They have come up with many theories about where we came from and how we got here. From the time they arrived, they have claimed that this is a New World simply because they were previously unaware of its existence. Today many people still call the Americas the New World. The Europeans knew about India but were not really familiar with its people. Columbus decided he had reached Asia, and thus the people on these continents were Indians. As a collective name it worked for them, because there were so many cultures, languages, and nations in the Americas that no one name would have been truly accurate.

The eradication of the Native American cultures and peoples began the instant Europeans set foot on these lands. It is evident from the vocabulary used to describe the Americas. To them, it was a new world where the quickest explorer could possess lands; all he had to do was chart a map and claim territory in the name of his king or queen, regardless of who lived in those territories. European immigrants never considered the land to be owned by the indigenous people who lived, farmed, and hunted in those particular territories. Pope Alexander VI in Rome, the Spanish Rulers, and Queen Elizabeth of England handed out deeds to American land.

According to Europeans, this was a new world devoid of humans; to them, the indigenous people were savages, because they were a different race with different cultures, societies, and religions. The fact that their societies were dissimilar to Europe's determined the degree to which they were considered human. Denying their human characteristics made it easier for the Europeans to justify their plunder and steal from the indigenous nations. It is easy to steal if you can make the claim that the objects you have stolen did not belong to anyone human. If you were a Christian, all you had to say was that those people were not human; they were savages. God sent the Europeans to prosper from the fresh bounty of the Americas; they had found a new life and abandoned the worn out, decaying world of Europe.

In order to accomplish this feat, it was necessary to deny the existence of human populations in the Americas; they spoke of the New World, but it was not a new world. It did not exist on another planet. It was just a new neighbor Europeans had never encountered before. Today many people continue to speak of the Americas as the New World. They still cannot admit the fact that these continents were only new to them.

The Europeans accomplished the feat of pretending it was a new world by giving different titles and names to these lands. The name America is attributed to a relatively unknown German mapmaker who thought Amerigo Vespucci was the first to see these continents. Early in history, some people claimed Vespucci had never set foot on the American continents, but today it is admitted that he did sail to the Americas. Vespucci's main contribution to the discovery of America was that he was the first to contradict Columbus: he claimed that America was not part of Asia as Columbus had believed.[68] These continents may have received the name America because Amerigo Vespucci wrote a book in 1503 called *Mundus Novus* (New World).

According to the letters Vespucci sent to Lorenzo de Medici, the people of the Americas could be viewed as rational animals: "Having no laws and no religious faith, they live according to nature. They understand nothing of the immortality of the soul. There is no possession of private property among them, for everything is in common." Vespucci's description, while recognizing that the indigenous people were rational animals, went on to deprive them of any real human attributes. Vespucci writes, "Let us come to rational animals. We found the whole land inhabited by people entirely naked, the men like the women without any covering of their shame."[69]

Thus, the belief that indigenous people were complete savages and had no concept of European ethics or of the immortality of the soul allowed Europeans to view the people of America as subhuman.

Today, the same sentiment prevails toward the Indians of Brazil: the Akuntsu tribe, which had only seven people in 1995, is now reduced to five after one of the oldest members died. The bulk of the tribe was killed by gunmen and ranchers who took over their lands in 1960s and 1970s.[70]

Thus, the Indians of South America continue to die in order for intruders to take over and possess the land. Genocide of the indigenous people continues, and the world remains silent. The Indians are not placed on the endangered list; they fare worse than animals, and they have no advocates for human justice. Their lands continue to be stolen. Nothing has changed since Amerigo Vespucci wrote *Mundus Novus* in 1503.

Vespucci's description of the people of the Amazon perhaps describes the people who still live there. However, if he had traveled to Mexico or Peru, where the Aztecs or Incas lived, he would have found entirely different societies capable of building sophisticated structures and temples. He would have found people who knew the art of weaving and made beautiful clothes. In Peru, Vespucci would have found convents of women who devoted their lives to weaving beautiful fabrics for the Inca emperor and his royal family, who was believed to be divine. Later, during the conquest, the Spanish would go into those monasteries, make slaves of the women, and send the fabrics to Spain. These women were overworked so much by the conquistadors that many of them died.

In Mexico, Vespucci would have found a patriotic society with kings and royal families who lived in palaces as well as an established aristocratic class. Localized land holdings were called *calpoltin*; they were ruled by a chief or lord. There were also the *teuctin*, a hereditary class of lords who took tributes from the common people and had serfs. They also had a *huei tlatoani*, the great speaker who ruled over all the people. In his nation, he was considered an emperor.[71]

In those days, Tenochtitlan (today Mexico City) had a population of about 200,000 people, making it one of the largest cities in the world during the time of the conquest.[72]

The polytheistic Aztec religion was complex; they worshipped the sun god Huitzilopochtli, provider of light and essential for the growth of plants, and the rain god Tlaloc, provider of water and god of agriculture. Quetzalcoatl or Ehecatl was the god of wind, creator of windstorms and our breath. Each god represented an essential part of nature. There were many gods, but Aztec religion was more complicated than just a religion of nature. Beyond those gods, there existed a higher being, Ometeotl, the god beyond all gods, a god that existed in the pantheon of gods above the twelfth level of heaven. This was the creator god of all things, the highest god, the god of duality, male and female, a supreme being, a type of transcendent god.[73]

The Aztecs had arrived at their theological metaphor of God through poetry, which they called "Flowers and Song."[74]

Nevertheless, it was Vespucci's version of the indigenous Americans that captured the European imagination, promulgating the idea that those people in America were just a notch above animals and had no notion of property rights or any theological concepts of God. Thus conquering these continents would be no worse than a hunting expedition. The people of the Americas were savages without souls.

Traveling into Mexican territory, the Spanish found a sophisticated culture; the Aztecs had a strong blend of religion and history. It was their belief that the gods created them and would return to destroy the earth. The world existed in the era of the fifth sun, and it would again be destroyed by the end of this cycle. The Aztecs feared the end would come in the form of a terrible earthquake.[75]

Michael Coe claims that they had two separate myths about their origins, one that had them coming from Aztlan (land of the White Herons) and one that had them coming from the land of the Seven Caves.[76]

Historically, Mexicas claimed they went to the valley of central Mexico from the north, from a place called the Seven Caves or *Aztlan*. Although the Aztecs mentioned this story repeatedly, there is no precise geographical area with a connection to this myth. Those seven caves are yet to be discovered. They could be in northern Mexico or the southwestern United States. No one knows how far from the north the Aztecs traveled to get to Tenochtitlan. We know from the legend that their god Huitzilopochtli told them to leave Aztlan. The Aztecs were a warlike tribe who went to central Mexico to fight as paid warriors. After an arduous trek that lasted over one hundred years they arrived at Lake Texcoco. There their god talked to a priest named *Quauhcoatl* and instructed him to show the people a place where they would see an eagle perched on a cactus eating a snake. This place, an island on the lake was the site to build their new kingdom, their promised land. In those times, it was a snake-infested swamp, which the Mexicas cleared and developed. When the Spaniards arrived two hundred years later, it was a beautiful city, capital of a large empire. Hernan Cortes claimed it was larger than most Spanish cities. It was well organized, teeming with businesses; city leaders would regulate the sales of goods to ensure fairness. The Mexicas also had a large trade market with their neighbors, travelling and collecting taxes all over their empire. The *Codex Mendocino* has pictorial representation on how they recorded their trade and kept their accounting.

Diego Durán, a missionary and historian of Mexico during the sixteen century, was the first to use the term Aztlan. According to Durán, "These people, like the others who populated the country, departed from the Seven Caves in a land where they had lived, called Aztlan." The name Aztlan means "whiteness" or "place of the Herons."[77] The term *white* does not really refer just to an ordinary white; it is more like the whiteness of a halo, a sacred white. When the Aztecs referred to their sacred visions, they often mentioned a white glow. The myth of Aztlan gave the Aztecs a feeling of being a sacred race, a proud people who had advanced the civilization in their kingdom. According to Fray Diego Durán, that was where the Aztecs claimed to have originated. A German explorer named Humboldt made the term Aztlan popular in Europe and in the United States.

When Cortes arrived in Tenochtitlan (Mexico City) for the first time, he was astonished at its size and architecture. He noted that the city was built inside a lake and surrounded by large bridges built to access the metropolis. The city had perfect streets, and the waterways were also used as means of transportation. Inside the city, commerce flourished. There were vendors of all types of birds, including chickens (probably turkeys), quail, and eagles. There were also vendors for deer, rabbits, fish, and other types of edible meats. There were stands where people could have their hair washed and trimmed and shops that sold jewelry, medicinal herbs, and sweets like honey, corn syrup, and agave syrup. Cortes also mentioned the abundance of vegetables in the marketplace and claimed they even had stands that sold prepared meals.[78]

According to other Spaniards who first arrived in Tenochtitlan, it was a beautiful city with all types of buildings and large markets with great assortments of merchandise. There was no lack of social structure, and the communities were well organized, but soon the Spaniards plundered the towns and villages and left the Aztecs literally without possessions and culture. They left them like wild savages.

According to Fray Diego Duran, after Tenochtitlan was conquered, the city was devastated by smallpox, a plague brought by a black man who accompanied the Spaniards. A large number of people died since they had no immunity or cure for this new disease.[79]

Juan Ginés Sepulveda, the church leader in Spain, denied the humanity of the Aztecs, the Incas, and other Native American cultures. These civilizations flourished for thousands of years, parallel and unknown to cultures in Asia, Europe, and Africa.

The American indigenous people were deeply religious. In Mexico, their temples attest to how religion played a central part of their lives. Nevertheless, their religions were completely different from Christianity. Judeo-Christian religions claim God made men in his own image, but Indians often suspected this god was really made in the image of Europeans. The truth is that people often make their gods in their own images. While the concept of deity varies from one religion to another, the human spirit always yearns for a god. The indigenous people of the Americas were no different than the god seekers of Europe, Africa, or Asia. They all had gods, many of them made in their own image; people always want their gods to act and be like them and reflect their own values. Looking at all the wars carried out in the name of the Christian God or Allah, we can see how we often make gods in our own image. We attribute to God our thoughts and prejudices. According to the Spaniards, the Aztec gods were flawed, and that justified their plunder and murder of the population.

In our American culture, we continue to prefer images of God that match political ideologies; we often forget that our God is a universal God and loves all creation. People often prefer to have a narrow political god dictated to them by their politicians.

In Mexico, the Spanish Catholic Church left Mexicans with the idea that people must suffer in order to reach heaven. People who believe this pie-in-the-sky creed believe everything in heaven will be better, but for now, they must bow, kneel, and obey the church, which allows them to be exploited and remains blind to their suffering. The high dignitaries of churches continue to live in splendor and riches. Modern human beings continue to worship a god made in their own image while continuing to enslave their brothers and sisters. Indigenous people in the Americas continue to be enslaved and to live in poverty, and our religious institutions remain blind to these injustices just like the early European immigrants.

This is all part of the Aristotelian philosophy according to which the only purpose of some people is to serve as slaves and not rebel.

This belief was combined with the idea that God had created the American continents so that Europe, which was becoming overpopulated, could settle its "poor and wretched" masses in the so-called New World, a free for all where everyone had the right to be regardless of whom they were displacing in the process. This concept of European immigration was popular until a few years ago in the United States. The embodiment of this idea is written on the Statue of Liberty. This idea was discarded when the poor and wretched started coming from south of the border and the huddled masses began to look like the indigenous people Europeans had removed in the first place.

At the time of the conquest, Spain was a powerful nation that had enlightened people among its elite. Some of these people were undergoing an ethical revolution. Among those scholars were church priests who held to a strict ethical code and who brought up the case of the nature of the indigenous people of America. As a result, the idea that the indigenous people were fully human often arose in the Catholic Church; unfortunately, the Spaniards who conquered America did not share the same sentiment. They considered the natives slaves and chattel, denying them rights to land and property. After the nature of the indigenous people of America was settled in the courts, the Indians of the Spanish conquest were subjects of the king and were supposed to be treated as such. Yet Spain was far away, and the Spaniards in the Americas did not treat the Indians as free men but as slaves. This long history of exploitation continued in Mexico and South and Central America for centuries.

In the United States, for the most part the indigenous did not serve as slaves; they were displaced and massacred based on the idea that the "only good Indian was a dead Indian." European immigrants also spread diseases, such as smallpox, and they killed the buffalo, an important food staple of many tribes. The buffalo provided food, warm clothing, and leather for shoes. Thus, the indigenous were left without land, food, and—after the Indian massacres—without warriors to defend their homelands.

Sarah Vowell, an American historian, writes that when King James heard about the terrible plagues in America among the Native population, he responded by thanking "Almighty God in his great goodness and bounty toward us."[80]

Historian Jill Lepore states that when the British saw the Indians torture Englishmen, they were considered "the perfect children of the Devil," while the Europeans were the antithesis, "the perfect children of God."[81]

It was this early version of Manifest Destiny that converted the American continents into a *tabula rasa*, a land without civilizations or history, a paradise where the Europeans could come and take possession of land, natural resources, and slaves. It was this doctrine of Manifest Destiny that was later spelled out in Theodore Roosevelt's policy toward Mexico and Central and South America. The policy continues to exist today. It omits the divine aspect, but the practice of the idea remains pretty much in place.

Today it is obvious that indigenous people are still not considered humans; in the Lacandon jungle of Chiapas, crimes against humanity have been perpetrated on the Maya people for many years. These crimes are just as evil as those suffered by the Jews during the Holocaust in Germany or by blacks during apartheid in South Africa. Mayan houses were burned, farms destroyed, and water supplies contaminated, and the people escaped to wander in the jungle without food or shelter. Many Mayas became ill and some died. Those returning to their villages were encircled by the army and detained like prisoners in concentration camps. While many Mexicans actually risked their lives to document those actions on video tape, most Americans did not view those tapes and remained silent about the Mayan suffering. They continued to deny the status of Mayas as real human beings.

Exploitation of indigenous people continues five centuries after the violation of these continents by the European aggressors. This intense, merciless plundering has never been compensated for by any European nation. No nation has ever admitted that their savage invasion devastated and destroyed two continents on which the original dwellers perished by the millions at the hands of plundering, bloodthirsty invaders. On the contrary, they view themselves as benevolent purveyors of civilization.

Today this doctrine of racial superiority is not limited to Europeans but is sometimes shared by other immigrants who also exploit the indigenous people. In Peru, Alberto Fujimori, a Peruvian from Japanese parents, was elected president. Soon his regime became a cruel and bloody dictatorship under the patronage of Japan and the United States. After many years, his government was toppled. He fled Peru and obtained refuge in Japan, which refused to extradite him to face charges for crimes against humanity. In the end, Fujimori went to Chile, where he hoped to launch a comeback, but his efforts failed, and Chile eventually extradited him to be tried and condemned to a long prison term for his crimes.

Europe was a Christian continent; as such, they claimed to believe in the sanctity of human life and the love of God. When they invaded the American continents, those Christian men committed savage and unspeakable crimes against the indigenous people and the African people they brought as slaves. They simply believed that anyone who was not of European stock was racially inferior. Historically, there is not a single European nation that did not help exploit the American continents and Africa and Oceania in the name of God. Nevertheless, Christian religious dogma or teachings never played a serious role in the settling of the Americas as history books would lead us to believe.

As Lepore notes, "Whether Indians were fully human is a question writers about the war would take up again and again but would ultimately leave unanswered."[82]

Indians in United States reservations still live in dire poverty, lack appropriate housing, and have poor health care. Many reservations get their health care from young interns who do not have experience treating serious problems. Many reservations depend on charity to provide food for their families. Young people lack education and cannot get jobs; their lives are no better off than the lives of those in third world countries, but the United States is one of the wealthiest nations in the world.

Mexican Americans also suffer under similar conditions in the southwest of the United States, living without good sanitation, housing, or adequate food. American Indians and Mexican Americans have no goodwill ambassadors in Washington, Hollywood, or the mass media to voice their suffering, because other Americans choose to ignore their inhuman treatment.

During the conquest of South America and Mexico, whenever

missionaries really took their religious calling seriously, the Church immediately reprimanded them. We must remember that the church also gained a great deal of wealth from the exploitation of the Americas. In the eighteen century, the Catholic Church ordered the Jesuits to close and disband their missions in what are today northeastern Argentina, Paraguay, and southern Brazil because they had tried to defend indigenous people from kidnapping and slavery.

It was sheer avarice that brought throngs of Europeans to these American shores; their mass migration was so great that it displaced and dispossessed all the nations of the Americas. The result is that the descendants of the original people have become aliens in their own lands. The goal of the invaders was to amass as much territory as possible in the names of their kings or queens. Spanish encomiendas gave lip service to the throne as far as treatment of Indians, but their actual goal was self-enrichment. To soothe their consciences, Europeans created the myth that the ruthless, bloody crimes committed against the American nations were done in the name of God. They claimed that their intentions were to convert and civilize the indigenous people, so their military atrocities and plundering were justified.

This was not a vacant land, and it was not a new world; it had been populated by many people in both hemispheres. To the north, in what is now the United States and Canada, there were many nations with unique cultures who spoke over three hundred languages; today there are still about fifty languages left among Native Americans.[83]

This land was never vacant; it was inhabited just like Europe. North and South America contained peoples of many cultures; those cultures formed many nations and spoke many languages and are still here. In the United States, many tribes still use their ancestral tongues. Navajo, Apache, Hopi are just a few. Likewise, in Mexico you can still hear languages like Nahuatl, Huichol, Quiche, Tzotzil, Zapotec, and Otomi.

Today Mexico downplays its indigenous population, often treating them as a dying people, non-existent, a branch of native Mexicans that no longer plays a vital role in Mexico. In truth, the indigenous population continues to increase in Mexico despite its poverty, and they continue to live voiceless and faceless, without political power or the ability to educate themselves and advance from slavery to freedom.

In present times, the worst and most unfortunate thing about the mestizos is that they have been taught to identify with the conquerors. Many traditions acquired from the conquistadors have become part of the mestizo mentality. Many of those who enforce the military order in Mexico are mestizos, and they protect the powerful *terratenientes*, or landowners. The manner in which Mexicans treat women—machismo—is inherited not so much from an indigenous tradition as from a Spanish one. Don Juan, representative of the macho image, comes from Spain, not Mexico. As a result of this attitude, women are often treated as having no rights. When the Spanish came to America, they did not believe that the people of this continent were human; women were just chattel to be used and discarded. To the Spanish, women were just objects to be traded and sold in the marketplace.

It was under this kind of slavery that Mexican mestizos and indigenous people became poor and landless peons. Today, this dire poverty often makes Mexicans sacrifice their lives in attempts to come to America to escape hunger and find work. This history of being poor and landless has caused them to move to America, where they often continue to live in poverty and misery. While most dream of being able to live as respected working families, they often find that they still do not have adequate housing, medical care, or education to live comfortably in this country. Many of these people are undocumented aliens and are treated as criminals. They do the jobs most Americans will not do; they do slave work for slave wages.

There has been a systematic extermination of American indigenous people since the landing of Columbus. The genocide started with Columbus and continues today all over the American continents. History books do not write about the terrible holocaust that took place during the conquest—the burning of people, the murder of children, and the extermination of whole populations.

Fray Diego Durán describes how the Aztecs were massacred by the Spaniards while they worshipped in their temple. Durán writes, "In this way the 'preachers of the Gospel of Jesus Christ,' or rather, disciples of iniquity, without hesitation attacked the unfortunate Indians, who were naked except for a cotton mantle, ... fleeing from those ministers of the devil. As they were unable to do so, all were slain and the courtyard was drenched with the blood of those wretched men. Everywhere were intestines, severed heads, hands and feet. Some men walked around with their entrails hanging out due to knife and lance thrusts."[84]

In North America, Indians in what are now Canada and the United States were also nearly extinguished by the European illegal immigrants. Immigrants in North America were no different from the Spanish Conquistadors; they too engaged in savage treatment of the Indians.

The British, like the Spanish, killed Indians in horrendous ways. For example, in one incident, the Pequot Indians killed an outlawed member of the Puritan community who had been exiled after he kidnapped two young pilgrim girls. The Pequot killed the Englishman, thinking he was a Dutchman who had stolen from them. It was a case of mistaken identity; the Indians could not tell a Dutchman from an Englishman. The Pequot returned the girls unharmed. The English decided to take revenge on the Pequot. John Underhill and John Mason decided to attack by night while the Indians slept. They surrounded the community and prepared to set it on fire. They entered the wigwams and started to torch them. The Indians who woke up and tried to defend themselves were killed with fire, swords, and muskets. The British were attacking at their wigwams' exits so that the Indians could not escape the inferno. All the Pequot Indians died. According to some of the men who witnessed the attack, "it was a fearful sight to see them thus frying in the fire, and the streams of blood quenching the same, and horrible was the stink and scent thereof."[85] According to Mason, many of the dead were women and children. In all, there were six to seven hundred people who died that night. [86]

After the attack at Mystic River, Connecticut, the British set out to look for more Pequot Indians. When they found them, they killed the men and took the women and children, selling them as slaves.[87] John Underhill used his skills at burning down Indians when he joined Governor Kiefft's war against the Dutch and the Indians of the Hudson Valley in the 1640s.[88] In 1675, the English army burned down the Narragansett village in Rhode Island. Several hundred Indians died that time.[89]

According to Sarah Vowell, what was left of the Pequot tribe was sold into slavery, and large numbers of those slaves went to Bermuda. Others remained in the United States as parts of other tribes.[90]

This cruel holocaust was very similar to the horrendous burnings and killings the Spanish committed in Mexico and in the southwest of the United States. The Europeans who came to America all had the blood of the American Indians on their hands. The Pilgrims were no better than the Spaniards. They all desired to see the Indians dead by fire or weapons. Those devastating acts were often done in the name of religion. According to the pilgrims, God had willed the crimes they committed.

Sarah Vowell writes that Mason praises the Lord for "burning them up in the fire of his wrath, and dunging the ground with their flesh: It is the Lord's doings, and it is marvelous in our eyes!" John Underhill claimed the Bible also condemned Indian women and children to death.[91]

In Mexico and South America, the Spanish and the Portuguese conquistadors committed harsh and violent crimes in their search for gold, slaves, and land.

In the United States, after the conquest of Mexican territory in the 1840s, many Mexican Americans were lynched by European Americans coming into the new land that had just been declared United States territory. For example, during the gold rush in California, many of the first gold miners were Mexicans who had staked land claims. A large number of prospectors were European Americans, Europeans, and even Australians. They were all newcomers to California. They often came and attacked the Mexican gold miners, destroying their camps and lynching many of them in order to claim their mining territory. In Sonora, a mob of two thousand recent immigrants came upon a Mexican gold mine campsite and burned it down. They rounded up hundreds of Mexicans in a corral and lynched and murdered over a hundred men.[92]

Another victim of lynching was a pregnant Mexican woman who was approached by an Anglo miner who had previously come to her abode and tried to attack her. The second time he came, she stabbed him. Her sentence was to die by hanging, and she proudly accepted her punishment, even adjusting the rope and bidding the crowd good-bye.

Today, the crimes are still violent and harsh, but they are also silent. Muskets, crossbows, and arrows no longer kill American Indians. Today, they are silently strangled to death by depriving them of fertile land and water. American Indian reservations have the highest unemployment rates in the United States, some as high as 80 and 90 percent. They also have some of the highest mortality rates. Many die before they reach fifty years of age. Some residents lack sufficient food, some lack water and electricity, and most lack medical care. Many die of drug overdoses, while others commit suicide over despair. These dire living conditions are factors that explain their short life spans.

The lack of good schools and health care postpone prosperity and extend the poverty of Native Americans in one the wealthiest nation in the world—a nation that became wealthy by exploiting Native Americans, stealing their lands, and killing their people. Today, this low-intensity genocide is taking place while other ethnic groups continue to grow. American indigenous groups continue to diminish.

In Ecuador, Chevron and Texaco went into the territories of the Cofan and the Secoya forest tribes to build oil wells, leaving a trail of pollution. They also drilled in other Indian lands and left the same polluted earth. Chevron and Texaco deny polluting or dumping hazardous waste. According to the *New York Times*, which has published several articles on this subject, this argument has been going on for several years. Juan Forero reported the pollution on October 23, 2003, while Simon Romero and Clifford Krauss wrote a similar article on May 14, 2009. The argument continues, and nothing much has been done to stop the contamination. People in those areas got sick from the oil and slush left behind, condemned to live in a polluted environment. They continue to get sick and die from the oil and chemical pollution left in their drinking water. Meanwhile, Chevron public relations people produce television commercials about how well they treat South American children.

In the United States, the Indian population is no better off. Some of the Navajo in Arizona raise sheep for wool and for weaving blankets. Their reservation is in the hot desert without water or electricity; they get their water by driving to a watering station miles from their homes. They depend on one source of water, which they need for their families, their herds, and to clean the wool they spin and use to make their blankets. Their meager income derives from the blankets they sell. If a place such as Grand Canyon National Park has water to serve tourists, why can't the Indians have water to serve their community?

Yet even the water under them is threatened. Uranium-mining companies use the water for the mining process. Extraction of uranium has been going on for several years; wealthy corporations know there is a great deal of wealth under the desert. People from the reservation who were employed to serve as miners have been exposed to radiation. Many have contracted cancer, and their families have been contaminated as well. Industrial operations use large amounts of water and produce large amounts of waste; placing uranium mines and power plants in Navajo lands does not benefit the people but detracts further from the little they have.

Among the Sioux, life expectancy is less than fifty-five years. Unemployment ranges from 80 to 90 percent. In America, no one should live under such dire conditions. It is a crime; it is genocide! We are killing God's children.

The Mexican indigenous people who come to work in the United States do so because they too lack land and water. They have only humble farms or live in tattered slums in urban areas. Most lack electricity, and they lack schools and medical care. They are jobless and cannot even afford food. They are not better off than the American Indians in the United States. If they try to come to the United States looking for work, they are treated as criminals by law enforcement, and in some places they are killed by racist gangs.

Sometimes those racist gangs are not even punished for crimes against people from Mexico or Central America. That happened in the case of Luis Ramirez, a Mexican national killed by a gang of white teenagers in Shenandoah, Pennsylvania. Although five teenagers allegedly participated in the crime, only two went through a legal trial, and they were later absolved. The two European American teenagers, Derrick Donchak and Brandon Piekarski, claimed Ramirez started the fight. The fact remains that someone punched Ramirez, and someone used a blow to his head to kill him. During the trial, a demonstration occurred outside the court. It was against the immigrant. Among the demonstrators, a man showed up with a sign claiming that self defense knows no race. That the teenagers acted in self defense is doubtful; as if one solitary person would take up against five men! Fortunately, some pro-immigrant groups have been applying pressure in the wake of this injustice, and the murder is now being investigated by the FBI.

If police officers do not enforce the law, there is no question that European Americans will continue to murder indigenous people with impunity. Another case of violence occurred against a fourteen-year-old boy from Honduras, who died. The responsible high school students were not even arrested.

It is important to notice that these events do not get a lot of publicity in the mass media; the death of the Honduras youth was aired on Spanish-language television. The death of Luis Ramirez was reported by Sean D. Hamel of the *New York Times*.

Our own government treats Spanish-speaking undocumented immigrants like criminals, sentencing them to two years in harsh prisons, such as the one in Maricopa County, Arizona, where inmates are subjected to extreme heat and poor diets. There, the sheriff Joe Arpaio feeds prisoners fifteen-cent meals and punishes them if they smuggle sugar or cigarettes. He makes sure that punishment makes the prisoner suffer, and his tent prison offers no major protection from the elements. There is no patriotic American protesting against this inhuman treatment, because many of the people are immigrants from Mexico or Central America. Movie stars, who are quick to protest against inhuman acts in other countries, remain silent about the civil rights abuses in their own backyard.

If an immigrant advocate tries to point out these injustices, anti-immigrant groups quickly respond with false slogans. For example, Thomas Saenz, a civil rights leader, was nominated to run the Justice department's civil rights office; he was quickly removed from the list of candidates after pressure from anti-immigrant groups. He was too good a lawyer, so they accused him of being pro-Mexico. President Obama took him off the list and substituted Mr. Thomas E. Perez, a man with a Spanish name but who was not known at the time for a strong stand on immigration. He does have a Spanish name, so Mexican Americans concerned about their brothers should be satisfied, right? We are destined to be invisible and silent in America.

The threat to Mexican Americans has reached Arizona with the recently enacted SB 1070. In spite of assurances to the contrary by those responsible for the bill, this new law essentially requires all Mexicans and Mexican Americans to carry papers to show whether they are citizens or legal residents. The question is, would the same treatment be extended to people who do not "look Mexican"? In other words, would it extend to the non-indigenous?

In Texas, the requesting of papers has also affected a young Mexican student. In June of 2010, a young man who attends Harvard University in Boston, Massachusetts, was asked for identification at the airport. He showed his student ID, but security agents continued to investigate him and found that he came to the country with his undocumented parents at the age of four. Hence, his stay was not legal. The fact that he had spent most of his life in the United States and knew no other city but San Antonio, Texas made him an illegal immigrant. Does our country, where he received all his education, now send this valuable, intelligent student back to Mexico even though he can become a great asset to the United States? We often go overseas to get what we call educated workers, but we reject Mexican students who are here simply because they came as young children of undocumented parents.

This questioning of undocumented students has also come up in California, where a young Mexican woman who was a senior at a university was not allowed to graduate because she had come as a child brought by undocumented parents. She was sent back to Mexico, where she had no relatives or a place to stay.

This type of hostility toward Mexicans can create a great chasm between American society and the Mexican American community when the latter sense that their people are not welcome in the United States.

Downfall of Mexico

This was the way it was told, this was the way it was related,
and for us they came to draw it on their papers
the old men, the old women.
They were our grandfathers, our grandmothers

— Miguel Leon-Portilla,
Los Antiguos Mexicanos a
Traves de sus Cronicas y Cantares

A nation is like a human mind; it has to have memory of its past if it is to comprehend its future. Mexico has suffered a case of amnesia. Spain was able to wipe out much of its language, its history, and its culture when it invaded Mexico.

Mexico has not been able to recover from the loss of its native languages, history, or culture since the conquest. This also occurred in South America, where Spain transplanted its language, history, and culture with the edge of the sword in the name of the Catholic faith.

In Mexico, the Spaniards sent the children of the wealthy leading Aztec families to study in newly established monasteries, where they learned the Spanish language. They learned the Western culture of the Catholic Church, which was rooted in Latin and Greek. They also learned the history of Europe; they became good Catholics and were loyal to the Spanish crown. The Spanish missionaries even tried to consecrate some Indians as priests, but the Catholic Church denied them the right to become priests for many years. They did not want them in leadership positions.

Priests like Bernardino de Sahagún, who wrote the book *Historia General de las Cosas de Nueva España* (*General History about the Affairs of New Spain*), did attempt to gather the history, culture, and even religion of the Aztecs. Today his book is very valuable when learning the culture and history of Mexico, but here again it is a Spanish interpretation done by a man not trained to do sociological or cultural studies; his goal was to teach Christian doctrine. Nevertheless, he left one of the greatest collections of ancient indigenous literature and history. He felt he needed to know what those people understood if he was to teach them a new faith.

It is said he established the rule of interviewing different communities about their religions and cultures and later comparing the accounts of the different communities to see what they held in common. He would then write down the cultural and religious ideas they had in common as part of their history. This was a very scientific method in which to do studies of cultures. Today he is considered a pioneer in the field of human and cultural studies. Many anthropology professors claim Sahagún was the world's first ethnographer.[93]

From Sahagún's documents, we have learned the names of the gods the Aztec worshipped and some of their beliefs. Sahagún claimed he learned the Nahuatl language so he could understand what the Aztecs believed; he claimed that in order to teach Christianity you needed to know what the natives believed. It is also very important that he recorded the history of the conquest of Mexico as narrated by Mexican natives, who spoke of the Spanish massacres and the deadly disease of smallpox that came with the European invasion.

Much of what we know about the history and customs of Mexico prior to 1521 we have learned from Sahagún and other friars who were attempting to communicate with the people they were charged to convert. On the other hand, there were priests like Bishop Diego de Landa, who ended up burning Mayan manuscripts because he deemed them the work of the devil. Bishop Landa was supposed to convert the Mayas, descendants of one of the most advanced civilizations in Mesoamerica. He dismissed their culture, causing irreparable damage to our knowledge of their culture and history.

Priests like Diego de Landa were the typical Spanish conquerors who did not have tolerance for the religions and cultures of the indigenous people. They viewed them as evil savages who needed to be civilized.

Those people who did not become enslaved and were able to escape the onslaught of the conquerors continued to follow their cultures and use their native languages. However, they did not have a way to preserve it, because they lacked the skills of the traditional keepers of knowledge, the scribes who wrote in red and black ink (Aztec and Mayan scholars and teachers). If one travels and meets those indigenous people today, in many cases they are ignorant of their past; while they may hold on to the language and to religious and cultural habits, much of their history and science has been lost: the arts of mathematics, engineering, architecture, and even the practice of preserving their history in writing.

By the temples and palaces left behind, we know that they were architects. By their art, we can tell they were great artists. By studying their mathematical skills, we know the Maya had developed the concept of zero independent of outside influences. The Maya also had skills in astronomy and were able to predict the movements of the celestial bodies. Atamalcualiztli, an old Aztec poem entitled in Spanish "Fiesta de Los Tamales de Agua" ("The Feast of Water Tamales"), refers to a time dedicated to the gods where tamales had to be made of pure corn and could not contain any fruits, vegetables, or meats. The poem told it was also a time to worship the heavenly bodies; the ancient astronomers followed the planets in their yearly journeys with great precision. This ancient poem traces the journey of the planets and gives them metaphysical and religious significance. People would gather at night to worship the heavenly bodies. Edward Seler, a German scholar who dedicated his life to the study of ancient Aztec history and literature, described the significance of this poem in detail. Seler's work was a classical study of the codices and the Nahuatl language. He wrote the *Commentaries to the Codices Borgia* in 1898.[94]

When we talk about some of the oldest ruins in Mexico, we usually think of the magnificent pyramids. Monuments like the famous pyramids of the sun and the moon of Teotihuacan are still admired by many who visit them.

Just as magnificent were the famous ball courts, which flourished all throughout Mexico and as far as New Mexico and possibly Utah. The sport, which could best be described as a combination soccer/basketball game, took place in a large court with small hoops on the wall through which the players were supposed to throw a small, hard rubber ball by hitting it with parts of their bodies, possibly their trunks and legs. Traces of this sport go back to the time of the ancient Olmecs. Among the relics found around Montalban, Mexico were reliefs showing thirty-two ball players wearing wide pants, knee guards, gauntlets, and visor helmets and hauling a ball.[95]

This game was not for wimps; the rubber balls were so hard that they left the bodies of the players bruised and bloodied. Professor Richard Adams, an archaeologist at the University of Texas in San Antonio, would say in his lectures about the Aztecs, "Those games were so popular that some of the spectators would get carried away and often gambled their life savings on the sport." The games were such a part of their culture and religion that wherever the Mesoamericans went, they took their sport with them. Today, archaeologists have found ball court ruins and digs not only in Mexico but also in New Mexico, Utah, and other parts of the United States.

These games were more than just a sport; they had strong religious significance. Among some of the ruins of sports arenas, one can find depictions of gods, such as Quetzalcoatl, one of the patron gods. The legends of those ball games are as old as the myths found in the Popol Vuh (an ancient Maya text) and the Aztec codices. In the cosmic poem about the sacred water tamales, those ball games were a symbol of the cosmic struggle; they had religious connotations. The poem describes gods representing Venus and other celestial planets as the players in the game. The travel of those planets though the sky was accurately and scientifically described. Festivities took place at night in order to have the sky and stars as a giant stage. The name of the poem reflects the time of the year when they ate only tamales made from solid corn and not with fruit or meat fillings in them. It was a time when people only ate certain foods they considered sacred.

Some anthropologists have suggested a theory for why certain civilizations flourish while others remain dormant. They believe that in order for a civilization to flourish, it needs to have a certain amount of leisure time, time to think abstract thoughts. A population that spends all of its time hunting and raising meager crops does not have time to devote to other endeavors. To produce a great civilization, the people in a society need to produce large quantities of food; they need agriculture. Therefore, such a society must have a large part of its population involved in farming and allow others to have time to meditate on religion, politics, science, and art. Darcy Ribeiro, an anthropologist, states that the high cultures are societies which have surpassed the stage of their agricultural goal of sustenance. In other words, cultures that produce more than they require flourish.[96] This allows these societies to have time to form hierarchies with different layers of authority. This type of civilization was typical of Mexico and Peru as well as many others in the Americas. The history of flourishing kingdoms in Mexico goes back to the time of the Olmecs, the Bajio phase, around 1350 BC. Dr. Richard E. W. Adams believes it was in this era that the Olmecs began to set themselves apart from other indigenous cultures in Mexico.

According to Dr. Adams, the Olmecs and some of their neighbors were the first in Mexico to set up societies with complex political, economic, and religious systems.[97]

The Olmecs existed in the region around the Tuxtlas in what is now the state of Veracruz from around San Lorenzo up to Laguna de los Cerros in Chiapas.[98] The word *olmec* literally means "the people of the land of olli" (rubber). They existed centuries before the Mayas and other Mesoamerican kingdoms came to prominence, but their civilization influenced all neighboring cultures in art, religion, and social order. They were one of the oldest civilizations in the region. They had an organized religion centered on jaguar worship, and they set up family hierarchies based on a myth that claimed their ancestors descended from marriages between Olmec women and jaguars. Those families made up the Olmec aristocracy.

The story about the Olmec women and the jaguars is a myth similar to that of Zeus among the ancient Greeks, who came down in the form of various animals and made love to women. The jaguar cult existed early and became widespread. Thus, it is not known if it originally came from Mesoamerica or if it traveled from South America. Artifacts with the symbol of jaguar worship can be found in both hemispheres. Dr. Muriel Weaver states that in religion, "According to Stirling (1943), the remarkable carvings depict a woman copulating with a jaguar, a union that might have given rise to a mythical offspring combining jaguar and human characteristics."[99]

The Olmecs left behind large monuments and relics with traces of a sophisticated religion and politics. Some of the artwork they left behind features infants with jaguar characteristics, such as snarling mouths, fangs, and "a deeply notched or V-shaped cleft on the head."[100]

Their impact on sculpture, farming, and sociopolitical organization were to have great influence on other Mexican civilizations that followed theirs. The Olmecs have long vanished, but they have left behind their art, which is found in giant stone heads and other types of stone carvings and artifacts.

The Olmecs influenced the Toltecs and some of the later prevailing societies, such as the Mexicas, Mayas, Tlaxcaltecas, Otomis, Tarascos, and Zapotecs. The Toltecs later became the elite civilization of Mexico; they were artists, architects, farmers, and business people. They left behind a splendid culture. The Aztecs probably defeated the Toltecs in war but continued their civilization; the Aztecs never lost respect for the Toltecs but actually admired them. Much of the folklore we presently know about the Toltecs we have learned from the Aztecs, who formed a mystical cult around them and left many poems in their honor.

The Aztecs built elaborate kingdoms; they had palaces, temples, and sophisticated schools or *calmecac*, academies where the noble families sent their young. The Aztecs had a highly developed language, Nahuatl (Mexica). Today there are Nahuatl scholars, such as Miguel Leon Portilla in Mexico and Frances Karttunen, a professor at the University of Texas in Austin. They are able to explain the grammatical rules of the Nahuatl language.

Mexico had a large number of societies, each speaking its own language and developing its own culture. Mexico shared its religion and culture with other peoples. Today archaeologists are still debating whether Mesoamerica was the mother culture of these continents, because they are believed to have developed the first crop of corn, which would become the Americas' primary food source.

Although racial intermingling has occurred over the last five hundred years, Mexico still has one of the largest Indian populations in the Americas, consisting of several million people who still speak the original languages and observe indigenous customs.

When the Spaniards arrived in Mexico, the Aztecs were the most powerful of the Mesoamerican kingdoms. They called themselves Chichimecs, meaning from the lineage of dog people. In Nahuatl, *chichi* means "dog," and *mecatl* means "rope" or "lineage." There is no question that during the Spanish conquest the Aztecs were known as the wealthiest, most powerful and culturally advanced nation in Mexico and possibly in North America.

They had networks of trading routes with their neighbors. Many of those neighbors had fought wars with the Aztecs and lost and were forced to pay tribute. According to Fray Diego Durán, some of the tribute paid to the Aztecs included deer; shells; honey; fruits, such as pineapple; precious stones; and *huipiles* (dresses). Some of these clothes were elaborately embroidered in all colors; some used dyes, and others used bird feathers. Other tribes gave blades and shields for war. Still others provided cacao, jewelry, jaguar pelts, and many other kinds of tribute.[101]

If a community was too poor to pay material tribute, they paid with their children, who were distributed among the Aztec lords. They gave their children as tribute, the males to be used as slaves and the females as concubines.[102]

This was important when the Spanish arrived in Mexico. The roads built by the Aztecs to receive tribute were used by the Spanish as well to travel and collect Aztec tribute. The fact that those tribes were paying tribute meant they were sacrificing their work for the Aztecs, which meant that they really wanted to revolt against the Aztecs. The Spanish would provide them with an opportunity to rebel, so many tribes joined the Spaniards, but after the defeat of the Aztecs came the slavery of all of the Mexican tribes. The greed of the Aztecs was their downfall and later the downfall of all of the tribes in Mexico.

Fray Alonzo de Molina, the author of the first Mexican-Spanish dictionary during the sixteenth century, titled his work *Vocabulario en Lengua Castellana y Mexicana* (*Vocabulary of the Castilian and Mexican Languages*); it could have been titled *Vocabulary of the Castilian and Nahuatl Languages*, since this was the spoken language of the Aztecs. This early dictionary is today used to translate the Nahuatl language. Molina's is the earliest, most authentic dictionary of the Nahuatl language. He probably called it Mexican because the nation was also known as Mexicas. As explained before, the Aztecs called themselves Chichimecs, a name they carried proudly. When they arrived from the North to the central valley of Mexico, some say that they acquired that name because they were despised by other tribes as nomadic barbarians; thus they were called dog people. But Chichimec just could have been the totem name they chose because they respected the dog symbol. Judging by how many people are willing today to have their dogs cloned or spend large sums of money on them, they too could be called dog people. Thus, the Chichimec might have just liked being dog people. In any case, they referred to themselves as both Chichimecs and Mexicas.

Their warriors' aggressiveness and self-determination were considered virtues, but if the Chichimecs lacked wealth and culture, they soon conquered the highly sophisticated Toltecs, who were known for their skills in art, agriculture, and science. The fall of the Toltecs is often attributed to the barbaric Aztecs, but there may have been other factors involved, such as droughts and lack of food and water.

The Mexicas might have conquered the Toltecs in war, but they also might have conquered by intermarriage. Much like the Romans in Europe who absorbed culture from Greece, the Chichimecs immersed themselves in Toltec society, and soon they too could claim to be a part of this elite culture. The Aztecs never forgot the greatness of the Toltecs, whom they admired. Aztec poetry shows their pride in having inherited the Toltec culture. The following poem is an example:

And in this manner [the Toltec] believed
in their priest Quetzalcoatl
and in this way they were obedient,
and given to the service of god[103]

But as the Chichimecs gained military control of Mexico's territory, they began to build a powerful theocracy in the name of their god, Huitzilopochtli. (The name could mean "the hummingbird from the south" or "the hummingbird from the left." Scholars are still investigating this term). Powerful priests and the military ruled this theocracy; the military controlled all the nations around them by threats. Their religion mandated human sacrifices of blood to keep the sun alive and moving in the sky.

There is no question that it was this terrible military obsession with death that finally brought them down to be conquered by the Spaniards, who often got rival tribes to fight with them against the Mexicas. At the same time, it was this military might that made it possible for the Aztecs to establish the largest commercial route in Mesoamerica. The *pochtecas* or traveling sales representatives visited all over the empire, setting up trading posts with all their neighbors in the area; those Aztec businessmen served a dual purpose as salesmen and as spies to learn whether the other tribes were rebelling against them.

These salesmen would dress down to hide their true wealth as they journeyed around the empire.[104]

Meanwhile, as the city of Tenochtitlan grew, so did the powerful Huitzilopochtli religious cult demanding human sacrifices to the sun god. Wars provided the opportunity to capture sacrificial victims. The military intimidated their neighbors by threatening to use their people as victims for the sacrificial altar if they did not follow the laws of the Chichimec kingdom. They used religion to control people and justify human sacrifice. This was not much different from more modern times when countries fight in the name of their faiths and try to impose their own religious ideas on other nations.

The resentment of tribal neighbors against the Aztecs prevented military unity among the people of Mexico. When the Spanish came, neighboring tribes readily took up arms against the Chichimecs. Tenochtitlan became the target of Spain because it had the one thing the Europeans coveted most: gold. After the fall of the empire, gold left the shores of Mexico by the shipload, and the invasion of Mexico continued until every tribe in Mexico was enslaved.

Communities like the Maya, who contributed so much to the culture of Mesoamerica, continued to exist as the least ravished by the Spaniards, perhaps because their contributions were of intellectual wealth and not gold. The Spanish had no desire for knowledge, so the jungles of Yucatan and Chiapas swallowed up the Maya, who had introduced architecture, astronomy, agriculture, science, mathematics, and art to Mesoamerica. Of late, foreign corporations are coveting their natural resources, treasures such as oil, water, and mahogany.

We may like to romanticize our Aztec heritage, but we are a multifaceted people, and our roots could extend to any tribe or nation in Mexico. Perhaps it is best if the majority of us can no longer claim just one Mexican tribe as our own. Just like the Aztecs, who claimed the culture of the Toltecs, we could take the best traits of our indigenous ancestors and claim them as our own. The fact is that we do not have only one ancestry in Mexico but diverse ancestries.

The century following the conquest of Mexico saw the largest loss of cultural identity. This loss of identity was justified by the Catholic Church as necessary to convert the Indians to Christianity. In reality, it mainly served to enslave the people of Mexico. With the defeat of the

Chichimecs, the Spanish army captured Tenochtitlan and destroyed the Mexica Empire.

The Spanish took the children of the noble Aztec families from their parents and isolated them in monasteries so that they would grow up without knowledge of their history, heritage, religion, and language. They did it in the name of God. Perhaps those zealots who often destroyed and burned codices, the written records of the Chichimecs and Mayas, really believed that all the written history of the Indians was the work of the devil. Yet depriving our ancestors of their culture was the true evil, committed by the invading Europeans in the name of Christianity.

Left without self-determination, without a country, without families, without a language, and without economic resources, the Spanish conquest damned the Aztecs and all indigenous people into slavery.

One only has to read Fray Diego Durán and Bartolomé de Las Casas to understand the torture and torment the people of the Americas suffered under the flag of Spain. The invaders amassed their wealth using indigenous people as beasts of burden and as slaves. They also destroyed their cultures, their heritage, and their languages. Those who fled to the mountains and jungles survived with their identity and language intact. Even today, Mexico has millions of indigenous people who still speak their languages and live their cultures without a country they can call their own. Today the conflicts of Chiapas and other regions of the American continent can trace their roots back to this conquest. Their history is the endless repetition of the merciless invasion of the Americas. European invaders with more sophisticated weapons and technology slaughtered the indigenous people, who at the time still depended on outdated weapons. Europe had not used bows and arrows since the Middle Ages.

Historians like to romanticize the so-called new world, but it was only new in the sense that Europe was ignorant of its existence. The people who lived on these continents had been here for as long as the Europeans had lived in Europe. The division in our planet was not between a new and an old world; it was only between European and American worlds. The biggest myth ever promoted by the Europeans is that there were not any inhabitants in the Americas except for a handful of roaming nomads. The fact is that in both North and South America,

Europeans were still fighting Indians in the nineteenth century. This was not an empty continent; Europeans declared it so because they preferred that indigenous people just disappear, remaining invisible and voiceless.

Today the battle against Indians continues; in Chiapas, in the jungles of Brazil and Peru, people are still suffering from land loss. In Europe, no single ethnic group has suffered such a systematic and prolonged genocide. The systematic extinction of the indigenous people of North and South America has lasted for five centuries.

Perhaps if Europe had not been overcrowded five centuries ago, the invasion of the Americas never would have taken place. Europeans never would have felt a need to emigrate. They would have found sufficient land, food, and material wealth so that they would not have had to risk their lives to come to this continent. The Europeans who came to this continent were desperate; they knew that their only salvation was to come across the ocean, risking death from sea storms and diseases. They were as desperate as Mexican, Central American, and South American immigrants are today when they come to the United States.

Europe had become so overpopulated that it no longer had room for economic development and expansion. The plagues of the middle Ages were a sign that something was going wrong in Europe. Europe's population grew at such a rate that it no longer could provide for the basic needs of its inhabitants. The crops that grew in Europe were not sufficient to maintain the continent. One has to remember that European crops were limited to a small number of vegetables. The Europeans were mostly carnivorous, while the Americans were mostly vegetarians. In Peru, indigenous people cultivated wide varieties of potatoes and corn. In Mexico, they cultivated squash, tomatoes, sweet yams, corn, beans, and many types of tropical fruits, such as mangos, pineapple, and avocado. The Americas, unlike Europe, never had any serious food crises except when they overpopulated their cities much as the Europeans did in Europe. When the Indians overpopulated, they just moved to a different region. Unlike Europe, North and South America were never overpopulated for long periods. The reality is that Europeans did not come here primarily for religious freedom; they came here for economic and material reasons. Religious freedom was secondary. Survival was primary, which is why they came from the dungeons and prisons. The Puritans were a small group; the overwhelming majority of Europeans did not come here escaping oppression and looking for religious freedom, but that is the myth historians like to propagate. Not all the Spanish conquistadors came to bring the faith to the heathens, but that is what they would have us believe. As years passed and new generations of immigrants started to come from Europe, they brought slaves and servants from Asia and Africa, and the population of foreigners grew. Vast numbers of people started to replace the indigenous population. In South America, a fight to increase territorial domain took place between Portugal and Spain. France and England, who were latecomers, took over what are now Canada and the United States; they also brought over a large number of African slaves. Their history in North America is the same as that of the Spaniards and Portuguese elsewhere on the continent. During early colonial times, the Spanish dominated the flow of immigration into South America, but centuries later, a large number of Italians and Spaniards also displaced the indigenous people in South America. In Argentina, the introduction of the Winchester rifle in the late nineteenth century eliminated a large portion of indigenous people. Today in Brazil, the elimination of the last of the indigenous people in the Amazon continues. In the United States, the Native Americans continue to be victims of the European Americans; their deaths do not come from bullets but by way of slow starvation and deprivation of basic needs. Mexico, with a large indigenous population, is now engaged in this type of war. It is relatively bloodless, because weapons are used only to maintain brutal concentration camps. This war is being waged by European Mexicans and mestizos who have been indoctrinated into believing that somehow their own people are subhuman and do not deserve to exist. The main reason they are able to keep the indigenous people of Chiapas prisoner is because powerful European and Asian nations have made the indigenous people targets of their greed for possessing more land and resources in Mexico. Some people claim Canada wants the silver mines, France wants to exploit hydroelectric power, the United States wants oil, and Mexican ranchers want land for cattle raising. Thus they plot to kill Mayas as if they were not humans; they treat those Mexicans as if they were invisible and voiceless. All the superpowers congregate around Mexico and, like children under a piñata, try to shake and break up Mexico and watch the goodies come out as they greedily scramble for its natural resources and cheap labor.

In Peru, a son of Japanese immigrants took over the government and soon established a brutal dictatorship with the backing of the United States and Japan. During those fateful years, indigenous people were sent out to fight a war against Ecuador over long-established boundaries. Why? Because it would eliminate indigenous men who might revolt against the dictatorship and its foreign sponsors.

These continents were so enormous that even five hundred years of systematic murder and persecution of the indigenous population has not been able to destroy them completely. Over the last five hundred years, a large portion of the indigenous population has mixed with other races, mostly Europeans and Africans. In Mexico, mestizos comprise the bulk of the population, but large communities of indigenous people remain. In South American countries, indigenous populations have been marginalized and continue to be used as slave labor. South American authors have written many books describing atrocities that still take place in their countries against the poor. It is the mestizos who make up the majority of the working poor, while the indigenous live under worse conditions.

Except for recent events in Bolivia, almost nowhere in the Americas can one say that indigenous people or mestizos lead their nations or that they are allowed to participate in the decisions of their societies or even to determine their own futures. Today most indigenous people live in dire poverty, and their dreams of living in prosperity and freedom are only dreams.

When the Americas become overpopulated, the indigenous suffer the most, because while they never immigrated to other continents, they are displaced to make room for immigrants; for five hundred years, their lands and territories have been confiscated. At no time in history have these people ever immigrated to Europe, Asia, or Africa; they have never invaded another continent. Recent migrations of indigenous and mestizo people from the Americas seeking to escape poverty and find new opportunities in Europe have been resented by Europeans, who keep passing more restrictive immigration laws. They think that their illegal immigration into the Americas was noble, while the reciprocal arrangement is criminal.

It has only been in the past few years that Mexicans, Central Americans, and South Americans have immigrated to Europe, where their fate is often not any better than when they come to the United

States. In Europe they still do the hardest work, and like in America, they are still seen as immigrants without rights.

Bob Libal, a *Sojourn Newsletter* reporter, wrote about a vigil held with Amnesty International and the League of United Latin American Citizens (LULAC) to bring attention to the conditions at the T. Don Hutto Family Detention Center in Taylor, Texas. This prison is a for-profit private prison, a place where illegal immigrants and their children are kept. Some of the children are infants. Others are older, but they all have one thing in common: they are all treated as criminals. They get very little medical care, their diet is poor, and they get very limited schooling.[105] Those children are getting only an education in crime. This is America, which is supposed to demonstrate justice and liberty, yet it imprisons children who have not committed any crime. They are only guilty of being born to poor immigrants who come looking for a better life, just as millions of Europeans came just a few years ago. The only difference is that they are not European, which makes them subhuman. Prisons like T. Don Hutto are now being set up in other places. They will increase in the United States as more immigrants without papers are imprisoned, and their children will not know what it is to live outside a prison; their lives will be scarred forever.

Today people in the United States from Mexico, Central and South America, and the Caribbean usually carry the immigrant label even when they are American citizens. They continue to live as abandoned people, voiceless and invisible to justice.

Our Roots Are in America

We are Americans with a long American history; we are the people who inhabited the North American continent for thousands of years. Yes, Mexico is also part of North America. The division is not a natural border; it was drawn up to separate Mexico from the United States after the United States appropriated Mexican territory as a result of the Mexican-American War.

At that time, the southern border of the United States was delineated using stone markers, a very controversial way to separate our territory from Mexico. The government in Washington DC also wanted the Rio Grande, so it gave Texas part of the former Mexican territory. They wanted to ensure that they would be able to use the Rio Bravo or Rio Grande for shipping traffic to transport goods and merchandise. President Polk declared war on Mexico and sent in troops; Mexico had no choice but to defend its territory. Unfortunately for Mexico, it was still weak after its war of independence with Spain. Mexico lost the war with the United States and signed the Treaty of Guadalupe Hidalgo in 1848; as a result, Mexico lost California, New Mexico, Nevada, Arizona, and parts of Colorado, Wyoming, and Utah. Since Mexico had never recognized Texas's secession in 1836, from its point of view the treaty also meant the loss of Texas.

Some Anglo Americans take pride in claiming they are descendants from the Mayflower Pilgrims; others take pride in their British, Irish, German, French, Polish, or Italian origins, claiming that their ancestors came to make America great. Mexican Americans were never viewed as true American citizens, despite the fact that our ancestors have lived in what is now the United States since long before the first waves of Europeans arrived. While it is true that today there is immigration from Mexico and other Spanish-speaking countries, the reality is that many of us never immigrated to the United States, and our families have lived here for more generations than the European Americans. It takes just one generation for European Americans to be called Americans, but Mexican Americans are rarely accepted as such. There are plenty of excuses for denying us our rightful place: our speech, our traditions, our language, our culture, and even our religion are not "American" enough. Some claim we are not Western in culture and do not share a language with the rest of the United States. While it is true that many Mexican Americans still speak Spanish—the older generation is typically bilingual—most of the younger generation speaks only English. The great majority of Mexican Americans worship in Christian churches (Catholic or Protestant), wear western clothes, and attend schools where they learn Anglo American history and philosophy and Western culture. The truth is that all the statements made by detractors of Mexican Americans are just excuses for exclusion; it is the color of our skin and our indigenous looks that make the real difference for a racist Anglo American culture. Although it is not always overt, racism is alive and well in our country. Many Anglo Americans claim Mexican Americans do not want assimilation when in fact we have been discriminated against and segregated since the time of the Treaty of Guadalupe Hidalgo. The early California Constitution granted voting rights only to white (Spanish) Mexicans, leaving out mestizos and Indians. The amended constitution read as follows: "Every white male citizen of the United States and every male citizen of Mexico, who shall have elected to become a citizen of the United States, under (Article VIII of) the Treaty of Peace." A delegate from Monterey proposed to add "white" in front of "male citizen of Mexico."[106]

The emphasis on whiteness is significant because it determined how people would be treated as American citizens. When we were declared white, we should have been able to attend white schools, eat in white restaurants, and not be segregated in churches, but the reality was that we were still segregated. Today we continue to be segregated in our barrios, where we attend exclusively "Mexican" schools. Mexican Americans look different from Europeans, and we are judged solely by the color of our skin. However, Mexican Americans are not just a color; we have a history, a culture that points to the fact that we are Americans with civil rights.

Mexican Americans are not aliens that flew on a spaceship or immigrants who sailed across the ocean. Many Mexican Americans were born here in the United States and have had family here for generations. The United States has become our stepmother; our mother died. She died when we were invaded by Europe, but many of our ancestors were legitimate sons and daughters of this country, not foreigners. Our roots are in the southwestern United States, the territories that were part of the Treaty of Guadalupe Hidalgo.

Historically, ancient Mexicans were in parts of the southwest before the Spanish brought them as slaves to build their colonial empire. Archaeologists have found ruins that predate European arrival; they have discovered Mexican ball courts and artwork. Recently, some thousand-year-old chocolate was found in a New Mexico cave. Chocolate was cultivated extensively in Mexico and Central America, not in what is now the United States. Ancient Mexicans shared their culture and traded with groups to the north.

This means that interaction between Native Americans from the United States and from Mexico existed for many generations. They had learned to live as neighbors, influencing one another and sharing culture. Mexican Indians were not considered criminals when visiting their American neighbors; they all belonged on the northern continent. There was nothing illegal about traveling the continents; it was not a crime to come north of the Rio Grande. The European powers were the ones who set up borders and territories and divided the lands according to their convenience. Mexico is part of North America; it is not on another continent. Those ancient indigenous people did not have to sail to the Americas; they just walked. Today Mexicans continue to walk north, but the consequences are different; they are not welcomed anymore. They are seen as inferior and treated as criminals because of their race and their poverty.

Today the term used for non–United States citizens coming from Central and South America is very often "illegal immigrant." This is a legitimate term but one that has taken on sinister and negative connotations when applied to people from Mexico and Central and South America who come to the United States without documents. The term implies that they are criminals for daring to step into the United States without documents. The price they pay if apprehended is prison time. Today being Mexican definitely means being a foreigner, someone who does not belong in this nation. What Anglo Americans do not acknowledge is that people from Mexico and other South American countries are running to the United States because so many European aliens have gone to their countries and taken their lands. Those Spanish-speaking people have no place left to live! American oil companies, such as Chevron and Texaco, have gone to South America and taken oil. In the process, they have ruined the environment, leaving land and rivers polluted. Other riches, such as aluminum, copper, tin, and silver, have been mined in Central and South America, where corporations take advantage of lax labor laws and pollute the environment.

Europeans claimed they came here by God's will. Manifest Destiny, Theodore Roosevelt's doctrine, is not God's doctrine. Our ancient ancestors had a different viewpoint; they too believed we were here by divine destiny. Is the European god an "Indian Giver" who first gave the land to the Indians and then took it away and gave it to the Europeans?

It seems all civilizations claim divine destiny when they want land. The borders drawn after the European invaders terrorized us into surrender were made by them, not God. God did not intend for indigenous people to live in the deserts and wastelands assigned to them by the foreign invaders. In the United States, Native Americans were herded into reservations; after the Anglo American invasion of the southwest, the Mexicans got to keep what the invaders considered the worst parts of Mexico. In the west, the United States kept San Diego, a great port, and took the gold mines of California.

President Polk allowed Mexico to keep what he considered the least fertile parts of Mexico. The United States tried to invade Mexico a second time during the Mexican Revolution, when they went after Pancho Villa.

Perhaps we need to reinvent ourselves, find a powerful new name to suit us as Americans who are racially different. During the sixties, a group of radical Mexican American civil rights leaders came up with *Chicano*, a racial term that was quickly picked up by many.

Unfortunately today, some of the people who claim to be *Chicano* never say or do anything that would alienate them from standard Anglo American political policy. Some act this manner due to ignorance of our historical past and others due to political expediency.

I once asked a Mexican American politician to be more assertive in his political role in school programs; he claimed he could not afford to lose his job. He had a family to support. Unfortunately, many Mexican Americans have always lived under that cloud. They cannot afford to be without a job or get involved in political causes due to their personal commitments to their families. It is not easy for young Mexican Americans who desire to speak up for justice but cannot risk their social lives and jobs. Maybe it is up to the Mexican American community to support these young political activists.

Yes, we are a mixed social ethnic group, not only in terms of race but also in terms of culture, language, religion, heritage, and politics. I heard from European Americans that we have a separate culture, but the so-called Mexican culture that is supposed to keep us apart is only a veil. If we live in the United States, we do not have a complete Mexican culture; we have a United States culture. We go to schools with Anglo American teachers and students, study a Eurocentric curriculum, and speak English. We attend Catholic churches with Irish or German American priests and Protestant churches with Anglo American ministers. We watch American television and movies and listen to American politicians who want us to follow their political doctrines. We have an American culture. That is why we feel we need to join the Army and fight for our American principles. We join the army but not the unions; we do not advocate universal health care, because politicians tell us it wrong. In school, we have been taught that the military is good and unions are bad. We have learned that capitalism is good and socialism is bad. We have been indoctrinated to believe that American health care is good and socialist health care in England and Canada is bad. We have been taught to write only in English, and some of our Spanish is terrible. Even our Mexican food is really an American version of Mexican food.

Our role in history as cobuilders and contributors to the creation of this nation and as citizens is totally obliterated from history books.

We cleared lands to win the west and built railroads to take the cattle from Texas to Chicago; these facts rarely appear in textbooks. One of the few writers who has documented the Mexican railroad workers is Carey Mc Williams. He writes, "Mexican labor was extensively used in the construction of the Southern Pacific and Santa Fe lines ..." and "Hundreds of Mexican families have spent their entire sojourn in the United States bouncing around the Southwest in boxcar homes."[107]

Through oral tradition, I learned about Mexicans and Mexican Americans working on the railroad going from Texas to Chicago; when I was a child, my uncle used to tell stories about his experiences with the railroad. Chicago has a large Mexican American population, and that did not happen by accident; many of the early Mexican settlers in Chicago came from Texas as railroad workers.

Mexican Americans cultivated the land, rounded up the cattle, and tamed the wild horses. That is why many English words associated with ranching and cattle come from Spanish. *Ranch* comes from the Spanish word *rancho*. *Rodeo* means "round up," and *lasso* comes from *lazo*, a word for a rope hoop to capture cows. A spotted horse is known as a *pinto*, and a light golden horse is a *palomino*. The Mexican *vaquero* literally means "keeper of cows"; this word for cowboy would later be adopted into English as *buckaroo*. So if a lot of cowboy vocabulary came from Spanish, guess who was taking care of the ranch? Guess who cleared the way for building highways? Mexican Americans have always worked in the country clearing brush, in the fields picking vegetables and fruits, in the railroad, and in construction. Mexican Americans have always worked in the heat of the southwest with the sun on their backs, helping build America. Today they continue to work in our hotel and restaurant industries cleaning up rooms, washing dishes, serving, and cleaning tables. Almost inevitably, they work as servants, making low wages and doing extremely hard work, and they are often cheated out of their wages. Workers in the clothing industry often work extra hours without pay. Workers in the restaurant industry do not receive their earned tips. Upper management often keeps all of their tips when they cater dinners. When some of those workers object, they are fired. I have personally attended union organizing meetings and seen how hotel and restaurant management has broken the union's efforts by quietly firing the leaders.

Today we continue to provide large real estate developers with cheap labor. We provide bricklayers, carpenters, and concrete construction workers. Some of the homes we build sell for millions. The laborers often do not make enough money to support their families with proper food and housing.

In addition to building a large part of this country, we have also helped to defend it in time of war. During World War II, most Mexican American families with young men had at least one son in the war, sometimes more. Those young people who were not drafted volunteered. They fought courageously, sacrificing their lives and dying for this country. Most films about war events ignore the contribution of our Mexican American heroes.

World War II was not the only war Mexican Americans fought in; there was Korea, Vietnam, the Gulf War, Iraq, Afghanistan— every conflict or invasion our government has been involved in. Any time we engage in war, our children are the first to serve, yet the nation still refuses to recognize us as citizens. We remain second-class, marginal citizens. European Americans lure us into wars, and as our children go to fight overseas, we remain at home, enduring the same prejudice that prevents us from having equal representation in politics and government. We have never had a Supreme Court judge from our midst, and we have had just a few congressmen. Nevertheless, we have fought in every major war America has had since the Civil War. President George W. Bush erected the border wall between the United States and Mexico, pointing out illegal drugs and other crimes and even mentioning the threat of terrorism, and Mexican Americans continue to be looked upon suspiciously by European Americans, who treat us all as immigrants.

While some countries in Asia bring in drugs, and Russians have established organized crime, Mexicans are often blamed for much of the crime in America. We only have to watch fictional television dramas to see how often Mexican Americans are portrayed as criminals.

While the excuse for militarizing our southern border since the 1990s has been to deter terrorists from the Middle East, it is a fact that none of the perpetrators of the 9/11 massacre or the shoe bomber or the underwear bomber came here through the Mexican border. They all flew here with legal visas issued by the United States government or came as students, tourists, or travelers. Most of them were welcome because they had money, unlike the poor Mexican and Central American farm workers who simply come to work and often end up dead in the deserts of Texas, Arizona, or California because they are denied legal entry into the United States.

Yet those who arrive safely are quickly put to work as gardeners, construction workers, field laborers, maids, or building janitors. They come to generate money to support their families, and they are despised and prosecuted as criminals. Their only crime is seeking work.

Business people in the United States keep outsourcing manufacturing and highly technical jobs to Asia, leaving people in America jobless. The Asians taking our jobs are not visible; they are not here. But the Mexican and Central American immigrants are here, so they get all the blame. Media corporations, such as CNN and Fox, profit from peoples' discontent; thus we have people like Lou Dobbs spewing hate every evening, encouraging Americans to direct their aggression against Mexican and Central American immigrants.

American trade has made China the strongest and most powerful Communist nation on earth; it keeps getting wealthier and stronger, while our citizens are left frustrated and jobless. Mao Tse Tsung was right when he said that the United States was a paper tiger! For years, we were taught to fear and hate China's Communist system, and we learned to consider them our enemy. Today they have really won the battle; they get our manufacturing jobs and our money, a precarious situation for us. Our corporations are China's best friends; the real villains are Wal-Mart, General Electric, Dell, and Microsoft, as well as banks and other industries that often outsource a large portion of their skilled labor to foreign nations. A few years ago, Vice President Al Gore declared that it was fine to take manufacturing jobs to Asia because our new job market was in computer-related jobs, but now even those jobs are being outsourced to India. After the American people bailed out Chevrolet, the company decided to produce its cars in China with American money. Where are the jobs they were supposed to build in America? Even low-skill jobs, such as customer service and telemarketing, are now being conducted overseas.

A few years ago, after the devastation of hurricane Katrina, there were jobs available cleaning New Orleans. These jobs were very hazardous and unhealthy. Undocumented immigrants from Mexico and Central America performed these jobs, which not many Americans wanted. No one bothered them, because no one else desired those jobs.

Generation after generation, we continue to be powerless, without a voice in this nation. We work for the lowest wages and attend inferior schools. The tradition of building inferior schools for Mexican Americans has existed in Texas and the southwest since they became part of the United States. Segregated Mexican American schools were substandard, with inadequate supplies and poor facilities. The teaching staff was also inadequate and received lower wages than the teaching staffs at white schools.[108]

Mexican Americans do not earn enough money for health insurance and do not earn enough money to have adequate housing.

They do not have a real voice in government or a place to request justice. Our government still refuses to nominate a Mexican American Supreme Court justice, although other significant American population segments have had Supreme Court justices. Our High Court includes Anglo Americans from all walks of life—Catholics, Jews, and women. Blacks have also been represented, but not Mexican Americans. If Mexican Americans try to discuss important issues, such as education, with Washington leaders, we are ignored; we are not included in major decisions. We have no voice in the courts even when we are tax-paying American citizens.

For many years, I have been advocating the need for a Supreme Court judge, a judge that would be knowledgeable about issues the Mexican American community faces in the southwestern United States. I have proposed that Mexican Americans demand a Supreme Court judge who understands their needs. I have attended Democratic Party election meetings and Mexican American political gatherings, but while they have voted to keep the idea as an issue, it has not seemed to travel far. The usual response has been that there are only a certain number of seats available and that we cannot take anyone out of the court in order to replace him or her with a Mexican American. Some of my friends have argued that Asians are not represented in the Supreme Court either. My answer is very simple: why not do what we have done to the United States flag—just add stars? The size of the population has increased; we have a large number of congresspeople, because we believe in making sure our diversity is represented. So why can we not increase the size of the Supreme Court to include more minority groups and even more Anglo Americans? Just add seats! Let us have fifteen court members. There is nothing sacred about the number nine.

At the present time, the president has nominated a Puerto Rican woman who is very qualified and trained to do her job as a judge. I applaud and respect Sonya Montemayor, but the fact remains that Mexican Americans still do not have a Supreme Court judge. Is there not a single judge from among us that can represent us in Washington?

Could it all have to do with the use of the terms *Latino, Hispanic,* and *People of Color?* All those terms which lump us together. The different subgroups that make up the Hispanic population in the United States include people from many different cultures. A New York Puerto Rican has not had the same experiences as a Mexican who is a migrant farm worker; their original cultures are different and their histories are different. Puerto Ricans do not have immigration issues; Mexican migrant workers do not have urban New York issues. Hence, we not only need Puerto Rican judges; we also need Mexican American judges. We need Cuban American judges and Chinese American judges who know and understand their respective cultures. Does it mean these judges would always have to rule in favor of their ethnic groups? No, it just means they would understand the cases they are interpreting better. There is no question that we need to make America a true melting pot, not just a figurative melting pot. However, in order to have more judges in court, we must demand to have representation in court. We need more young Mexican American lawyers attending law school. We need more Mexican Americans in Ivy League schools studying law.

In October of 1996, there was an event called the Coordinadora 96 March, which included Mexican Americans; citizens of Mexican, Central America, and South American origin; and immigrants from many countries. People came from all over the United States to highlight the need for equality, justice, and fair treatment. This was during the years of California's Proposition 187 amid a wave of anti-immigrant hysteria that spilled over against Mexican Americans as well. It also became the best example of how our government refuses to listen to citizens that they do not accept as Americans. One hundred thousand people congregated in Washington DC from all over the nation, but only a single Latino congressman from Chicago attended the affair, Mr. Luis Gutierrez. No other congressperson or major political leader attended the rally or even sent a letter recognizing our march or welcoming us to the nation's capital. We were totally ignored; Washington continues to consider us invisible and powerless.

We are American citizens who wish to have a role in the shaping and forming of this nation just as other Americans do. We want our history told in history books, and we want to be recognized as American citizens. We want no favors, just recognition of our true significance as American citizens.

Racism against Mexican Americans is nothing new; while today most archaeologists tell us that Mexico and Central America had very advanced civilizations before the arrival of the Europeans, some people make claims attributing the rise of those ancient cultures to foreign influences. Those people feel that the Mexican and Central and South

American civilizations were too advanced to have been created by indigenous people. Some even make outlandish claims, such as the idea that these cultures were the result of a visit from space aliens (von Danikken).

Americans are xenophobic; they fear anyone who is different, especially if that difference includes speaking Spanish. Many Americans view speaking Spanish as a second language as increasing the power of the so-called Hispanic. The implication is that if a school teaches Spanish as a second language, it is betraying its nation. They believe America is going to become weak by speaking Spanish. In other words, speaking Spanish in the United States appears to many Americans as unpatriotic. Here in Texas, even department stores threaten to fire Mexican Americans if they speak Spanish to each other or to customers. The paradox is that in large cities, such as San Antonio, Texas, large department stores have learned that many of their customers come from Mexico. Those customers are wealthy and often only speak Spanish. Those stores need Spanish-speaking clerks if they want Mexican customers.

The paranoia has reached high levels in some places. Recently, a Mexican woman in Dallas was given a ticket for violating a traffic law and another for speaking Spanish. In California, undocumented immigrants cannot get drivers licenses even when that can result in serious accidents when drivers don't know highway regulations.

English is the international language of diplomats, scientists, and businesspeople, but this fact does not seem to impress America. People in other countries learn English in order to trade with the United States. Our country has many resources that the world needs, and Americans happen to speak English. Yet some Americans still fear that Spanish will take over the United States.

Some American businesses are busy learning Chinese. China is changing the language of the United States fast. We are heavily indebted to China and are trading heavily with them every day. Perhaps the United States might one day change its primary language to Chinese, since it is the wealthy and powerful businesspeople who do business with China who have an interest in the Chinese language. Who knows? China already owns a large part of the United States. We owe our souls to China. Maybe we will someday end up speaking Chinese in order to keep up with China.

But just as America is blind to the power that English as a language has, it is also blind to the fact that is just a stone's throw away from fifteen or more heavily populated Spanish-speaking nations that are growing in population every second. How long will the United States ignore the heavily populated country across our southern border? It is a neighbor who speaks a language the United States does not care to speak, a neighbor of many nations with political and economic interests that are often aligned with those of the United States. When the president of the United States has a world conference, he always goes to Europe and consults with France, England, Germany, Italy, and other European nations. Mexico and Central and South American countries are generally omitted.

For many years, those Central and South American nations have been providing the United States with a variety of raw materials, including copper, bananas, oil, tin, minerals, and produce. Today we get tomatoes from Mexico, grapes from Chile, bananas from Guatemala and Honduras, and flowers from Colombia. We also depend on Central and South America for cheap labor, such as the factory workers who often produce tools and clothing. We should not fear learning Spanish; we should use it to our advantage. We need to learn Spanish the way Mexican immigrants learn English. They spend a great deal of time and money learning to speak English. They view videos and attend English classes. Therefore, many adults and children learn English. They want the whole family to speak English so that they can get better jobs and their children can succeed in English-speaking schools. For them, English is not a luxury; it is a necessity. These Mexican immigrants are aware of a need to speak English, and they wish to speak it. It is a myth that Mexicans do not want to speak English. It is a myth propagated by those who wish to give Mexicans a negative image.

My mother used to tell me that the Anglo community did not want Mexican Americans to speak English because they would compete for the higher paying jobs. She was not completely wrong; farmers and growers believed that "Educating the Mexicans is educating them away from the job, away from the dirt."[109]

Why do the people in the United States have such a poor image of Mexicans and other people who come from Central and South America today? Is it because they have learned to identify them with drugs? Drugs, which Americans of all races buy by the ton. We need to teach our children about the harm of drugs, and we need to stop the flow of drugs into the United States. Dealing in drugs on a large scale has been going on in North America since the sixties, and no one has been able to stop the flow from entering the United States. Who is dealing drugs in the United States? We know who sells them—the small-time dealer in a rundown house who is arrested and appears on the news nearly every week. However, do we know who buys them in large quantities when they arrive in the United States? There is no question that drugs destroy our children. In order to stop the traffic of drugs, but we must find more appropriate ways to solve the drug problem. Past efforts have all failed.

Nevertheless, we need to do legitimate trade with Mexico, Central America, and South America. Today, many of our medical drugs come from India; we have no idea of their safety. Could we not monitor those drugs if they came from Mexico? Why can we not buy safe drugs from Mexico and monitor their production?

We forget that if we are to pursue legal trade with our neighbors to the south, it is to our benefit to learn Spanish and not fear it.

If we are too arrogant to learn Spanish for the purpose of trading and selling, we should at least learn to speak it in order to intercede in drug crime across the borders. How can we deal with our neighbors if we do not understand them? Therefore, the question of speaking Spanish in the United States should be relevant to all American citizens who come in touch with Mexico and Central and South America.

In Europe, Europeans often know the importance of speaking not only one foreign language but up to five or six. Why? Because they are neighbors and have to speak to each other in order to stay at peace and trade.

People who live on the border between the United States and Mexico could profit at the diplomatic table. The Spanish language could facilitate better relations. Instead, we rant about how Mexicans want to make the United States a Spanish-speaking nation.

American propaganda keeps telling people on the radio and on television that Mexicans are increasing in population and will soon take over. The question that does not come up is why Mexicans are still a minority when they lived in what is now the United States over a hundred years before it existed. The United States Census Bureau counts Spanish-speaking people as Hispanics or Latinos of any race.

Therefore, Mexican Americans are not counted separately; they are all part of the larger group that includes Mexicans, Argentineans, Guatemalans, Hondurans, Cubans, Puerto Ricans, and others. Thus, the true numbers of Mexican Americans remain hidden in states like California and Texas, where they have lived longer than any other ethnic group.

Fairy Tales and Stereotypes

Fairy tales have a reputation of unjustly stereotyping stepmothers as evil, self-centered women, interested only in the welfare of their own children. In many cases, this stereotype is not applicable to the many wonderful women who love their stepchildren or at least show sympathy and kindness to them, but in other cases, the stereotype of the cruel Cinderella stepmother is true. In those other cases, a bad stepmother can make life hell for her stepchildren, because those mothers feel stepchildren threaten their own children and their inheritance.

Indigenous people are the stepchildren of the American continents. They are the children of the land and the legal heirs by birthright; they have an evil European stepmother who has moved into their home and completely disinherited them.

The European immigrants are the ones who have taken away the rightful inheritance of their indigenous American stepchildren. They fear and hate native people because they are afraid someday they will reclaim their inheritance. Like stepchildren, they are hidden when company comes. For that reason, in places like Argentina, some people claim there are no Indians left, while in places like the United States, indigenous people are rarely seen.

The stepmother fears that someday those children will come back and claim their rightful place; that is why she wants them out of their home. She feels she needs to deny them so they no longer can have any claim to their home, where they were born and to which they have legal rights. By giving them false names and denouncing them as strangers, she thinks she will keep them powerless.

In the United States, she calls them illegal immigrants, aliens, Latinos, Hispanics, and colored. She calls them every other name but their legal name, which is Americans, legal heirs to their homeland.

In other nations of the American continents, natives have seen their homes destroyed and taken over by European immigrant settlers. Today those natives remain landless, poor, uneducated, and powerless.

Richard H. Immerman claims that by the twentieth century, Guatemala was made up of an upper class and the very poor. The wealthy made up from 1 to 2 percent of the population. They were primarily of European and Anglo American extraction. The poor indigenous lived in primitive huts with insufficient food to eat. The wealthy elite lived in modern houses with Western appliances, drank imported wines, and ate delicacies; they also owned most of the land.[110]

Indigenous people live in poor conditions all over the American continents, often under tyrannical governments propped up by large corporations and the United States government.

These stepchildren might be unable to defend themselves today, but children grow up and do not forget that once they had a home that was their birthplace and where they were once lords and masters. No banishment from their homes will ever make them forget. This is true of all indigenous people; they want to feel free to live on their land. They want to have legal rights to live in their land as heirs. They want to claim land for their homes, they want to get justice in their courts, and they want to be workers who earn wages and not slaves. This goes against all the stepmother's wishes, because she has no intention of acknowledging those children as legitimate heirs; that would mean that they would be entitled to part of the land's wealth. Retribution would be needed, and that would mean acceptance of the indigenous people of North, Central, and South America. Today, many of those people live in nations where they are treated as aliens in their own lands. If their lands were returned, they would not need to migrate to seek better opportunities. Asia has recently joined Europe as the evil stepmother conspiring to keep the legal heirs of the Americas in servitude.

There were theologians and church leaders who argued the case of the Spanish Conquest and its legal rights in America, such as Francisco La Victoria. According to Jill Lepore, he disagreed with Pope Innocent IV "and claimed that difference in religion could not justify wars."[111] La Victoria also claimed that Christians had no right to deprive heathens of property that they owned because they were not Christians. In addition, quoting St. Thomas Aquinas, he said that "all forms of dominion derive from natural or human law; therefore they cannot be annulled by lack of faith."[112]

This was a very interesting ruling, since La Victoria had some experience with Jews, who, according to Spain, were heathens. La

Victoria had come from a converted Jewish family and could identify with the Jews of Spain who owned property and the Indians who owned property in their countries. While this settled the issue between the church and Spain, in the Americas, Europeans continued the massive slaughter of indigenous people. In the name of Christianity, Spaniards and other Europeans set out to ruthlessly eliminate natives in order to take possession of land and gold. In spite of intellectual debates, Indian slavery continued in the Spanish colonies. In Mexico, early missionaries considered the indigenous people human, converted many of them, and even ordained some as priests, but the hierarchy of the Catholic Church did not accept them and discouraged missionaries from using indigenous priests. For many years, indigenous people could not be ordained as priests in the Catholic Church.

In the legend of the Virgin of Guadalupe, Juan Diego was the humble Indian who witnessed her apparition in Tepeyac. This story proved very important in the missionary effort to convert Indians to Christianity. Recently, the Pope consecrated Juan Diego as a saint, but in reality, there is no proof that he even existed. Spaniards had a disregard for Indians; hence, they did not keep good records of indigenous people. Many Spanish priests referred to Mexicans as devil worshippers and destroyed their codices, which contained ancient Mexican history, literature, and culture.

Nowadays the church claims those people as part of its flock, so they considered elevating an Indian to sainthood. At the time of the canonization of Juan Diego, the head of the basilica of the Virgin of Guadalupe in Mexico City was a German priest who claimed that the Pope could not make Juan Diego a saint because there was no proof he ever existed.

Thus, up to this date, the people of Mexico have been in European custody. Did Juan Diego exist? One can never know, because the church has never allowed indigenous people to become custodians of their own church. Did the church actually need Juan Diego to convert the Indians to Christianity? Some Spanish priests stood up for the Indians; Mexico and Spain have records of those priests. Unfortunately, none of them have been canonized or considered for sainthood. It seems as if the Catholic Church has never really recognized Indians as human; the argument for the humanity of the Indian people of America never left Spain. We have to remember that the dialogue between Bartolomé de Las Casas and the Catholic Church took place in Spain and not in Rome.

In 1588, the Jesuit priest Jose de Acosta wrote a book entitled *De Procuranda Indorum Salute.* The first chapter dealt with how to preach Christianity to the Indians and not giving up hope on them. In later chapters, he also refuted Sepulveda's Aristotelian argument about slavery. Without mentioning Sepulveda's name, he stated that Aristotle's theory of slavery had been proven invalid by the University of Alcala and Salamanca as well as by the Council of the Indies.[113]

Bartolomé de Las Casas had earlier stated that his case needed to be approved by the Council of the Indies, and by 1588 the council had approved his argument. However, in territories captured by the Spaniards in America, the slaughter and enslavement of Indians continued; the evil stepmother continued her greed for gold and land.

In the United States, the stepmother slowly created the myth that Indians were illegitimate children, that they were the ones who had invaded her sacred abode. Why did the evil stepmother set up reservations and send the legitimate inheritors to live in squalor and poverty while her own children took and inherited the most fertile and abundant land? European Americans have always felt that people who were not white were a threat to their race and culture. The number of Native Americans who lived in North America cannot be accurately determined, because there was no way for them to be counted when the Europeans first arrived, and there were no attempts to count Indians. It is estimated that by the early twentieth century, only 250,000 Indians had survived extermination from cruel wars, hunger, and diseases.

Today, Native Americans continue to die of malnutrition and to suffer physical and social ailments related to extreme poverty. A majority of immigrants coming from Mexico and Central and South America are also descendants of indigenous people who have suffered a fate similar to that of their North American cousins. In the United States, Native Americans are foolishly called "Red Men" and the improperly labeled "Latinos" are referred to as "Brown Men." Ethnicities are defined by color, as if that is what makes people inferior or superior; in reality, most of the people who use these terms could not tell a North American Native from a Central or South American indigenous person. All American natives belong to the same race and share similar traits, just as Europeans share similar traits in spite of regional differences.

Today some indigenous people have mixed with other ethnicities, and there might be some changes in their DNA. Nevertheless, they all belong to a common race; they all lost their lands, their freedom, and their identities.

When the United States Constitution was being written, slavery was discussed not as a moral or ethical issue but as a purely economic one. During the Federal Convention of 1787, John Rutledge stated that slavery should not be discussed as an issue of morality or humanity. According to him, "Religion and humanity had nothing to do with this question."[114] Mr. Ellsworth went on to say that every state had the right to import what they pleased. "The morality or wisdom of slavery are considerations belonging to the States themselves." He added, "What enriches a part enriches the whole, and the States are the best judges of their particular interest."[115]

Unlike Spain, which spent years debating the issue of whether the Indians should be considered human beings or slaves, Britain and later the United States saw slavery not as a moral issue but an economic one. Today many Americans see the coming of immigrants not as a human issue but as an economic issue.

There have always been politicians who do not like immigrants from Mexico or Central or South America. According to Jean Pfaelzer, a professor of English and American Studies at the University of Delaware, "During the Great Depression, two million Mexicans and Mexican Americans were deported under Herbert Hoover's Mexican reparation campaign." Many of the children were born in the United States. They were citizens, and many of those Mexican American families had lived here for many generations. They were American citizens who were too poor and powerless to protest.

Conservative commentator Lou Dobbs and others still claim that rapid immigration from Latin America is causing a population explosion in the United States. This is not new propaganda; it has been going on for generations. During the Great Depression, politicians also blamed the so-called Latinos for America's financial and social woes. Today CNN is one of the most influential and powerful television stations and was well aware of Mr. Dobbs's ranting; by promoting him, they were accomplices of his racist doctrine. In their quest for ratings, they treated the coming of immigrants as an economic issue, not a human issue.

In 2004, a Harvard professor named Samuel Huntington, authored and copyrighted a book stating that it could not be reproduced or quoted in any way or form. I suppose he was anticipating the harsh criticism he would get from Mexican Americans and other Hispanic Americans in the United States. His premise was that the United States, founded by British settlers who spoke the English language and had Protestant values, was in danger of losing its identity with the coming of Hispanic immigrants. While it's true that those invading Europeans did speak English, their so-called Protestant ethics were a little murky, unless coming to America with Protestant values meant stealing food and land, introducing slavery, and devastating game like buffalo and deer that provided sustenance to Native Americans.

Many Puritans did praise God when Native Americans died by the thousands from foreign illnesses, such as smallpox. The Puritans also praised God for helping them burn and kill Native American families whom they considered savage heathens or the scum of the earth. This is a chapter of history rarely found in our textbooks.

This Harvard professor has recently died, so there is no way to hold dialogue with him. His book claimed that European and other immigrants to America assimilated into the American Anglo Protestant culture. According to this professor, it is the coming of Hispanics immigrants that is eroding these Puritan ethics and the fabric of our culture.

What this professor did not recognize is that Puritan ethics did not truly figure very strongly in the slave markets, on the Trail of Tears, in the expulsion and genocide of American natives, or in the taking away of land grants from Mexican citizens after the Mexican-American War. Let us not confuse capitalism with religious ideals. The early British invaders were not religious Puritans; they were hardcore capitalists.

This professor complained about Mexican Americans who are citizens as well as Mexican immigrants. He implied that Mexicans come to this country to live and take advantage of the generosity of America. He manipulated statistics to prove that Mexicans are destroying America's culture and therefore the fabric of society. He claimed that Mexican immigrants were more likely to live in poverty and to be on public assistance than any other groups. This type of distrust for Mexican Americans is not new. The reality is that most immigrants from Mexico and Central America come to the United

States to work. There are situations when some of those people are likely to go on public assistance, such as in the case of farm workers. Big agribusinesses lay off the laborers for the winter season. Since farm workers do not earn enough wages to cover winter expenses, some people have to depend on food stamps. If we were really looking for the truth, we would find that it is the big corporations who are truly on welfare. When American taxpayers supplement migrant workers' wages during the winter, the months when the farm fields lie dormant, what we are really subsidizing are the giant agribusinesses that don't pay adequate wages. Propaganda has always portrayed Mexican Americans and Mexicans using and abusing public assistance in large numbers. However, the fact is that Anglo Americans constitute the majority of welfare cases.

According to the big lie, we have failed to incorporate into mainstream America because we prefer our Mexican culture. We refuse to speak English, and we have a culture that is different from the rest of America. We also refuse to assimilate. Therefore, the real reason we sit on the periphery is because we are ignorant of the ways of the rest of the United States citizens and refuse to accept allegiance to the American flag. Let us dispel those hideous myths in a few sentences.

We refuse to assimilate. In the history of the United States, Mexican Americans have never refused to serve in the military or betrayed the nation in time of war. Mexican Americans went to fight in World War I, even if the history books do not record it. During World War II, Korea, Vietnam, the Gulf War, and the wars in Iraq and Afghanistan, Mexican Americans showed up in large numbers. If the Selective Service did not draft them, many of our people volunteered. Such was the case of one of my cousins, who was slightly underage and had to get special permission. He saw the last of World War II and later served in the Korean War. We have earned our citizenship many times over. Our brothers' war stories are just as heroic and painful as those of other ethnic groups.

Our devotion to this nation is so strong that even when we receive orders to shoot our fellow Mexican American brothers, we do it without questioning. This happened in the case of a soldier named Villa who fired on a young man at the Texas border. This soldier remained so loyal to the United States that he never even apologized for the death of the young American citizen named Ezequiel Hernandez. This was extreme, bordering on insanity.

Mexican Americans have never betrayed the United States, even when they were prisoners of war in Germany, Japan, or other places. We have proved our allegiance many times over. Why is it, then, that Mexican Americans are the least recognized? Why does the movie industry refuse to recognize them when they produce war movies, documentaries, or television shows? During World War II and Vietnam, we saw our largest numbers of casualties, yet their heroic acts do not appear in American history.

Other criteria for assimilation into American culture as proposed by Samuel Huntington include language, education, occupation, income, citizenship, intermarriage, and identity. This set of criteria is arbitrary and unscientific; the early European immigrants did not come to the United States educated and with high incomes. Most came illiterate and penniless; being poor was the major reason they risked their lives to come to these continents. Intermarriage has nothing to do with being an American; that is a contemporary concept. We must remember that up to the 1960s, interracial marriages were illegal in some places in the United States. At a time when the Anglo American community had built a social barrier against Mexican Americans, there could be no intermarriages.

As for language, Mexican Americans in the 1920s were discouraged from speaking English because Anglo Americans did not want them to compete for higher paying jobs and feared that they would not remain farm workers. Ignorance of the English language had the added advantage of barring Mexican Americans from politics. "Mexican Americans refuse to speak English," that is one of the most mean-spirited lies that has been propagated by the mainstream European American society. The truth is that the reason our elders did not speak English was not lack of desire. As a child, I remember an elderly man asking me how I was doing in school and teasing me that when he was a child all his schooling consisted of learning about Mama cow and Papa cow; he would ask me if that was all I was required to learn to graduate from school. The reality is that what he said pretty much summed up what took place in the Mexican American community. Schools just did not exist, and where they existed, they barely covered the elementary level.

Another of the Harvard professor's criteria is education. Mexican Americans did not have a choice as to where they could live. As Texas expanded its agriculture, railroads divided towns. Mexican Americans knew where they had to live and attend schools: in their segregated neighborhoods.

Children of Mexican Americans were expected to work from the time they could carry working tools. Girls were expected to help wash dishes in the homes while their mothers did laundry and scrubbed the floors for the European Americans. The story line about the European frontier women who came to the southwest suffering a great deal because of all the hard work they had to endure on the frontier is another myth. Even poor European and Anglo families had one or more Mexican women or mestizas who worked for food to take home and maybe a few cents. The women who worked for those frontier families were usually the wives and daughters of the mestizo men who worked on the farm or ranch. The mestizo women who did not work in the homes worked in the fields. The whole family was expected to work in the fields from sunup to sundown. The reason it is so easy for modern American women of Mexican descent to work outside of the home is that they have done so for generations. There has never been a time when it did not take the whole family to survive. So if they have been working so long to survive, why are most of them still living below the poverty level?

The only profession available to a poor migrant worker was working on farms. Without education and without the English language, they did not have a choice of professions.

It is clear that supposedly educated people have a very poor understanding of Mexican American history. For example. in Texas in 1919, to discourage Mexican Americans from voting, the Texas Rangers in Corpus Christi warned them "that if they could not read, write and speak the English language and they voted, they would be put in the penitentiary." Many people did not vote out of fear of not being able to meet such criteria.[116]

When my mother was a child growing up in a small Texas town, Mexican American children attended segregated schools that only went up to the third grade. High schools usually did not exist for them except in large cities, such as San Antonio, Texas, or Los Angeles, California.

Today in San Antonio, Texas, there is a Mexican American mayor (a Harvard Law School graduate), the third in the last thirty years; there are many city officials, such as the director of the public health care system, who are Mexican Americans. The presidents of the University of Texas at San Antonio and the University of Texas Medical School are Mexican Americans. There are also a number of state representatives and state senators who are Mexican Americans. The founders of one of San Antonio's largest car dealerships and a large national advertising agency are Mexican Americans. I am sure other places in the southwest, especially large metropolitan areas like Los Angeles, Phoenix, Albuquerque, Houston, or Dallas, also have outstanding Mexican American citizens.

Apart from some elderly people, most Mexican Americans speak English as their first language. They send their children to college whenever they can afford it; however, the very poor still lag behind. Among Mexican, Central American, and South American immigrants, there are many people who do not speak English, yet they are no different from many other immigrants from other parts of the globe who also often arrive without speaking English.

The Harvard professor had no business preaching hatred, fear, and racism to students. His actions should have been grounds for dismissal. He alleged that as Hispanic populations continue to grow, they are establishing beachheads in the United States. *Beachhead* is a military term, a position on an enemy shoreline captured by troops in advance of an invading force. What exactly this professor meant when he used that term is not clear. Was it that Mexicans are immigrating into the United States with some grandiose invasion in mind? Nonetheless, his allusion leaves a bitter taste in the mouths of Mexican Americans. It is true that many Mexicans and Central Americans are now working in the south, but it is also true that they tend to be guest workers brought in by American farmers to do agricultural work. Samuel Huntington died in 2008, so we will never know what he meant by *beachheads*.

I only hope Harvard will not replace him with another racist professor. Many intellectual Mexican Americans refuted his arguments when his book came out. His work dealing with Mexican immigration was very negative. He claimed that other nationalities have adopted the Protestant work ethic, implying that Mexican Americans do not. If this was the case, what accounts for people like Bernard Madoff stealing billions of dollars? Where is the Protestant ethic he is supposed to have adopted? Is being rich the only criteria used for being ethical? British Petroleum comes from a Protestant nation; nevertheless, it does not seem to be very ethical in the way it conducts its business. If this is true, this Harvard academic had no knowledge of what it means to have ethics. My poor Mexican American mother had a better understanding of what it meant to be a Protestant; for her, it meant that if you worked cleaning a bank and found a dime on the floor, you laid it on the countertop and did not take it. That is what "Thou shall not steal" meant. My Protestant mother taught me that.

The claim that the coming of people from Mexico and other Central and South American countries will destroy Protestant ethics ignores the fact that such ethics never actually existed. Judging from our past history of injustices toward Native Americans, Mexican Americans, African Americans, and the poor, we can say without hesitation, What Protestant ethics?

During the last hundred and fifty years, there has been a great deal of immigration from all over the world—Russian Jews who escaped Tsarist persecution, European Jews who escaped the Holocaust in fascist countries. We have also seen people come from China, India, Japan, and the Middle East. All of these immigrants imported their own cultures and religions. Some may have similar religious ideas, such as the Italian Catholics, while others have very different religions, such as the Hindus and other non-Christians. Those religions are tolerated as fitting into our secular nation. These large numbers of immigrants will have a great influence on America's culture. Will they accept Protestant ethics any better than the indigenous people of the Americas, who are for the most part Christian?

While some immigrant Catholics might not speak English, it is still a Western Christian faith based in Rome. There are also a large number of so-called Latino populations, both immigrants and American-born, who are increasingly joining Protestant churches, to the dismay of the Vatican. This phenomenon is not particular to the Unites States but is also spreading in countries like Mexico, Guatemala, and Brazil.

Fears about the faith of Mexican Americans are completely unfounded; many are Protestants and have been Protestant for generations. The population of the United States includes many different dogmas and radically different worldviews, but as different as the Spanish-speaking Catholic Church may appear, it is still closer to Protestant Christianity than non-Christian faiths. In other words, both Catholics and Protestants derive their ethics from the same Christian traditions.

Some academics and politicians use graphs and data to show poor development among Mexican Americans. They also speak with alarm about the number of illegal Mexican immigrants coming to the United States. The reality is that the indigenous and mestizo people of the Americas are not causing the overpopulation problem in the United States. The ancestors of those people have lived on the American continents for thousands and thousands of years. Overpopulation was caused by immigrants coming from Europe and other continents, who for over five hundred years have not ceased arriving in large numbers to our shores, leaving their impoverished and overpopulated lands behind. However, when mestizos come from the south, moving within their ancestral continent, they become a problem. The problem of overpopulation in the Americas is not those people; they are not the invaders. They have never invaded Europe, Asia, or Africa; they have rarely emigrated outside of their continents. Because of their past history, they are landless, poor, and degraded. When they come to the United States, they become illegal aliens. This label means that they are considered criminals, because it is considered a crime to come without special documents. Their much-revered pilgrims did not have any legal documents to invade America and leave all the natives homeless and on reservations. When the English, the Spaniards, and the French came to these continents, they had royal grants and deeds given to them by their monarchs (who did not own land in America). This was mockery at its worst! All they had to do was to claim territory in the name of their kings and queen without regard for the natives already living in the land.

The Americas did not have borders before Europeans came and forcefully divided the continent. They are responsible for landlessness and powerlessness among the indigenous people, the true heirs, who are left homeless, landless, and without wealth. I witnessed poverty in the Andes, where a young girl was selling pottery in the desert; I also witnessed poverty in Brazil, where a young barefooted mother with her child in her arms was beading rosaries to sell to tourists. They have nothing! That is why many sacrifice to come to the United States in search of food and shelter.

Why is it that a caste of people who have spent most of their lives working from sunrise to sunset and even on weekends are still living under the most devastating conditions in America? The answer is simple. They have never worked for their own benefit but to increase the profits of the ruling class, the Europeans who a few centuries ago arrived on these lands and now refuse to allow the survival of the indigenous people. This scenario is not limited to the United States but exists from Canada to Tierra del Fuego; the abuse is systematic and endemic. Carlos Fuentes recognized these abuses but offered no solution, maybe because he too is part of the society that oppresses. In Mexico and the rest of Latin America, this oppression is sometimes carried out by mestizos who have been taught to hate their indigenous roots, creating schizophrenic monsters who often hate their own people just as much or even more than the European Americans.

It is ironic that Popes are always encouraging the rights of the unborn while completely ignoring the right to life of the indigenous people of the American continents. Probably the reason is that the Pope belongs to a European church and a European world that stands to gain material wealth from the downfall of the American indigenous people. While the poor of North and South America suffer, the church remains silent and does little for them.

The displacement of indigenous people started immediately after the arrival of Europeans in these lands. Initially, there was a profusion of immigrants from every imaginable country in Europe. They came from Spain, England, France, Italy, Holland, Ireland, Germany, Russia, and other nations. Then they enslaved African people and brought them to America to perform free labor.

Later in history, immigrants also arrived from Asia, usually coming as servants; Europeans brought all types of cheap labor to America. Those immigrants also increased the population of America along with the Europeans. Mr. Ellsworth, during the argument about slavery at the Federal Convention of 1787, claimed that Virginia and Maryland already had so many slaves that they no longer needed to bring more, because "it is cheaper to raise than import them"[117] General Pickney stated that Virginia would gain by stopping importation because her slaves would rise in value. He argued that slaves were needed because

"The more slaves, the more produce to employ the carrying trade; The more consumption also, and the more of this, the more of revenue for the common treasury."[118]

Mr. Rutledge stated that North Carolina, South Carolina, and Georgia would not agree to become part of the Union "unless their right to import slaves be untouched."[119]

European immigrants did not just bring themselves but actually brought involuntary labor to America. Now they want to blame the population explosion on Mexicans and other Spanish-speaking immigrants

The invaders from England risked a great deal to journey to America. Looking at the geographical size of the British Isles, we see that they had a small territory and were growing desperate and aggressively claiming new lands. Poverty in England and Europe was pervasive. By the fifteen century, nations had become overpopulated. The majority of the population of Europe was made of serfs and peasants ruled by iron-fisted lords who ruled their fiefdoms.

Historically, the Romans invaded England, and then centuries later the Saxons (a Germanic tribe), and then the Normans, and eventually they engaged in war with Spain. The territory occupied by England was very small compared to that of other European nations. They coveted the lands found in the Americas. The immigrants coming to these continents were poor peasants who could not read or write and only owned the rags on their backs.

The pilgrims did not come solely for religious freedom; they also came to escape the blight in Europe. They came the same way the poor of Mexico and Central and South America come today, hungry and desperate.

Spain claimed it was out to seek a new trading route to spices and other materials when its ships sailed looking for a new way to reach India and China. Spain did not know the Americas were in between, but the discovery of gold made it more attractive than spices. After that, what Europeans really wanted was gold and the lands on which they found it.

Spain and England were not the only nations in Europe seeking more territory and more wealth; there were others, including Portugal, Holland, Russia, and France. With the exception of Russia, they were small in territory and locked in a perpetual struggle to seize more from their neighbors. When they heard about the Americas, they instantly coveted the land.

Spain had lost land and political power with the invasion of the Moors, who remained in control for nearly eight hundred years. The fact that many Spaniards mixed with the Moors, who were non-white and non-Christian, made other Europeans consider Spaniards inferior. Ironically, the Moors introduced a great deal of cultural and scientific knowledge into Spain, which eventually made its way into the rest of Europe. In 1492, Spain had won its freedom from Moorish influence and established its own Christian culture and kingdoms. Later on, it had a prosperous Golden Age, during which it excelled in literature and underwent a period of enlightenment. Spain launched its conquest of the Americas during this period.

Some of the Spaniards who came to the Americas eventually mixed with the natives. This new mixed breed was considered even more inferior in the eyes of other Europeans. In the United States, this view affected foreign policy toward Mexico and Central and South America; in Latin America, it drove ethnic cleansing attempts. For instance, Domingo F. Sarmiento, an Argentinean intellectual and at one time the president, wrote in his books about the inferior races of people who lived in Argentina, namely Indians, mestizos, and Africans. His policies favored European immigration and eradication of Indians in the late 1800s.

European explorers were so relentless in their pursuit of territory that they also conquered lands in Asia, Africa, and Oceania. A British king arrogantly declared that the sun never set on his empire.

Spain and Portugal took over large parts of the Americas thanks to a Pope who felt he had the authority to give away land that did not belong to him! I suppose he felt God had awarded him the land so he could dispose of it in any way he wished.

What really made the Europeans strong and wealthy was gold. Spain stole gold from the Aztec and Inca empires, and British pirates often stole the gold from the Spaniards. Spain controlled the major gold mines of the Americas in Mexico and Peru. Both England and Spain exploited the indigenous people of America in order to increase their political power in Europe. Perhaps if the peoples of Peru and Mexico had not invested so much of their cultural heritage in gold, the

Europeans would have not stolen most of their culture and would not have melted it into ingots to empower their kings.

Today we would have more artifacts and archeological remains from those cultures if European immigrants had not plundered them. The conquistadors of Spain and the pirates of England took many golden treasures from the Americas and melted them down to make their own jewelry. Thus, much American art was lost forever. Spain and the rest of Europe did not have much gold and silver until after the conquest of the Americas.

Bartolomé de Las Casas wrote that on Darien (today part of Panama), Spanish soldiers and Indian slaves under the command of Vasco Nunez de Balboa were carrying so much gold that the men were tired and no longer had the joy of finding so much treasure; instead, they were hungry because they had not eaten. They had abandoned food supplies and other necessities in order to carry the gold.[120]

In another episode, Bartolomé de Las Casas narrates that one soldier got so carried away with hoarding gold that he even abandoned his weapons. This made it easier for Mexican warriors to slay him.

The exploitation of the Americas did not stop after the conquest and subsequent colonization of the continents but continued among the new independent nations. One example is the Mexican-American War, in which the powerful United States invaded Mexico, which had just spent many of its resources gaining independence from Spain. During the Texas secession and Mexican-American War, Mexico had insufficient resources, so it was defeated. Once victorious, the United States claimed territory from Mexico in what is now Texas, California, Arizona, Nevada, New Mexico, and parts of Colorado and Utah. They drew new borders and made sure they got the best lands. The real immigrants to those territories were not Mexicans, who had lived there for nearly two hundred years. The new immigrants who started pouring into the new territories were Anglo Americans and Europeans.

Could the large number of Mexicans who stayed in their homes after the United States took over their territory explain the large number of Mexican Americans living in the southwestern United States today? The fact is that those Anglo American and European immigrants came into territories Mexico had to cede under the Treaty of Guadalupe Hidalgo. The treaty promised to allow Mexicans already in those territories to keep their property, but the reality turned out to be different; Anglo immigrants did not keep the treaty's terms and seized Mexican-owned lands.

Congressman James Slayden of San Antonio, Texas made a comment in the Annals of the American Academy in 1921 that exemplifies Anglo American fears and prejudices. He stated, "large planters short of labor ... welcome the Mexican immigrants as they would welcome fresh arrivals from the Congo, without a thought of the social and political embarrassment to their country."[121]

The taking of land from indigenous people continued in all parts of the Americas. The United States plotted to take land by dividing the nation of Colombia and creating Panama, where they could build a canal to use for moving freight faster between oceans and keep a military base, thus establishing a real beachhead. For many years, United States managed the Panama Canal, free to do business and establish a military base there so that it could control both hemispheres of the Americas. Other European American capitalists participated in the ruling and managing of Central and South American territories. Minor Keith from Brooklyn, New York went to Costa Rica to build railroads. He also established banana plantations alongside the railroad to increase his wealth. When Minor Keith became rich and powerful, he married the daughter of the president of Costa Rica. He was so powerful that he was dubbed the uncrowned king of Central America.[122]

He soon went into Guatemala and set up the United Fruit Company, a banana company that exploited the people of Guatemala. He acquired large parcels of land, leaving the people landless. He later set up a mail service to be provided by his railroad and again set up banana plantations along the tracks. He became so rich and powerful in Central America that he was compared to an octopus swallowing up most other businesses.[123]

Guatemala's dictator, Jorge Ubico, maintained a close relationship with the United Fruit Company and helped exploit his nation. The United Fruit Company was virtually exempt from taxes and duties and was Guatemala's largest landowner. Its total property was more than the combined holdings of half of Guatemala's landholding population.[124]

Is it no wonder that people from Central and South America are immigrating to the United States today! They have nothing left in their own countries, not even enough food to feed their families. The United States became concerned when the newly elected government of Jacobo

Arbenz Guzman wanted to reclaim the land for the people of Guatemala. The United States secretary of state accused Guatemala of becoming communist and promoted the overthrow of this democratically elected government in 1953. The United Fruit Company "owned Guatemala" as well as the American politicians and the law firm of Secretary of State John Foster Dulles, who started the propaganda that Guatemala was a Soviet satellite.[125]

John Foster Dulles was one of the authors of the documents that allowed the United Fruit Company its exceptional status for ninety-nine years. According to Paul Hoffman, author of *Lions in the Street,* Dulles was a "businessman with a law degree."[126]

President Dwight Eisenhower helped overthrow President Jacobo Arbenz Guzman of Guatemala with the help of the CIA. In his place he installed General Enrique Castillo Armas, a United States–trained military leader, who reinstituted the old iron-fisted dictatorship.[127]

Guatemalan Nobel prize-winning author and poet Miguel Angel Asturias penned his critically acclaimed book *El Señor Presidente* in 1933 while in exile. He was not able to publish it until 1946 in Mexico. His public opposition to dictatorial rule led him to spend much of his life abroad. In this esoteric work, he wrote about the oppression and dehumanization of the people under a ruthless dictatorship. The novel is a fictional allegory, describing the seemingly supernatural evil powers of the country leaders and their minions, and how that evil spiraled downward to the people. Although the characters are fictitious the city he described actually exists in Guatemala, it is assumed that the plot represents the iron-fisted dictatorship of its president Manuel Estrada Cabrera.

When the British took possession of Guyana as a colonial power in South America, they imported slave workers from Africa and servants from India to work in their sugar cane plantations. Later on, these impoverished workers tried to make their nation independent from Britain, and just as in the case of Guatemala, they were accused of being communists. Repeatedly, when people in Central and South America have been left landless and tried to regain possession of their lands, they have immediately been accused of being communists by the powerful.

When Manuel Lopez Obrador was running for the presidency of Mexico, the New York Times claimed that if he won the election, the American business community would be uncomfortable. If they objected to his election, it was because they believed they would not be able to continue the exploitation of the Mexican people. Maybe they would have set up an artificial conspiracy to destroy him as a politician who opposed their capitalist goals, as was done in the past to Arbenz in Guatemala. Eventually, Lopez Obrador lost the election by a very thin margin, so thin that it became a point of contention in Mexican politics. Mexico needs to find a truly honest politician who will not be controlled by the United States if it wishes to become a democratic nation with children who are educated and healthy and no longer need to emigrate and perform jobs no one else wishes to do. Mexico needs to become independent from the United States so that it will no longer remain invisible and voiceless as a nation. Unfortunately, as long as only the wealthy European Mexicans control the country, Mexico, like the rest of the Americas, will remain poor and helpless, and the United States will continue to manage its affairs. We will see more Mexican immigrants coming into the United States. This human traffic may cease some day if wealthy European and Anglo Americans stop the exploitation of Mexico, Central America, and South America.

Today we do not call people like Lopez Obrador communists; we call them leftists or some other name. Why? Probably because today we do almost all our business with China, which continues to be a real communist state, still flying the red flag with the hammer and sickle. It remains faithfully communist, but at the same time it has become our closest and best trading partner. While vigilante groups sit at our southern border on the lookout for immigrants, the country that is taking jobs from America is China—jobs in the textile, shoe, computer, electronic, and furniture manufacturing industries. There are very few jobs that have not gone to China yet, taken from our red-blooded Americans. If those vigilantes worry about their jobs, they need to set their sights on bigger prey. Our dollars are making China rich and powerful while they vent their frustrations on smaller targets.

The United States has been picking on Cuba for decades because it embraced communism. We are now also picking on Venezuela and Bolivia because they are leaning socialist; among some there is even talk about boycotting their products. If we really hated communists and wanted a boycott, we would stop buying products that come from

China—dishes, shoes, plastic flowers, radios, computer chips, and thousands of other common objects that we no longer manufacture.

Job losses are not the result of so-called Latin American immigration; they are the result of outsourcing to China and India. Some of our leaders like to say that China is becoming more democratic, but in reality, it is continuing to repress and exploit its poor people. On the other hand, India, although imperfect, is really a democracy and now has more educated people to provide goods to the world, while we are sinking into more debt and poverty. Soon we will have more people on the streets and without jobs than India or China. While we point at Cuba and call it communist, China is in bed with our powerful politicians and their capitalist masters who are betraying our nation. Our own bankers and businesspeople who take our industries to Asia are the ones destroying our country, not the powerless immigrants.

Some years ago, our business leaders brushed away concerns about the flight of blue-collar jobs overseas and told us we no longer would need to work in factories because we were becoming workers in service industries. We would concentrate on computer occupations, and our jobs would pay well. Instead, we found that even those jobs have been gradually evaporating and that those same business leaders no longer need American workers in service industries. American capitalists discovered India and its lower wages. Our computer age dissolved and went to Asia where poor workers are willing to do our jobs for much less money. At this point in history, countries like India and China hold the fate of our nation in their hands. Those workers we cannot see are the ones who take our best jobs; they are also the ones who handle our private credit information and know the value of everything we own. The poor, uneducated immigrants from Mexico and Central America just get to pick our food and clean up after us.

Today America does not condemn China, because we are heavily indebted to them, but we will continue to send CIA agents to influence Mexican and Central and South American governments.

The United States' real threat is not Mexican and Central American immigrants but treaties like NAFTA that allow a small but powerful group of corporations from the industrialized countries to control wages, health care, property and human movement. Therefore, it is not just the old colonial powers, such as Spain and England, that have left people in the Americas landless. Multinational corporations have replaced the old empires, corporations run for the most part by European Americans and Europeans. They continue to invade and steal land in the Americas; they continue to exploit our indigenous populations, leaving them landless, invisible, and voiceless.

Our History as Americans

"Do not find it strange if there has been no manifestation of joy and enthusiasm in seeing this city occupied by your military forces. To us the power of the Mexican Republic is dead. No matter what her condition, she was our mother. What child will not shed abundant tears at the tomb of his parents?"

Governor Juan Bautista Vigil y Alarid, 1846
—Gregory Rodriguez,
Mongrels, Bastards, Orphans, and Vagabonds

In order to understand our historical heritage, we must learn who we are as Americans and why we are citizens of the United States. Our history began in the heart of Mexico. We are the descendants of the ancient Olmecs, who disappeared before newer tribes arrived in Central Mexico; the Olmecs were very influential among the later civilizations of Mesoamerica—Mayas, Toltecs, Huastecas, Totonacs, Tarascans, Zapotecs, Otomies, and Aztecs, just to name a few of the many diverse indigenous groups that are known to have existed in Mexico when the Spanish arrived. Nevertheless, our heritage stretches farther than just Mexico. These groups had close relationships with their brothers and sisters in South and North America, and their bloodline is long and complicated.

The arrival of the Spaniards in America makes up part of the terrible and cruel history left in our oral and written records pertaining to the conquest of these continents. The first thing Columbus did when he arrived in the Caribbean islands was to kneel down, thank the Lord, and start rounding up Indians to take and sell as slaves. Thus began the history of slavery in the Americas! The Caribbean islands saw the beginning of slavery in America by Europeans.

Other Europeans, wherever they went, left a trail of blood and destruction, repeating the same history of slavery, bloodshed, and destruction inflicted upon the indigenous people by the Spaniards over the entire continent. It did not matter what nation in Europe those invaders emigrated from; their legacy in America was one of violence and devastation. They plundered and killed indigenous people in North, Central, and South America until nearly half of the original population was extinct.

In places like Cuba and Puerto Rico, the Spaniards nearly wiped out all the indigenous Taino people. After the eradication of the Taino, the Spaniards took indigenous slaves from Mexico to those islands to do their work. Europeans were the true illegal immigrants; their conquest was criminal injustice.

People from England, Portugal, Spain, Germany, France, Italy, Holland, and other European countries came to the North and South American continents to acquire territory; they massacred and displaced the inhabitants of those lands without mercy or compassion. The Indians who survived the merciless killings became slaves in other territories of the Americas or in Europe.

Those European immigrants also brought their slaves from Africa. By separating them from their tribes and their families, slave owners ensured that those slaves could not rebel and create fighting units. Those people suffered violence and often died on the slave ships. This made it easier for the Europeans to manipulate them. White plantation owners often created distrust between their slaves and other neighboring slaves in order to keep them from uniting as a group.

Although at the beginning Europeans used American indigenous people as slaves, they exterminated so many that in order to raise crops and produce goods they had to bring more slaves from Africa. Later in history, they brought workers from China and other nations. Today, the overpopulation in the United States is not caused by the indigenous natives. It seems that the number of Native Americans on reservations is declining, while the number of immigrants from Europe and other nations is increasing.

Today many immigrants from Central and South America are coming to the United States because Europeans have taken possession of their lands. Those people are homeless and in dire poverty; they have nowhere to turn. Today America is still bringing in large numbers of people from Europe and Asia. These immigrants often come with their elderly relatives and their young children and increase America's population. American businesses claim they bring them in because they do not have sufficient workers in the field of computers and other technological jobs. The truth is that many large corporations are bringing these immigrants to replace American workers. They hire workers from Europe, India, and China because they do labor for lower wages. There is no lack of educated Americans; there is just a lack of high-paying positions. Thus, many Anglo Americans have lost their jobs to European, Chinese, and Indian immigrants, not poor indigenous farm workers from Mexico and Central and South America.

In America, there is a deep and profound racism against Mexicans and Mexican Americans. At the creation of the Texas Republic, the Anglo population consisted of mostly Southerners and some Northerners. These people never intended to settle and raise their families under the Mexican flag. They came to form an independent republic and continue their slave trade. They came in pursuit of territory, as they had done in the rest of the United States.

Today, new groups of immigrants from Mexico and Central and South America come because they no longer have productive lands or jobs in their countries. The United States treats these people as criminals; when apprehended, they increase the prison population, where they live non-productive lives. These families often have children; some of those children spend their young lives as prisoners, wearing prison garb. Children's rights are not protected, and they may have to live among criminals. In other cases, babies have been put up for adoption, meaning the parents will never see their children again. All of this imprisonment costs money, contributing to the fragile United States economy. The cost of maintaining the prisons is enormous; nevertheless, America is determined to make them pay for the crime of coming to seek jobs. The truth is that while we enjoy many inexpensive vegetables and fruits from Mexico and Guatemala, families in those countries are starving. They do not even eat off their land; even their food is imported to the United States. Mexican television reports that some people are so poor they often only drink tea; their poverty is no secret.

Americans claim immigrants from Spanish-speaking nations increase the population of the United States. However, the population explosion can be attributed to a large European immigration that has taken place since 1492 and the work force the European immigrants have imported from Africa and Asia. This population has come to America from Europe for over five hundred years. Those Europeans have come in large numbers and increased the population of the United States. In Europe, the population at one time had increased at such fast pace that even the rivers were running out of fish.

In the United States, Native Americans were not able to survive without land and food. Many of the men died in battles against the intruding Europeans, who often raided villages and killed men, women, and children. Their food supply was also destroyed or stolen; that was the reason so many buffalo were destroyed in the United States. Tonkahaska (Tall Bull) to General Winfield Scott Hancock: "The buffalo are diminishing fast. The antelope, that were plenty a few years ago, they are now thin. When they shall all die we shall be hungry; we shall want something to eat, and we will be compelled to come into the fort. Your young men must not fire at us; whenever they see us they fire, and we fire on them."[128]

It was not just buffalo furs that the Europeans wanted; they also wanted to starve the indigenous people in order to take possession of their lands.

Europeans fought and killed many indigenous people and did not stop the murder until they had left them completely powerless, without land and without children to defend what was theirs. Today Native Americans who survived the holocaust often live in extreme poverty in barren areas of New Mexico, Texas, Oklahoma, Arizona, Utah, and South Dakota. They live on reservations, which typically are arid and not very productive. They do not participate in justice or in wealth in their own country. Although these lands are supposed to be sovereign, federal and state governments still control their existence. Some Indians were fortunate enough to discover oil on their lands, while others have found they can make money by owning gambling casinos, but by large, most Native Americans still live in dire poverty.

Some Indians may question why it is that their populations have remained the same for many years, while other populations in the United States keep increasing. Is it because they continue to live in dire poverty and lack sanitary conditions? Today many Native Americans have no electrical power or water on their reservations. I met a middle-aged Navajo man who spoke about growing up without electricity and water. This poverty makes it hard to live on the reservations. They live in very hot climates, such as Arizona and New Mexico, or in freezing states, such as South Dakota, without proper protection against the weather and are often malnourished. They often lack jobs, water, electricity, and even stoves to heat their homes. Many become so hopeless they commit suicide. Some take up drugs and alcohol as a form of escapism and end up with violence in their homes. The unemployment rate among Native Americans is very high, the worst among minorities.

Just a few years ago, the Republican lobbyist Jack Abramoff cheated Indians out of large amounts of money with the pretense of lobbying for their casinos. Abramoff defrauded Saginaws and Chiawas from California, Choctaws from Mississippi, Coushattas from Louisiana, and Tiguas from Texas. Today Abramoff sits in jail for crimes against the federal government but not for crimes against the Indians. He stole tens of millions of dollars from the Indians, but this crime was not prosecuted. The exploitation of Indians continues up to the present; they continue to be invisible and voiceless in America.

Europeans came plundering and stealing the birthrights of the indigenous people of the Americas. Most European nations participated in the slaughter in one way or another.

After the Spanish reached Hispaniola, they branched out to Cuba, Puerto Rico, and Jamaica in search of slaves. From those islands, the Spaniards went to the coast of Central and South America, where they continued to capture and sell Indians.

It was during their explorations of those coasts that Hernan Cortes discovered Mexico in 1519. He found this nation to be strong and wealthy, and to his delight, he discovered that they also had gold! Thus began a terrible, bloody war; the Aztecs had weapons, but they were no match for the iron weapons of the Spaniards. Their armory was for hand-to-hand combat; their weapons were made of obsidian designed for fighting at close range. The Europeans had muskets, canons, and swords made of steel. Finally, the Europeans' horses allowed them to move swiftly and plow into crowds of people.

It would be those weapons and those horses that allowed them to conquer Mexico. However, there were also two more factors: before the arrival of the conquerors, the Aztecs had already been involved in wars with their neighbors. The Aztecs had demanded tribute, slaves, and sacrificial victims from their weaker neighbors. When the Spanish arrived, they established alliances with those Indians who were hostile toward the Aztecs and persuaded them to fight on their side. Finally, the Spanish unwittingly brought to the Americas one of their deadliest weapons—a biological weapon, smallpox. This was a new disease for Native Americans for which they had no immunity; consequently, thousands of Mexicans died of smallpox.

Although conversion to Christianity and assimilation were part of the conquest policy toward the Indians, the bloody, horrendous acts of cruelty committed by the Spaniards were recorded repeatedly in the journals kept by some Spanish priests who traveled and lived alongside the conquerors. Once these priests converted the Indians, they saw them as God's children and denounced the conquistadors for their atrocities.

Antonio Montesinos was the first to denounce the acts of the Spanish soldiers and went as far as refusing to serve them communion. He witnessed the conquistadors' eradication of the Taino Indians in the Caribbean. Bartolomé de Las Casas, who originally was an encomendero, later joined the priesthood and spent the rest of his life denouncing and recording the cruelty of the Spanish against the Indians.

Fray Diego Durán stated that twelve priests from the order of Saint Francis were sent to convert the Indians. As imitators of the twelve apostles, these men went barefoot and with humility. Eventually, they won the respect and love of the Indians. Five years later, Mexico received a group of Dominican priests coming from the island of Santo Domingo or Hispaniola. However, the Dominicans of Cuba and the Caribbean had already become known for the defense of the Indians. Some of those priests recorded the evil doings of the Spaniards.

Mexico was an agrarian society; the basis for their lifestyle was producing food from the soil. One of their most revered gods was Tlaloc, the god of rain. When the Spaniards landed, they brought cattle with them, and one of the ways of dispossessing the indigenous people from their lands was to allow the cattle to graze on the land and destroy the crops, which forced the people to abandon their homes. These were Mexico's first displaced inhabitants; the practice of using cattle to get people out of their homes and fields is today alive and well in Chiapas, Mexico. Wealthy landowners continue to let their cattle graze on Mayan cornfields so that the indigenous people will have no choice but to abandon their homes; in addition, other foreigners go to Chiapas to harvest the wealth of those lands. The difference today is that those invaders are mainly looking for oil. However, the practice remains the same—taking land that belongs to the American indigenous people.

History records that in Mexico indigenous people also lost their lands to the Spanish by fraud. The Spaniards would force some natives to sign deeds to lands that did not belong to them, pay them some insignificant amount of money, and later take possession of the land and dispose of the real owners by killing or enslaving them.

In the United States, the Native American lot was the same, with the exception that there were no Protestant or Catholic clergy to record the injustices as precisely as Bartolomé de Las Casas or Diego Durán. It was not a question of whether the Spaniards or other Europeans treated the natives of these continents any better or worse. The Spaniards have the Black Legend reputation because there were priests and missionaries who actually recorded those atrocities. Bartolomé de Las Casas not only recorded those events but actually defended the Indians in Spain and presented their case before the Spanish Catholic Church and king. In North America and Canada, the natives never had a European to defend their cause.

Bartolomé de Las Casas deserves to be recognized and perhaps canonized into sainthood. Although in modern times some Protestant churches have accepted Bartolomé de Las Casas as a saint, the Catholic Church has not chosen to introduce him to sainthood in spite of the fact that he personally was a hero for saving the lives of many indigenous people of Mexico and other places in the Americas. While his work did not entirely stop the mass murder of indigenous people, it probably slowed it down for some time. The Roman Catholic Church remains partial to its European culture.

The fate of the Americas was sealed with pieces of paper. Pope Alexander issued a Papal Bull in 1493 dividing South America between Spain and Portugal. Queen Elizabeth doled out deeds to British immigrants. The Treaty of Tordesillas was supposed to solve the dispute between Spain and Portugal regarding claims to newly discovered lands; being Catholic nations, both went to the Pope for mediation, who awarded the Portuguese explorers large land grants and gave the rest to Spain—as if any of these territories were the Pope's or Queen Elizabeth's to give.

At the time of the conquest of Brazil, the Portuguese settlers raised cattle, requiring large plots of land. Land and slaves became so valuable to them that they raided Jesuit missions among the Guarani Indians in the triple border region in South America (where the borders of Brazil, Paraguay, and Argentina are all in close proximity). They took the indigenous people as slaves and had the church expel Jesuit priests who helped the Indians defend themselves.

According to the British invaders, Queen Elizabeth granted them documents that gave them rights to lands in America. The Pope also granted the Spaniards and Portuguese lands in the Americas. As if kings and Popes had any authority over these lands. It seems that every powerful nation in Europe had rights in America, but not the Indians, who were the true owners. Meanwhile in the United States, the old adage that the only good Indian was a dead Indian remained the dominant philosophy; the number of Native Americans dwindled to a handful by the 1890s. Even then, they put up a heroic struggle. The battle of Little Big Horn and the Ghost Dance rituals are manifestations of their desperate efforts to remain free.

Today, history sometimes glorifies and romanticizes the vanished tribes, while the actual Indians who remain in North America are generally despised as lazy, ignorant drunks who have the arrogance to demand that their territories not be exploited for commercial purposes. Corporations constantly covet their hallowed grounds for exploitation, and developers desire their fishing waters for private recreational use. However, if this is true of the United States and Canada, it is just as true of Mexico and Central and South America. In all of the Americas, there is a constant push to drive Native Americans out of their remaining territories. A recent and graphic example is the treatment of the Mayas of Chiapas.

Today, the airport of Mexico City is not large enough to handle the large amount of air traffic; consequently, there is an effort to drive people off their lands to build an airport. Here again, the rich are taking land from the poor when they want to build projects, projects that often involve foreign businesspeople.

In Central and South America, the natives did not die out in such large numbers; maybe Las Casas's work was not completely in vain. In Argentina, southern indigenous people fought the War of the Desert until the late 1800s. Native people who were still living in Patagonia saw their demise with the building of railroads and the introduction of the Winchester rifle. Those who survived the battles became captives, and their families were parceled out all over the country as laborers and as servants. Those Argentine natives would never see their families again; the idea was to isolate them so that they could not rebel against their masters, the same policy that was used for centuries with slaves from Africa. The enslaved people were isolated from their original environments, tribes, and families. That way, they were easier to manipulate and subjugate. In Argentina, some people claim there are no Indians left. Perhaps that is their wish. In reality, there are indigenous people, only they do not have political power.

On the reservations, many Native Americans do not even have running water or electricity. Likewise, many Mexican Americans live in abject poverty as second-class citizens. This translates into not having political power locally or in Washington. Their poverty disqualifies them from having a voice in their destiny.

This lack of voice encompasses Indians as well as their descendants; I am referring not only to people living in reservations or within the confines of a tribal society but also to people scattered all over our society in big cities and in small towns. Many are not even able to trace their original roots, especially the mestizos. I am part of this group. We are referred with many names—people of Mexican descent, Mexican Americans, Latinos, Chicanos, and Hispanics (although many of our children do not even speak Spanish).

We must recognize and honor our indigenous roots, because we share an American indigenous history and blood. Our ancestors were made slaves by the invading Europeans; our women were abused, giving rise to our mestizo or half-breed heritage. Through generations, the Spaniards taught our people to be ashamed of our indigenous heritage. We are not Spanish or Hispanic; if we were truly Spanish, we would have been accepted into European American society long ago. Indigenous people and mestizos have not integrated, because they are racially different; their features make them different in the eyes of European American society. People of Mexican descent in the United States are different not because of their culture, their language, or their Catholic religion. They are different only because of their race.

People from all over Europe came from different cultures and religions, and they fully assimilated into America's mainstream society, which has rejected indigenous people as Americans purely based on race. Many people of Mexican descent have been on this continent a lot longer than European Americans. The truth is that they are just one of many indigenous American peoples displaced and marginalized by the European invaders. We never invaded Europe; Europe invaded us, from Alaska to the tip of Tierra del Fuego.

In our modern society, Mexican Americans cannot live without taking the whole cycle of history of the Americas into account, because as long as we are racially mestizos, we remain bonded to the rest of the Americas from Alaska to the tip of Tierra del Fuego. We have the same history, the same roots or *raíces* in our indigenous bloodline or *raza* (meaning people or race in Spanish). We speak of race because we are aware that it is race that makes us different from European Americans.

Some people mistrust Mexican Americans and question how well they assimilate into mainstream culture and how faithful they are as American citizens. The loyalty of Mexican Americans and other Hispanics toward the United States is suspect.

During 1915–1917, some Mexican Americans who had become tired of the Anglo American oppressors created a document called the Plan de San Diego. It was an effort to unite Mexican Americans, African Americans, Native Americans, and Japanese Americans into a "Liberating Army for Races and People." Their main aim was to declare independence from "Yankee Tyranny" and to form an independent country made up of California, Texas, Arizona, New Mexico, and Colorado.[129] In other words, they wanted to take the land Mexico had lost with the Treaty of Guadalupe Hidalgo. Perhaps they were weary of segregation, lack of respect, and landlessness. During the revolt, they raided companies and farms, caused derailments, and burned bridges. Many Mexican Americans lost their lives when the United States suppressed the revolt. Maybe historians with racial biases use this event as a reason to be suspicious of all Mexican Americans. However, outside of this isolated event, the great majority of Mexican Americans have fought in American wars for generations; they have helped defend the United States with honor and dignity. How much more faithfully can these young men act?

My grandparents were Mexican Americans; my grandmother's father was Marcos Jimenez, born in Texas during the time of the Mexican-American War. My great-grandfather was a merchant who traded goods between Texas and Mexico; at other times, he was a peon who worked as a farm laborer in the fields. As a child, he saw the end of the so-called Texan revolution and saw Texas become a state and adopt slavery. He claimed to have witnessed the sale of slaves in front of the Alamo. As an adult, he also saw the movement of American Indians pursued by the United States cavalry and witnessed the desperation of the warriors who mourned for their children's future. He claimed that at night some of those Indians would come to his home and use owl hoots as secret codes to indicate they were waiting to visit the poor Mexican families. He remembered how one warrior asked him to take his daughter as a bride for fear she would not be able to find a husband, since most of the young men had been killed on their journey to Mexico. My great-grandfather had to explain that he already had a wife and family; according to my grandmother, he always remembered those American Indians with great affection and sadness, because he identified with them. My great-grandfather had also lost his country and was now part of a new nation that did not accept him any more than it accepted the American Indians.

One of my cousins had a great-grandfather who immigrated to Texas from Germany. Once established, he became a sheriff and was instructed to shoot any Indian he could find but not to shoot Mexicans. They were protected by the governmental. He then asked how he would be able to distinguish them, since to him they looked pretty much alike. He was told to ask them their names, and if they had a Spanish name, they were Mexicans. He claimed he did not shoot any Indians because everyone claimed to have Spanish names. It seemed those Indians had caught on to the Anglo trick.

Growing up as a child, I remember seeing some Hollywood films depicting Mexicans abusing American Indians, but I also remember the oral stories regarding Native Americans that my grandmother passed down to my mother. That made me rebel against the distorted history in American movies that portrayed Europeans and Anglo Americans as heroic and benevolent while portraying Mexicans and Mexican Americans as being cruel to the Indians. Very early in life, I began to see that there were different versions of history—my mother's oral history, the textbook history, and finally the movie history.

Today, I still have to sort out my ideas about America and who I am. During my lifetime, I have read in newspapers and books how Mexican Americans have failed to stay wealthy because our ancestors refused to adopt the European culture and the English language. However, in my heart I keep hearing my mother's voice over and over saying, "the gringos always get the best jobs because they speak English. They never wanted us to learn English, because if we did, we would have been able compete with them for better jobs. As long as we do not speak English, we will continue to be poorly paid. We never had schools that went beyond grammar school." She would say, "When I was a child, there were no schools beyond second and third grade for Mexican American children who lived in ranches or small towns."

My mother worked for the WPA, which Franklyn D. Roosevelt created to make works for the poor and unemployed. Her job was to make low-cost dresses; it turned into a sweatshop where Mexican Americans sewed and worked long, hard hours as seamstresses under the supervision of Anglo Americans who spoke English and thus could be managers. Thus, my mother's failure to learn English was not the result of a desire to maintain a Mexican culture but of strict segregation; Mexican Americans had no contact with European Americans outside of worker-manager relationships.

We have been so conditioned to accept our role in history that we consider ourselves inferior. As a teenager, I remember going to see the movie *Pale Face* with Bob Hope and remarking that I would like to grow up and be a comedian like Bob Hope. My friends immediately replied that I must be crazy. They said that I looked like an Apache, that I couldn't be a movie star because I wasn't pretty. In our youth, we learned that there were certain professions we could not pursue. Many years later, when I returned to college for a second master's degree, the professor asked the class to develop a project having to do with racial dynamics. I agreed with my professor to develop a project in which I would ask Mexican American students on our campus if they would consider becoming movie stars. I developed a list of questions and passed them out; when I compiled the answers, I learned that their mindsets were similar to those of the teenagers I had encountered forty years earlier. They claimed they did not have the talent or looks to be movie stars and answered that if they were to become movie stars they would only be given negative or menial roles as criminals or maids.

The relationship between Anglo Americans and Mexican Americans goes back to the time of the Republic of Texas and the Mexican-American War; even since the Treaty of Guadalupe Hidalgo, relationships between the United States and Mexico have not always been tension-free.

During the time of the Texas Republic, the hostility of Anglo Americans toward Mexicans revealed itself. This open hostility continued and increased during the Mexican-American War. Years later, when United States troops went into the interior of Mexico, they attacked Mexicans without mercy, leaving many casualties. Historian Bancroft states that the United States invaded Veracruz and bombed it for four days without cause. Historian Livermore claims that the Americans killed all the wounded and that prisoners were burned alive.[130] The pro-slavery press encouraged the annihilation of Mexicans, inciting the military to carry destruction and loss of life to every family and to weigh on them an iron yoke to inspire respect.[131]

Carey McWilliams writes that it is important to remember that "Mexicans are a 'conquered' people in the Southwest, a people whose culture has been under incessant attack for many years and whose character and achievements as a people have been consistently disparaged."[132] Mr. McWilliams is correct about the Mexican dilemma as a conquered people; it has been over a century and a half since the Mexican-American War, yet some Anglo Americans still seek to justify their actions against Mexican Americans. There is an overt propaganda campaign against all things Mexican; by inference, Mexican Americans are also affected.

Lieutenant George C. Meade, who later fought in the Civil War, stated that American volunteers were "driving husbands out of houses and raping their wives ... They will fight as gallantly as any men, but they are a set of Goths and Vandals without discipline, making us a terror to innocent people."[133]

General Winfred Scott claimed that American volunteers had "committed atrocities to make Heaven weep and every American of Christian morals blush for his country. Murder, robbery, and rape of mothers and daughters in the presence of tied-up males of the families have been common all along the Rio Grande."[134]

The Mexican newspapers also protested. According to Lloyd Lewis, they referred to the American volunteers as "vandals vomited from hell, monsters who bid defiance to the laws of nature … shameless, daring, ignorant, ragged, bad-smelling, long-bearded men … thirsty with the desire to appropriate our riches and our beautiful damsels."[135]

Two days after the United States declared victory over Mexico, it also declared that there was gold in California. This produced a mad rush to California; it brought Anglo Americans from all over the United States as well as an undesirable element from Europe and Australia. Some Mexicans who had not accepted the surrender of Mexico also went to speculate for gold in Sonora. Along with them came miners from Chile and Peru. They all spoke Spanish and got along with each other.[136]

Meanwhile, the California legislature enacted a foreign miners' license tax. This tax was meant to discourage Mexicans, Peruvians, and Chileans from mining.[137] After the Guadalupe Hidalgo Treaty, Mexicans who stayed in the United States were supposed to become American citizens. How were they to impose a foreign tax on Mexicans unless they were unwilling to accept them as American citizens?

Maybe in their greed for gold, the Anglo Americans decided to eliminate the Mexican competition. Suddenly, two thousand Anglo Americans invaded the mining town of Sonora and burned the camp down. The Mexican miners were lynched and murdered.[138]

"On July 5, 1851, a mob of American miners in Downieville lynched a Mexican woman who was three months pregnant." It seemed that after a drunken miner had accosted her several times, she decided to defend herself and stabbed the intruder. She was promptly sentenced to death and brutally lynched by an angry Anglo American mob.[139]

Ever since, Mexican Americans and Anglo Americans have had stormy relations. Today the negativity is not usually that violent but continues silently in many ways, including the supposedly humorous jokes of Jay Leno and more serious cases, such as the closing of schools in predominantly Mexican American neighborhoods.

In modern times, the racism directed against people of Mexican American descent has been very subtle; it does not take the form of cross burnings or other traditional KKK intimidation techniques but instead takes the form of ignoring Mexican Americans' existence and diluting their political power. During President George W.

Bush's administration, we witnessed the gerrymandering of Mexican American communities in Texas so they would have less representation in government and less political power.

Unfortunately, many of our Mexican American politicians, instead of fighting the redrawing of the political map, resign themselves to fighting among each other instead of against the political machine. Many Mexican American and African American politicians embrace the Anglo American political machine and abandon their fight for social justice. Big mistake! Those politicians are often discarded once the European American political machine accomplishes its goals. They are discarded, their political careers are often tarnished, and they fall like a house of cards.

The Lyndon B. Johnson library in Austin, Texas, contains a section dedicated to the civil rights era of the 1960s, a very important chapter in Johnson's presidency. However, the participation and impact of Mexican Americans is completely omitted; in California and Texas, there were many leaders and youth who joined the fight for equal rights long before it became the dominant issue of the sixties. In Texas, Congressman Henry B. Gonzalez filibustered the Texas legislature for days to prevent Jim Crow laws from being enacted; his fight was not only for Mexican Americans but also for African Americans. However, no one outside our community has fully recognized these heroic people, because we have yet to gain the status of being recognized as Americans. We have existed in the southwest since before it was annexed to the United States, yet we are always considered outsiders; is it because of our indigenous roots?

Mexican Americans are not immigrants who arrived in the United States and overnight overpopulated the nation. Mexican Americans have a long and legitimate claim on United States territory that gives them a two-hundred-year head start on European, Asian, and African immigrants. They came with the Spanish explorers and are descendants of indigenous people.

A large percentage of them came over as peons, soldiers, and semi-slaves to do construction work and other manual work for the Spaniards. They came with the rich and powerful Spanish lords who explored and settled the southwest.

John L. Kessell, in his history book *Spain in the Southwest*, narrates how in an expedition through the land of the Zuni, probably in New

Mexico, the Spaniards traveled with new recruits from Spain and about a thousand Mexican Indians.[140]

Those peons were Mexican indigenous people or mestizos; they had no rank and were brought over as soldiers to help defend the Spaniards from the Comanche, Apache, Zuni, and other Indian tribes. They also came as *vaqueros,* or buckaroos, to take care of cattle, to clear the land for farming, and to do manual work for Spaniards. Those Mexican workers would also bring their wives to do work for the Spanish women.

After the Spanish lost the Mexican War of Independence, they also lost all their territories in what is now the United States to Mexico. The Spanish had often given their soldiers and other servants land granted by Spain. The Mexicans who owned land in what would eventually become the United States stayed on their ranches after the Treaty of Guadalupe Hidalgo in 1848. After the Mexican-American War, Mexico had to surrender a very large portion of its original territory. The United States guaranteed that the Spanish-speaking people who had settled those territories and had legal deeds could become American citizens and remain in the United States.

The reason states, cities, rivers, and other landmarks in the southwest often have Spanish names is that Spain was the first European nation to invade those territories. For instance, *Nevada* means "the snow capped state," *Colorado* means "the red region," *Florida* means "the place of abundant flowers" (after the Virgin of Flowers). All these places have Spanish names as a testimony to the fact that Spanish has been spoken in these lands since the sixteenth century. After the annexation of these territories into the United States, the Spanish language continued to co-exist with English for over 160 years.

Yet today some Anglo Americans claim that Spanish is taking over, that a language crisis is looming in the United States, and that eventually Spanish will destroy the English language. These people are completely ignorant of their own history and the dynamic of languages. The English language has already been "corrupted" by Spanish. Whenever two cultures clash, it is inevitable that language will adapt to the new realities. English was originally a Germanic language spoken by the tribes invading the British islands during the first centuries of the Christian era. During that time, they picked up vocabulary from the Romans and the Celts. French-speaking Normans also invaded

Britain, and this new encounter also resulted in the incorporation of alien words into the English vocabulary. When the British invaded American lands, the English language incorporated Native American words. When this nation started receiving immigrants from all over the world, our language changed again.

Some of the people decrying the Spanish language today may live in *ranch* homes, wear *chaps*, raise *broncos*, keep those horses in a *corral*, and take them to a *rodeo*. At the rodeo, they *lasso* the *pintos*. Some may live in *Palo Alto, Los Angeles, Amarillo* or *Las Cruces*. All those terms are Spanish words used before the United States conquered those formerly Mexican territories.

Thus, if those people wanted to return to a pure English language, they would have to purge not only Spanish but also Latin, French, Celtic, various Native American languages, Yiddish, and many other foreign influences that make up what we now know as English. It would be impossible. They would have to change the names of their ranch homes and many words in the cowboy's vocabulary. They would have to change the names of streets, cities, and states in the southwest. Los Angeles would become The Angels, Palo Alto would change into Tall Tree, and Santa Fe would become Holy Faith.

What is important here is not that the Spanish language is coming to change the face of the southwest, a historically Spanish-speaking territory. The reason so many of these terms originated in Spanish is that some of the first ranch owners and ranch hands in the southwest were Mexicans and Mexican Americans who lost their lands after the Treaty of Guadalupe Hidalgo. It was those poor Mexican workers who helped build the big ranching empires like the Texas King Ranch, which not only hired workers from among the Mexican American population but also actually took their lands.

In California, Mexican Americans and Mexicans met a similar fate. If they owned land and an Anglo settler wanted it, the Mexican or Mexican American owner could not even go to court to claim ownership. The courts usually did not recognize Mexican Americans as citizens.

The disrespect the Mexicans in the United States received from Anglo Americans was totally the opposite of what the Treaty of Guadalupe Hidalgo stated. It begins, "In the name of the Almighty God: The United States of America and the Mexican States animated by a sincere desire to put an end to the calamities of the war which unhappily exists between the two Republics and to establish upon a solid basis relations of peace and friendship, which shall confer reciprocal benefits upon the citizens of both, and assure the concord, harmony, and mutual confidence wherein the two people should live as good neighbors …"

Mexico accepted this treaty because it could no longer afford to continue a war with the United States. Mexico also feared the United States would try to conquer the rest of its territory.

According to the peace treaty, Mexicans who stayed in the new United States territory would be considered American citizens and have equal rights. Most of the Mexicans who remained were landowners, which was their reason for staying in the United States. Nevertheless, they soon began losing their lands to European and Anglo American invaders. For example, newcomers to Texas could buy land at auctions, and some of that land belonged to Mexicans who owed taxes. The authorities would sell the land and pay off the taxes. The problem was the price paid to the Mexican owners.

For example, in 1877, the Hidalgo County sheriff auctioned off three thousand acres of the Hinojosa grant for a total of fifteen dollars. At another time the sheriff sold a ranch of four thousand acres for seventeen dollars and fifteen cents.[141]

This situation was not very different from what had happened to the Indians who had tried to assimilate before the Trail of Tears in the United States. The Chickasaw tribe no longer had deer, bear, or buffalo to hunt, so they settled down and became very successful at farming; they raised cattle, pigs, sheep, and goats. They had large crops of cotton and vegetables. When the Europeans and European Americans saw their success, they decided to enact the Indian Removal Bill.[142]

This bill took away all the Indian farms and sent the Native Americans on the horrible Trail of Tears, where many of them literally froze to death and others died of starvation. It was clear that the European Americans did not want Mexicans or Native Americans left in the United States.

The question of why there were so many Mexicans in states like California, New Mexico, Arizona, and Texas is easy to answer; they were traveling with the Spanish explorers.

John L. Kessell writes that on one occasion, a Spanish cavalry army of two hundred traveling through Pueblo Indian territory was accompanied by an army of a thousand or more Mexican Indians on foot and hundreds of supporting Mexican cooks, herders, and muleteers. The Spaniards also brought some monks, Franciscan priests, black men, and other servants.[143]

There is no question that after the Spaniards conquered Mexico they used the Mexican Indians and mestizos as warriors in their conquest of the southwest. They used Mexican people as well as local Indians to build houses, churches, and roads; to carry food; and to help them fight their battles against other Indians they encountered during their conquest. Some of the Spanish had common-law Indian wives who came along as servants. It was those Indians and mestizos who would later inherit the lands left by the Spaniards after Mexican independence from Spain. Those Mexicans received land grants in payment for their services or because they were related to the Spaniards.

The reason so many Mexicans had land in the southwest is important. They were living there after the Mexican-American War when the Treaty of Guadalupe Hidalgo was signed. Most Mexicans in the new United States territory did not want to abandon their ranches, where they had sheep, cattle, horses and crops. Therefore, they stayed, and they were promised that they would be treated fairly. Some Mexicans who fought on the side of the Texas Republic found out that the Anglo settlers and authorities did not trust them either and ended up segregated and alienated.

Mexican families lost their homes, their cattle, their horses, and their lands just like the Native Americans.[144] Those Mexicans were left homeless and powerless. David Montejano, in his book *Anglos and Mexicans in the making of Texas, 1836–1986*, states that Mexicans had learned the concept of white supremacy from childhood. "Anglo and Mexican children, for example, understood that separate schooling meant separation of superior from inferior. This meaning was taught to them in countless lessons—the Mexican school was physically inferior, Mexican children were issued textbooks discarded by Anglo children." Mexican children were brainwashed to feel inferior from childhood, while Anglo children were taught that they were superior and learned to act superior.[145]

In Texas, many Mexican American people and organizations fought segregation for many years, and there were several court cases seeking to remedy inequality. Dr. Hector P. Garcia, the American GI Forum, state representative Henry B. Gonzalez, LULAC, and many brave individuals were among the leaders for desegregation in schools and other public facilities.

In my hometown, integration of public schools took place around 1947. My older cousins tried to enter the desegregated high school. They were happy, because they felt they were going to get a high school diploma; there had not been any high school for Mexican Americans in my small town before. One of my cousins—she was dark skinned and heavy set—attended the white high school for several weeks. One day she came home and said she could not tolerate the humiliation by the other students, who pushed her down the staircase and called her names. Her youngest sister, who was very attractive and fair skinned, received less harassment. Therefore, my oldest cousin, who was actually the most intelligent, had to quit school because of racial harassment, while the younger one went on to graduate. They were the only Mexican American children who integrated the high school that year; two were too many for the Anglo school.

In my case, my second grade teacher asked me if I planned to change schools in the fall. I remember it was a hot summer day, and I was standing on an empty lot close to my mother's Mexican café. The teacher approached me and told me that if I stayed in the segregated school, she would promote me a grade. Without hesitation, I informed the teacher I had decided I would go to the Anglo school, because there I would not be insulted for being Protestant.

My teacher knew that she and other teachers were going to lose their jobs if we changed schools. Our small town did not need two schools, so they promised the kids to skip them a grade. That fall I was the only Mexican American to show up at the white school. The girls remained quiet, but the boys immediately started to shout at me to leave because they did not want "dirty Mexicans" in their school. The teacher I was assigned was very polite and accepted me without any resentment. The girls followed the teacher's example, and the boys were the only ones who called me names. Those who knew me from Sunday school were more tolerant, since I had already attended church with them. As for the kids in my neighborhood, they heard my glowing reports about the new school; it had toilets with running water and bathrooms with towels to dry your hands. The following year, all the students from the segregated school showed up at the Anglo school. The teachers kept their promise and the children from the old school were now a grade ahead of me.

However, at that time, school administrators declared that those Mexican American students were not able to perform at the same level as their Anglo counterparts. Perhaps the fact that they skipped a grade might have accounted for the slower performance. Nevertheless, it was enough to re-segregate Mexican American students. Although the school was now integrated, the classrooms were not. They found a novel way to segregate, maybe moving the students in the segregated school a grade ahead was part of a scheme. Teachers decided that the majority of the Mexican American children needed special education classes, which meant they would have to go into separate rooms, have recess at different times, and eat on a different schedule. In other words, they would never mingle with the Anglo students, except for a handful of Mexican American students who would stay in the Anglo American classrooms, in order to comply with the new state regulations about integration. Since I did not skip a grade and had no academic problems, I stayed in the regular integrated classroom.

In Texas and all over the southwest, most schools in Mexican American neighborhoods still remain inferior; some of those schools are overcrowded and lack playground space and science labs, while the opposite is true at a great number of schools in predominately white neighborhoods. In San Antonio, Texas, they have even decided to close high schools in the barrio and make a single large high school to save money. Have Mexican Americans protested? The answer is no! The poor feel they do not have the power to demand better schools, and many middle-class Mexican Americans who have left the barrio are not concerned. Here again, our community lacks unity and remains brainwashed to believe our children are just inferior. The justification I last heard was that larger schools could have larger school bands. The truth is that this type of lame propaganda is just to make peace with the children's families.

Poor Mexican American children are often discriminated against in Texas. In the past, discrimination was even bolder. Montejano documents a case from a Mexican consul in El Paso, describing an incident in which an Anglo American seven-year-old child fell and hurt her face. The mother asked the child if a Mexican boy had hit her.

The child lied and said yes. The result was that the Mexican American boy and his brother were shot as a way to teach them to stay away from Anglo American children.[146]

Although the author did not date this event, it probably occurred prior to 1940. This event shows the deep racial hatred that existed among Anglo Americans. Montejano states that according to Anglo Americans, "Mexicans were untouchable inferiors, and disciplining those who stepped out of place was no offense."[147]

"The stability of the segregated order rested on Mexican recognition of their own inferiority. Mexicans had to be taught and shown that they were dirty and that this was a permanent condition—that they could not become clean."[148]

In some cases, newly arrived immigrants from Europe quickly learned and shared these racist attitudes toward Native Americans and Mexicans.

Mary Jaques, an English woman who visited Texas for two years in the late 1880s, wrote in her journal that it was hard to convince Texans that Mexicans were human. She wrote, "seems to be the Texan's natural enemy; he is treated like a dog, or, perhaps, not so well." She was upset that her British educated friends had such a savage attitude about killing Mexicans as a sport.[149]

The hate against Mexicans was so prevalent that many Anglo Americans claimed that Mexicans were so impertinent and well protected by the government that the Anglo Americans needed to get together and run them out of the country.[150]

Between 1920 and 1940, when Texas became more of a commercial state, northern Anglo Americans started to move into the state. David Montejano writes a humorous story about a woman who had moved to Riviera, Texas. He relates that in a letter to a friend, Mrs. J. B. Womack wrote about her first encounter with Mexicans. She stated that one day while staying home alone, she spotted a group of Mexicans approaching her house on horseback. They knocked and called out what seemed to be the word *carta*. She did not know if they wanted a cart or to put her in a cart and take her away. She locked herself up and did not respond. Finally, one of the Mexicans who spoke some English cried out, "We are here for our mail." The men were coming for their mail; Mrs. Womack's home was also a post office. She said that maybe what scared her so much was all the knowledge of Mexicans she had learned from reading history and war stories: "I had the impression that all Mexicans were cruel and treacherous like those I had read of."[151]

This folly remains in place today. What people learn about Mexicans and Mexican Americans comes from literary fiction and television. Television and films are our worst defamers. They consistently depict us as thieves, murderers, and rapists, lazy and of low morals. Television does not show Mexican Americans as doctors, professors, or other highly skilled professionals. Our children get a bad self-image from these depictions, and perhaps these shows even negatively impact their futures in the same manner that good programs like Sesame Street help children learn reading and writing skills.

As long as movies and television continue to show only negative depictions of Mexican Americans, our families must be vigilant and not allow children access to these negative stereotypes of Mexican Americans or other Spanish-speaking characters. In some cases, such as in *Law and Order* or *CSI*, Hispanic characters do not even appear physically. It is sufficient to mention the Spanish-sounding name of a criminal and the jail in which he is incarcerated. The invisible and silent character never shows his face but becomes a dangerous maniac. Why is he invisible? They did not even want to hire a Mexican American actor for a role as a criminal! Mexican Americans often get credit for things that are negative but are never given credit for the positive things they have done for America.

Usually textbooks and films convey the idea that American railroads were built exclusively by Chinese labor. As a child, I remember my uncle talking about working in the railroad and the adventures he experienced. He claimed many Mexican railroad workers on the Texas to Chicago track left Texas and did not return.

My uncle also claimed that when the railroad needed to take cattle from Texas to the slaughterhouses in Chicago, they hired Mexican and Mexican American workers to build the railroads, which explains the presence of a sizeable Mexican American population in Chicago today. This migration dates back to the late 1800s and early 1900s. I learned this from oral history when I was young and not from any history book. America does not recognize the hard work that Mexicans and Mexican Americans have contributed to this nation; their deeds do not generally appear in history books.

In Texas, Mexican Americans worked in every possible position on farms from picking onions to picking cotton; in the ranching business, they did everything from herding to keeping sheep and taming horses. Many of the terms used today on ranches come from Spanish words: *lasso, corral, rodeo, bronco, pinto,* and *patio.* Mexicans learned the art of ranching from the Spaniards, who brought horses, cattle, sheep, donkeys, chickens, and other domesticated farm animals to the southwest. Mexicans have contributed a great deal to the American southwest.

In the United States, Mexicans and even Mexican Americans are treated as criminals. In California, the police apprehended a man named Pedro Guzman, who was fifty-five years old and a United States citizen from Los Angeles, and deported him to Mexico. The man was mentally incapacitated and could not defend himself. However, because he looked Mexican, he was immediately labeled an illegal alien and deported. This was not the first or only time in America's history that Mexican Americans were deported. During the Great Depression, the government deported many poor Mexican Americans under the Mexican Repatriation Act, which required Mexican nationals to be returned to Mexico. In reality, many Mexican Americans who had lived in the United States for generations and were not Mexican nationals were also deported; they were just poor Americans. However, it seems that no matter how many generations Mexican Americans live in the United States, they are still not considered Americans. That is why they are given so many labels, such as Latino or person of color, but are never called Americans.

The legal status of undocumented immigrants varies depending on the political winds. Those who cross over from Mexico and Central and South America are imprisoned and receive cruel and unusual punishment, such as losing custody of their children. Some time ago, a woman came from Mexico with a young child and died in the crossing. The motherless child was immediately repatriated. During the Clinton administration, a Cuban child and his mother embarked on a raft to the United States. The mother died at sea, but the child arrived safely. The case became a political game; the government argued he should be returned to his father in Cuba, while Florida Cuban organizations and Republicans insisted the child should remain in the United States because he had relatives in Miami. We do not know if the baby from

Mexico had relatives in the United States; no one bothered to ask or cared.

Today many African Americans have attained power in the United States; they have demanded to be treated with respect and dignity. They demanded that civil rights be granted to their community. As the white community sees themselves losing political power, they feel they need to find another racial group they can oppress. Immigrants from Mexico and Central and South America have become the new victims of extreme and violent racism. These immigrants feel powerless because they are strangers in a new land. They are poor and cannot even defend themselves, because they do not speak English. As of late, many violent crimes have been committed against them. The problem is that this poisonous venom could also flow against Mexican Americans. The Mexican American community cannot stop being vigilant.

Recently, CNN television news reporter Lou Dobbs ranted on a daily basis about the evils of Hispanic immigrants. He kept pointing out how they were ruining the American economy. As wealthy American companies go to Asia and other parts of the world seeking cheap labor, Lou Dobbs and CNN kept pointing their fingers at the lowly Spanish-speaking immigrants who come to do hard, cheap labor. When American jobs go to China, India, and Japan, we applaud their cheap labor and cheap goods. We have been told our workers are not as good as Chinese and Indian workers, so we do not complain when our jobs go overseas. We accept what CNN indoctrinates us with while we lose more and more jobs and the wealthy corporations get richer and richer, and then we blame it on immigrants and Mexican Americans. A group called Democracy Now approached CNN and demanded that they take Lou Dobbs's daily propaganda off the air. CNN would never admit that they succumbed to pressure from a citizen's group, but they actually fired Lou Dobbs! Mexican Americans need to protest negative propaganda; we must hold accountable those who create negative images of our community.

Even toy companies create games for children with negative stereotypes. Mattel produced a card game in 2006 called Lie Detector in which all the cartoon-like characters wear normal clothes except for the one who looks like a Mexican. He has sleek black hair, a moustache, and is short and brown; he is depicted wearing prison garb. Let us keep indoctrinating the young people with racist attitudes! Mexican

Americans must put pressure on Mattel to stop this hate mongering masquerading as innocent children's games.

They must also put pressure on their congressional representatives, their senators, and their president to demand inclusion in the nation's government and decision-making. Mexican Americans pay taxes and vote; they are loyal Americans and must be treated as such! They must create a revolution for human justice.

Some police departments in the United States have abused immigrants. In three recent cases in East New Haven, Connecticut, police tasered Yadanny Garcia three times and ordered him to "go back where he came from." Jose Luis Albaraccin was pepper sprayed and beaten on the ground. When Edgar Torres threatened to denounce the officers who had used a taser on him, an officer stated that if he denounced them he would kill him. All three men had one thing in common: they were not sure why they had been arrested. In East New Haven, immigrants do not have to go to the police station to be arrested; all they have to do is just go to their Spanish-speaking grocery store to be ticketed and have their license plates removed by police. Because of all the harassment on individuals and businesses, federal agents are presently investigating the police department in New Haven.[152]

Today Mexicans and Central Americans are undergoing many types of persecution in the United States. Unlawful entry into the country is considered a crime, which often requires prison time. A crime requires court appearances, a judge, a lawyer, and sometimes a jury. Many immigrants are not aware of how the American judicial system works and do not appeal the judge's decisions.

Names I Have Been Called

European Americans keep chipping away at our roots, sculpturing and reshaping our identity according to their political agendas. They have called us aliens, Mexicans, dirty Mexicans (a popular Texas term), greasers, beaners, Mexican Americans, Latin Americans, Latinos, Chicanos, Spanish, Hispanics, brown people, and lately people of color.

In the United States, we are still called by any other name but American. We are not Hispanics, not Latinos, not Mexicans, not people of color. We are Americans who happen to be of Mexican descent. Many Mexican Americans, as well as many Mexicans, are descendants of slaves; they are mestizos, half-breeds who are part indigenous and part European (Spanish). The Spaniards taught our ancestors to shun their indigenous roots, but today Mexican Americans are no longer expected to be flattered if you call them Spanish. If Mexican Americans were truly Spanish, they would have long ago been accepted and integrated into European American society. Indigenous people and Mestizos have not been accepted and integrated, because they are racially different from European American society. It is not our culture, our language, or our Catholic religion that makes us different; it is only our race. People from all over Europe, including Spain, bring different cultures and religions to the United States, and yet they are easily assimilated into America's white society. The United States has rejected indigenous people as Americans purely based on race. This discrimination is certainly not based on origin, because they have been on these continents longer than European Americans.

In order to justify their treatment of indigenous people, European Americans came up with the theory that our prehistoric ancestors crossed from Asia by way of the Bering Strait, thus giving us an alien air. Maybe we went to Asia via the Bering Strait. Nevertheless, the effort to make us immigrants in America continues. Scholars have never debated alternative theories or offered other explanations, because it justifies calling indigenous people immigrants.

Hispanic is a term that loosely describes the heterogeneous group of natives and immigrants who in one way or another have acquired a "Spanish" culture. The federal government probably started using this term for convenient bureaucratic purposes, to lump together in a category all those people who just did not fit into black or white. This term really includes people from a variety of racial groups but unfortunately does not accurately describe Mexican Americans, because it denies our indigenous and mestizo roots.

Phoenicians, when they occupied parts of the Iberian Peninsula, named the area *Hispania*. In their language, it meant "land of many rabbits." Most likely that had to do with the number of rodents they saw there. By contrast, indigenous Americans should really be from the land of many jaguars; these felines inhabited both North and South America, and many nations on these continents worshipped the jaguars.

Another term that has been in use for quite some time is Latino, supposedly based on language origin; in the United States, it describes those who speak Spanish. In a strict sense, Latino could mean those who speak a romance language or who come from countries that speak a language with roots in ancient Latin, such as Italian, Spanish, Portuguese, French, or Romanian.

This is also a misnomer, since most of the people so called do not descend from the Romans, who spoke Latin. To make matters murkier, in the United States, Italians or people of Italian descent are not Latinos. This term is usually reserved for people from Mexican or Central or South American descent, whether they speak Spanish or not. It is a polite term used for half-breeds.

The term Latino or Latin American originated in South America; Chilean Francisco Bilbao coined the term Latin America.[153] Hispanic was a name appropriately given to all the Spanish-speaking people in South America. After gaining independence from Spain, South Americans did not identify with Spain but preferred France, which considered itself Latin. France was the center of the intellectual activity that gave rise to the independence movements of Latin American countries. In turn, France liked the Americas in a different manner; Napoleon III sent Maximilian to invade Mexico in 1863. Their occupation lasted four years, and the Mexicans eventually defeated France and executed Maximilian. That was the end of the French moment in Mexico and the end of the Latino illusion. The French invasion did not impress Mexico.[154]

Hence, Latino is not a racial category. Yet many years ago, during the first O. J. Simpson trial, either the Los Angeles Police Department or the media mentioned it as a racial classification in DNA testing. Since such wide varieties of people speak romance languages, I guess a Latino DNA could belong to anybody in the Americas—indigenous natives, mestizos, descendants of Europeans, Africans, and Asians who came to settle the continent.

Lately, we have finally faded into a blob: people of color. Strangely enough, this is a term accepted and used by many activists, but it has completely dehumanized us. Now we are not a race, a culture, or a society; we have become a thing, like a red car, a blue dress, or any item to be used and discarded.

The term *people of color* dehumanizes every race that is not white. It is as if only those who are of European stock have the right to call themselves Americans, because they do not belong to the subhuman race they consider colored. This labeling makes the identity of individuals depend solely on color and not race, culture, history, or national origin. Elite European Americans, who historically have classified people solely based on political biases and not on any scientific basis, arbitrarily determine color. The most evident example is the labeling of North American indigenous people as red men and labeling the indigenous people of Mexico as brown people. This political labeling had a very important goal: to separate the indigenous North Americans from the Spanish-speaking mestizos who are also indigenous. If one were to look at the DNA of these groups of people, the similarity would be astonishing. There are no biological differences between the indigenous people of Mexico, the United States, Canada, or South America. This labeling does not have any scientific basis; it was solely a political label intended to keep indigenous groups from uniting to fight discrimination and injustice. Those superficial terms have kept the North American indigenous people from forming alliances with other indigenous American groups in Central and South America. It is true that American Natives and Mexicans have mixed with Europeans, but their genetic code remains the same.

Tohono O'odham is a reservation in Arizona that borders on Mexico. The people who live there experience racial discrimination when they are asked to identify themselves and produce documentation proving they belong on their reservation. This happens because they look like many Mexican immigrants. They say they are asked what they are doing on the reservation; their response is that they have been there for four thousand years. Then they ask the federal agents what they are doing there on their land! Those federal agents have no respect for the environment or sacred Native American places. They are only seeking Mexican aliens who happen to look like American natives because they are all brothers.[155]

This Machiavellian term, *people of color*, serves only to make the water murkier for all minorities. For instance, when there is housing, educational, or other discrimination, no one minority can say who is suffering the most discrimination, because everyone is in one pool. For example, if statistics show that a college is admitting 10 percent students of color, there is no way to know out of that ten percent how many students are of a particular ethnicity, such as Mexican or Cuban. Everyone is buried under one color banner instead of having a defined ethnic group. This designation could lead to hiding the lack of opportunities for several groups who might be of the lowest educated and lowest paid American ethnic groups.

The fact that many migrant farm workers are Mexican Americans also means that they have the lowest paying jobs, jobs that require them to work from sunup to sunset five to six days a week without any health insurance, job security, or opportunities for education. When Mexican Americans are lumped into a single color category, it helps to disguise the blatant discrimination they are suffering, because statistics are averaged out over all ethnic groups. Today racism toward Mexican Americans is on the rise, masked by immigration issues; it subjects all American citizens who are mestizos to a sinister suspicion that somehow this ethnic group is plotting a takeover of the nation. In reality, many of the Mexican Americans who live in the United States have been in this country since the southwestern territories were annexed to the United States using military power.

Today the term *people of color* has been accepted by many Mexican Americans without questioning its philosophical and practical implications. They do not realize that when different ethnic groups are lumped together, the government and other institutions can hide discrimination by not having to account for numbers by ethnicity; this label is just another way to deny who we are as citizens, a way to make us forget we have lived in North America for centuries; it is designed to take away all our history and our past as Americans.

Some time ago, I asked a young man who referred to himself as a person of color why he chose to be called a person of color. He stated it was because he was colored. I asked him if white was a color. He said yes, so I asked him why white people do not call themselves colored. Is it because white is actually a code-word for superior? It is similar to Aryan, a term used in Nazi Germany to denote German racial superiority. White seems to have a similar interpretation, so if you do not belong to the white race, you default to being inferior. Outside of calling himself colored, this young man could not justify who he really was; he was just part of the color blob. As a young man, he accepted the colored label.

The term *people of color* is reminiscent of the colored designation the South African regime used to segregate Africans and East Indians. It was also used by southern segregationists in the United States to maintain their racial dictatorship. It is a term that denies our ethnicity and cultural identity and our rights as Americans.

I personally dislike a term that takes away my identity as a person, a dynamic and unique being, a term that blurs my personality into a nonentity by reducing me to an inanimate object, a color. I have a rich cultural history; I belong to a unique race of people with unique features, a unique language, and a social past. Mexican Americans have living roots that allow them to grow and flourish. They have a social milieu; they are not a color or objects that can be possessed like a blue car, a white wall, red roses, or any other material substance. Today the wealthy corporations think of people as material things they can own and dispose of, and *people of color* becomes just another way to refer to anyone who does not belong to the European supreme race. Yes, America continues to be racist.

Now that we have received many different names, politicians and demagogues claim that Mexican Americans are not patriotic because they do not claim to be Americans. Children do not learn about their labels at home; they learn them from teachers and Anglo American society, in schools, and in the media. Our children learn they are not

Americans but hyphenated Americans who only create problems for society.

A major medium used to propagate labels and stereotypes about Mexican Americans has been the movie industry. Between 1908 and 1915, Hollywood actually used the term *greaser* in several of its film titles, such as: *Greaser Gauntlet* and *Bronco Billy and the Greaser.* In these movies, Mexicans and Mexican Americans were divided into "good greasers" and "evil greasers." This stereotype of Mexican Americans continues to exist today. As a child, I remember how Anglo American children who wanted to insult me would just call me a greaser, and I suspect there are still European Americans who whisper that term behind our backs, still portraying us as evil, ignorant, and rude greasers. From 1908 to 1925, during the Mexican Revolution, American troops sent to capture Pancho Villa sang the following song:

> *It's a long, long way to capture Villa;*
> *It's a long way to go;*
> *It's a long way across the border*
> *Where the dirty greasers grow.*[156]

For generations, people of African descent have struggled for social justice and economic power in the United States. They learned that there is power in numbers, so they use the term *people of color* and are satisfied to see all Americans divided between people of color and whites, with them carrying the color banner and leading the way. The problem that we have seen is that when they carry the banner, many of us are still left behind. For instance, when African American leaders advocated for more people of color on television, the results was that a great deal more blacks have been on the screen but only very few token Mexican Americans and other Latinos, including people from Spain. Why is this important? It is important because television is a wealthy industry. When consumers buy items like Nikes, Dr. Pepper, Dell computers, Jeeps, or other advertised products, they spend money that pays for television commercials. Mexican Americans are a large segment of the consumer population, but they are discriminated against when it comes to getting jobs in English-speaking ads; they are not hired for television commercials. Somehow, Mexican Americans are seen as inferior and are not allowed to participate in American culture.

Mexican Americans, Mexicans, and Central Americans can be discarded without guilt or a sense of justice. Crimes against undocumented immigrants can be ignored by the police and the European American community that controls the courts. When mestizo immigrants are despised, by association Mexican Americans are not respected as human beings. We will not stop the injustice until we come out with our banner and fight racial injustice directed against our community. We have to come out under our own banner, the Mexican American banner; otherwise, we will continue to suffer discrimination, and our families and children will suffer for it as racism increases against Mexican and Central American immigrants.

European Americans label us according to their political situation; our identity has always depended on the ruling classes. Our people have been labeled according to the political winds depending on how strong racist sentiments are at the time. We have been denied the right of self-determination. According to my birth certificate, I was classified as white. Some Mexican Americans believe that the reason we used to be called white is that Mexico was protesting the subhuman treatment of Mexicans and Mexican Americans. Texas was trying to amend for the treatment of braceros. Mexico demanded rights for its citizens living in the United States, so Texas came out with a Caucasian Race Resolution in 1944, declaring that Mexicans were to be treated as white, and that was supposed to include Mexican Americans. This bill endorsed equal rights in public places, businesses, and leisure places. It was a bill that granted rights to Mexicans but still segregated African Americans, who did not have an advocate like the government of Mexico. It was a political move to keep Mexico satisfied with the treatment of Mexicans. David Montejano states that the Mexican Consul General Miguel Calderon politely stated that it was "merely exceptional measures for protecting Mexican Nationals in view of exceptional circumstances prevailing [in] this State."[157]

Being considered white was important not because our skin was really white but because of the political significance of the term *white*. Being considered white meant that we had equal rights as Americans; for that reason, European Americans did not want to accept us as whites. As racism increased, we were no longer considered whites. We had to change color.

Some Mexican Americans claim that we were once classified as white to beef up the political power of Anglo Americans, who wanted to have a larger part of the population in the United States classified as white. Another theory is that Mexico classified its citizens as whites and we did not want to change Mexico's classification. Mexican Americans do not want to be classified as whites; they just want to be recognized as a people who have a historical and cultural background and who are United States citizens.

Thus, we can say our racial name-calling remains political and is not biological or sociological. I was born before 1944, and my birth certificate still stated I was white; I think Texas used to call us white because in Mexico all mestizos were qualified as white. Therefore, Mexican Americans were white on paper, but in reality, they continued to be segregated until the civil rights movement.

There is one exception to the statement that we received all our names from others. In the 60's and 70's, during the Civil Rights era, and with the emergence of the Farm Worker and Brown Power movements, young Mexican American activists decided to call themselves Chicanos. This was a term used to express pride, dignity and independence; to denote acceptance of our indigenous roots and unique culture. Although several explanations have been offered for the meaning of this term, there is no consensus as to its origin. The most accepted etymology is that it is a shortened form for *Mexicano* (Mexican) that derived into *Xicano* or Chicano. Unfortunately this term might have limited long-term effectiveness, because it is associated with the civil rights era. Today the term is not as popular as it was during the 60's and 70's, it is usually associated with radicalism, and not everyone accepts it. Today some young Mexican Americans prefer this term, it is their choice.

The name that many people of Mexican descent still prefer is the old term Mexican American. It is a direct link to our Mexican historical heritage, culture, society, and indigenous race. I prefer this term because it shows a direct connection to what I consider myself to be.

Many Anglo Americans still claim their ancestral roots. They are descendants of the Mayflower Pilgrims, sons of George Washington, Englishmen, Frenchmen, Germans, or members of other European groups; they are proud and celebrate their heritage. On the other hand, we are supposed to be simply people of color. They too should be people of color; they are white. However, color is what separates superior from inferior in America. Why else is it important that we be classified by color?

We want to be identified based on our historical and social roots as citizens who were born and raised in this country. We desire to be identified by our historical heritage as Americans who built this country side by side with the European and other immigrants. We want to be recognized by the national origin of our ancestors. *Mexican American* defines our historical origin and culture. We want to be recognized as legitimate American citizens. We want to be proud of our heritage.

According to the missionary Fray Diego Durán, who lived in Mexico during the conquest, the Aztecs called themselves the people of Aztlan, the "place of the white heron." *Aztlan* is a term that means "whiteness." This term does not have anything to do with skin color; it seems to be a term having to do with sacredness, akin to a halo in Christian religions. They considered themselves a sacred race and claimed to have come from the land of Seven Caves.[158] I suppose we could be called Aztlan-Americans.

The Aztecs did not think of themselves as dirty Mexicans or people of color; they were sacred, dignified children of God. This idea was expressed in many Aztec poems.

When I was in first grade, I was Mexican. By third grade, I was Mexican American. By sixth grade, I had become a Latin American, and when I reached college age I was a Chicana. By the time my oldest son was in college, I was a Hispanic, and by the time my youngest child enrolled in college, he had become a person of color.

I called the school that had sent the pamphlet and told them they might as well continue to call us greasers or dirty Mexicans, names we know we have historically been called. I asked them not to call us by a derogatory name such as colored, a term used by southern segregationists and by the South African apartheid regime. This term takes away our Mexican American identity.

As a child, when I attended the recently integrated elementary school in my hometown, Anglo boys in my third-grade class often used the terms *dirty* and *greaser* to address me. What this term really reveals is the hate and aggression toward anyone who may resemble a Mexican; that is, anyone with indigenous features. Carey McWilliams claims that according to Vizetelly, *greaser* was originally "California slang for a mixed of race of Mexicans and Indians."[159] The name was based on the fact that most Mexicans have thick, dark black hair, giving it the appearance of being shiny and greasy. Today the term is still in use to denote Mexican Americans in a derogatory manner. White supremacists still apply terms like *greaser* and *dirty* to refer to Mexican Americans.

The so-called politically correct crowd uses the term *people of color* to refer to all non-white minorities. According to Geoffrey Fox, Benjamin Chavis, at one time executive director of the National Association for the Advancement of Colored People (NAACP), asked Spanish speakers to join their organization under the banner of people of color. He stated that Spanish-speaking people had a similar culture and history, and some even descended from blacks.[160] By a similar rationale, we could say that blacks should have Anglo leaders, because a large number of African Americans have European blood.

In seeking a voice for Mexican Americans, blood is not an issue; social issues, such as schools, housing, working conditions, and health, are what are important to Mexican Americans in their communities. The people who have grown up within our community must address those living conditions that require change. Blacks and Anglo Americans have rarely taken an interest in Mexican American issues, such as civil rights and the Farm Worker's Union. Historically, the people who have lived and worked in our communities have been the ones who defended our civil rights. We have fought for schools, unions, and health care. Congressman Henry B. Gonzales, Dr. Hector P. Garcia, and Cesar Chavez are just a few of the leaders who have made a difference in our society. Anglos and blacks are not familiar with our struggles, because they have never lived in our communities and are not familiar with the needs in our schools and in our places of work. Mexican Americans should not delegate defense of their rights to outside civil leaders if they are to maintain a strong political presence in the United States; they should not wait for others to carry their banner. Mexican Americans make up two thirds of the so-called Hispanic population; they should not allow anyone to be condescending to them.

We all come into this world with baggage. Mexican Americans happen to have Mexican heritage baggage. Yet our baggage does not come in matching sets; it comes in a mix-and-match set that includes the American indigenous heritage and culture and the European Spanish heritage and culture. Nevertheless, most Mexican Americans also have an Anglo American culture. Those of us born in the United States never studied Mexican culture, but we studied the culture, language, history, and government of the United States. We know the story of George Washington but do not know the story of Moctezuma. We can spell and write in English but have never studied Spanish grammar.

Sometimes people trying to define Mexican American culture claim that it is different because it is not Western. They forget that the Spanish Catholic church heavily influenced Mexican culture. In Spain, Roman Catholicism is a faith influenced by Greek, Roman, Moorish, and Sephardic Jewish philosophy; in other words, Western philosophy. As Christians, Mexican Americans follow Catholic doctrines that are based on Aristotle, Plato, Thomas Aquinas, and the Bible. We inherited the soul of Cervantes' Don Quixote, a man so in love with the legends of knighthood that he became insane. Mexicans also often become insane with legends of heroism in the United States, and the result is that they are willing to sacrifice their lives to come to this country. Sure, we also have cultural baggage from our indigenous roots, just as Europeans have historical and cultural baggage from their ancient pre-Christian past.

How much more Western can Mexican Americans get? The language is Western; Spanish is a Romance language akin to Italian and French. It is not an Asian or African language. It is language that determines the mindset and philosophy of a human being. Most Mexicans are Catholic, and a few are Protestant. Again, these are Western religions. But more important to Mexican Americans is the fact that the latest generations actually speak only English and attend American schools and actually acquire white American ideals, dressing habits, eating habits, and even patriotic habits. Most Mexican Americans after one generation in the United States feel no different from other immigrants who come to the United States, except that they are not accepted as Americans because of their physical appearance. They look like most other indigenous American natives. This is a clue as to why they are never assimilated into American society. Poverty is determined by our racial heritage. It is what determines our culture. We live in a culture of poverty and racial discrimination. We are the victims of imperialism and of European Americans who are afraid we might reclaim our lands, which we lost to the United States when the Anglo immigrants invaded Mexican territory. In over a hundred and sixty years of imperialism, we have been faithful to the American government and have never betrayed it in war or in peace. All we have asked for has been equality and justice. We have only gotten justice and equality piecemeal.

Mexican Americans eat French fries, pizza, and hot dogs as much as they eat tamales and tacos, just like the rest of America. They buy as many blue jeans and sneakers as other Americans and like to tinker with computers as much as the rest of America. Yet one rarely sees commercials in which a Mexican American writes on a computer while sitting in his jeans. Chewing gum is an old Mexican tradition. The ancient Aztecs already used chewing gum, but one never sees Mexican Americans advertising gum. Mexican Americans also love television and movies, but outside of a handful of actors, they rarely see people who resemble them on the screen except as criminals or maids. Separating them, ostracizing them, is a way of committing total discrimination against Mexican Americans.

Unfortunately, discrimination is not limited to the United States but is common in all of Mexico, Central America, and South America, where European immigrants have taken over. Where poverty reigns, usually the natives are at the bottom layers of society. Our nations are divided along racial lines. Skin color becomes what matters instead of intelligence, strength, beauty, or moral virtue. White is superior because white has more wealth and therefore the power to regulate our futures! It is still Hitler's evaluation of the supreme white race, the Aryan race. The myth was that they were smarter, stronger, and had desirable physical traits, such as blond hair, blue eyes, and freckled skin. Aryans had many colors, but their skin was pale.

People are intelligent regardless of skin color. Different ethnic groups are skillful in all types of sports regardless of race. However, people are still marginalized, and it seems to be related to skin color. Skin pigmentation is still the determining factor in what is considered the superior race, even if this is never mentioned in public. It would not be politically correct to mention an Aryan superior race in the United States.

The United States prefers to consider itself a colorblind nation but continues to persecute Mexican Americans because they look different. The United States is under the illusion that African American people have broken the chains of discrimination, but many of them still live in poverty. Although some people may have "made it," traditionally segregated and impoverished communities are still pretty much the same. Today Mexicans as an ethnic group are openly subjected to racism in this country. Segregation still exists; Mexican Americans continue to have inferior schools and it is still acceptable to make jokes about how ignorant and stupid they are. They remain voiceless and invisible in the United States.

Before the Mexican American War, some Mexicans were wealthy landowners and were respected by the Anglo Americans who arrived with land grants from the Mexican government. The Anglo immigrants called them "Spanish" or "Castilians." When the Mexicans had their lands taken away by illegal methods, they became poor half-breeds and Mexican Indians. It seems that the richer the Mexicans were, the more they were treated as white. The poorer they became, the darker they got, so when their territory became the United States, the census renamed Mexicans the "other race."[161]

When Samuel Huntington claims Mexican Americans refuse to assimilate, he fails to tell the whole story. Our assimilation has not depended on religion; many of us have belonged to Protestant denominations for generations. It is not our clothing; in the 1940s when our men went to war, the women stayed home and tried to dress like Betty Davis; we danced the jitterbug, we attended movies featuring Clark Gable, and we bought Frank Sinatra records. However, after we ate our hamburgers and drank our cokes, we went home to our segregated neighborhoods, our old "Mexican" barrios. While many of our men came back as war heroes wearing military medals and commendations, they were still segregated. Segregation was so strong that in large cities, property deeds and land titles had clauses stating that they could not be sold to Mexican Americans. In San Antonio, Texas, we may still find those discriminating clauses in some old deeds; they are now invalid, but they exist. In some American cities, schools were segregated until after World War II.

Even when Mexican Americans died fighting in World War II, they were segregated and discriminated against. Such was the famous case of Felix Longoria, a World War II veteran. When he died, his wife Beatrice tried to have a funeral service in her hometown, and she asked that he be placed in the chapel. Mr. Tom Kennedy, the owner of the mortuary, told her that "Mexicans" were not allowed in the chapel. He suggested that instead her dead husband should be placed in her home.

Dr. Hector P. Garcia, who had also served in World War II, heard the story and was upset that after Mr. Longoria gave his life for his country he continued to be segregated in death. Dr. Garcia took the case to court and won. Eventually, Mr. Longoria was buried in Arlington Cemetery in Washington DC.[162]

Hector P. Garcia visited the Mexican American communities in the Valley region of southern Texas as a medical doctor and saw the appalling poverty his people lived in. He then decided he had to organize the people so they could have a voice in their community. He gathered war veterans and organized the American GI Forum so that people could gather and express the grievances they had against segregation. Dr. Garcia called upon Texas to modernize and to become democratic by allowing thousands of Mexican Americans to vote without paying the poll tax of $1.75, which was too much money for people who often earned no more than three dollars a day and had to feed their families.[163] Could the reason that they did not assimilate have anything to do with the fact that they could not even vote?

Although American citizens, Mexican Americans have received the label "Mexican" for generations, so it is no surprise that in interviews and surveys, a large number of them respond that they are Mexicans. As a child, I was never called American. Historically, our schools have called us Mexican Americans, Latinos, and Hispanics, and now they wonder why we call ourselves Mexicans. Filling out papers at school and at work, there is always a place we have to write "Mexican American." It was not our parents who taught us to call ourselves Mexican or Mexican American. America's racist culture always wanted to know our ethnic origin; what they really wanted to know was our indigenous origin, not in what nation we claimed citizenship.

In order to have more jobs in the film industry and on television, we must speak out and demand those jobs. We must get professional training to be included in the high-paying work force. To achieve this, we must demand more college admissions. In order to have better schools and colleges, we must demand that the nation not leave us out of the field of education. To prevent exclusion, we need to train our children for college. A typical excuse for leaving us out is that we are not qualified, not prepared, or that we would take the place of more deserving students. Only Mexican Americans can strive for those actions in their communities; they need to speak up.

Several centuries ago, our indigenous ancestors were architects, mathematicians, astronomers, and agriculturists; they built their civilizations on their own without influence from outside of these continents. Today, when our youth try to enter colleges, their qualifications are questioned. Therefore, it is necessary that they speak up and be visible. They must speak up and be seen in schools, in the courts, and on the streets. We can no longer afford to remain invisible and voiceless in America. There is too much racism and discrimination against Mexican Americans. This racism can be seen in television commercials and the media, where Mexican Americans do not appear as part of the American community; the message of the media is to stay away from Mexican Americans.

There is a saying that a language is a dialect with an army and a navy. Language follows the triumph of a military victory. British Americans had the power to decide the borders and the official language of the United States, displacing the indigenous tongues. Today, indigenous communities are for the most part bilingual. Likewise, it was the Spaniards and the Portuguese who decided the languages of Latin America. Those indigenous communities that resisted and endured the assimilation of the conquest also remained bilingual.

Mexican American communities, which have existed in what is now the southwestern United States since the time of Spanish colonization, have always employed Spanish as their language. After the incorporation of the southwest as part of the United States and the imposition of the English language, those communities became bilingual.

Immigrants from Latin America, especially Mexicans, are often accused of not wanting to learn English and thus refusing to adapt to the American society. These two ideas, that Mexican Americans speak Spanish and have difficulty speaking English, are used by Anglo Americans like Samuel P. Huntington as evidence for some vast conspiracy to replace English as the primary language.

The fact is that most native Mexican Americans today are more fluent in English than in Spanish, since their schooling has always been exclusively in English. Immigrants are eager to learn English, judging by the amount of advertising for English lessons of all kinds on Spanish television and radio. It is also a fact that people descended from immigrants are not only fluent English speakers but often lose their ancestral language after the second or third generation.

169

Why have some people become so paranoid about the Spanish language? Why is speaking more than one language going to disintegrate our nation? Switzerland is a country that has existed for over seven hundred years and is composed of three major ethnic groups. Today, it has four official languages: German, French, Italian, and Romansh. Most people are fluent in at least two of those languages. There is no known threat of disintegration in Switzerland due to the existence of several languages. Speaking multiple languages did not make the nation weaker, just smarter.

People in the English Only movement fail to realize that we live only a few miles from Mexico, to say nothing of Central and South America, vast continents populated by Spanish-speaking people with whom the United States has to deal daily. We need to know Spanish to trade, to have diplomatic relations, and to understand our neighbors to the south, just as we need to have people fluent in other languages when we interact with other nations in Asia and Europe.

The need to interact with Latin America is not only economical or political but also cultural; in spite of being neighbors, we are for the most part ignorant of their artistic, literary, and scientific talents.

Brief History of the Mexican American Migrant Worker

To understand the dilemma of the Mexican American migrant worker, we must revisit the history of the United States and the conquest of the American West. It is a history of powerful armies taking possession of territories, lands that prior to the Treaty of Guadalupe Hidalgo of 1848 were settled by Spaniards and Mexican mestizos.

First, it is necessary to go even farther back in history to a time before the arrival of the conquerors. The time before Europeans arrived on this continent, before the massacres of the indigenous people of America. That is, the people European Americans now politely call Native Americans.

After the conquest of Mexico by the Spanish crown, the indigenous tribes of Mexico and Central America were enslaved. Those indigenous people came from many tribes and nations and spoke a multitude of languages. Most people, when referring to Mesoamerican Indians, think of the Aztecs and the Mayas; they are the most well known because they developed elaborate civilizations, but there were many other societies in the area. The ancient Olmecs were the first major civilization to develop in Mexico. Michael Coe and Rex Koontz state that the Olmec civilization probably existed from 1800 to 1200 BC.[164]

The next advanced civilization was that of the Toltecs. Later the Mayas, the Aztecs, the Mixtecs, the Totonacs, the Tarascans, the Otomies, the Zapotecs, and many others developed, each with their own society and culture. They all left their impact on Mexico's history and culture. Many indigenous communities in Mexico and Central America still use the languages of these societies; they are not extinct.

Native communities had several things in common. They had highly developed agrarian economies and religious traditions. Their religious beliefs and cosmology were centered on farming. They developed accurate calendars that they used to plant their crops each year; they had to know when to plant and when to harvest. The ancient Mexican calendar was precise and enabled them to plant crops on a yearly basis. Thus farmers in ancient Mexican societies did not depend merely on religion. They had a calendar, and they also relied on scientific knowledge about planting crops and where they should be planted.

One of the major Aztec gods was Tlaloc, the rain god. In order to harvest good crops, it was necessary to acknowledge and respect a higher being. Aztecs performed sacrifices and offerings to this god and built temples in his honor. Many of the old Aztec songs or poems were devoted to him. This god was also revered in Mesoamerica and the United States southwest with different names.

The farmers not only worshipped the rain god but also knew how to plant and how to harvest their crops. It was this knowledge that allowed them to cultivate and breed maize, which became the main food staple for all of the Americas. The cultivation of corn was the result of people from Mesoamerica experimenting with a type of wild grass called *teosinte,* possibly as far back as 5100 BC. Maize spread to every place in North, Central, and South America. Thus, corn became the sacred plant of the Americas, growing in every corner of the continent by 3000 BC.[165]

Recent investigations by Dr. George W. Beadle and John Doebley using DNA typing have revealed that all maize is genetically similar to a teosinte from the region of the Balsas River Valley of southern Mexico. Beadle and Doebley have also calculated that domestication probably occurred about 9000 years ago. Native Americans domesticated nine of the most important food crops of the world; maize alone provides around 21 percent of human sustenance across the planet.[166]

Dr. Richard E. W. Adams, an archaeologist at the University of Texas at San Antonio, cites a Spanish witness in the missions of Guatemala: "If one looks closely he will find that everything [these Indians] did and talked about had to do with maize; in truth they fell little short of making a god of it. And so much is the delight and gratification they got and still get out of the corn fields, that because of them they forget wife and children and every other pleasure, as if their corn fields were their final goal and ultimate happiness."[167]

This Spanish priest was correct, corn was a god, and the Aztecs' name for him was Centeotl. The Centeotl cult was devoted to raising corn and other agricultural products.

Mayas knew how to plant in ponds and the Aztecs built *chinampas* designed to grow plants in the river. Dr. Richard E. W. Adams writes that the Aztecs used dry farming with irrigation systems of both floodwater and canal types, but the most famous were the *chinampas* in the southern basin; they covered about 25,000 acres. The Aztecs anchored the *chinampas* to cypress trees and used stakes to hold them in place until they became attached to the ground. It was an ecological farming system using the natural water resources of the lake surrounding Mexico City.[168] There is no doubt that ancient Mexicans were actually scientific farmers who used specific methods to grow crops. The Aztecs were not just savages who accidentally dropped seeds and got a crop. Farming for crops was a science to them. They planted crops to feed their families and to sell to the community. Consequently, farming crops such as cotton and vegetables was an old tradition that would later provide the Europeans with experienced farm hands when they enslaved the Indians.

Before the Spaniards arrived, the Aztecs had developed a sophisticated aristocratic society. The *huei tlatoani* (literally "great speaker"), or king, ruled for life and belonged to the royal lineage; he was chosen by a council of high nobles from among the members of the royal family.[169]

The Aztecs organized the land into *calpoltins*, localized landholdings, with their own temples and schools. The *calpoltin* had an aristocratic landowner who oversaw his land and his serfs. Here the common people had their own land holdings. If they took care of their land they owned it for life, but if they failed to cultivate it for two years, they lost the land.[170]

The ancient indigenous people had been growing crops for many thousands of years and knew the science of farming before Europeans arrived. The Spaniards used the enslaved natives as farm hands to clear the land and plant and harvest crops.

In South America, indigenous people did not fare any better; they too became slaves. In northeastern Argentina, southern Brazil, and Paraguay lived the Guarani. The Jesuits established missions among these people as well as in other parts of South America. These missions flourished, and the Indians proved to be intelligent and creative and accepted the Jesuits' Christian religion.[171] However, these communities proved tempting to slave traders, who were able to take slaves that could speak Spanish and were familiar with Western culture. The Spanish and the Portuguese hunted for indigenous slaves. The Bandeirantes, based in Sao Paulo, Brazil, traded in Guarani slaves and hunted for precious gems. They were the first members of the wealthy families of Sao Paulo.

The film *The Mission*, although fictional, used some actual historical events for its plot. The movie depicts the treatment of the indigenous people around the missions near Iguassu Falls. Those people were taken from their ancestral lands into slavery, their communities were burned, and often they went for refuge at the Jesuit missions. The priests were sympathetic to their plight, but soon the church became irritated with the Jesuits and made them leave their missions in that area.

In modern Brazil and Argentina, things have not changed for the native people. When visiting Iguassu Falls, I witnessed indigenous women living in dire poverty, selling arts and crafts to tourists. A particular young lady was barefoot and holding her baby on her lap while she made simple crafts. She was beading rosaries from shells and beans. Other women sold woven cotton purses and other knick-knacks. Poverty remains rampant; these women are hoping to get enough money to keep from starving. They were all wearing badges authorizing them to enter the park and sell their wares; they needed a permit to enter their ancestral lands.

In the Andes, one can travel along dry, lonely *cordillera* roads and find people sitting in the desert selling pottery to the few traveling tourists. Those people are also living in dire poverty and risking their lives in the hope of making a few cents. It is not hard to understand why they escape into cities hoping to find nourishment, a roof over their heads, and work. They are landless, living in harsh environments that do not even have water, much less a place to farm. The indigenous people in South America continue to live voiceless and invisible to justice, so they continue to migrate in order to look for work. At Iguassu Falls, one can see Indian women selling their goods while they work on making more crafts. They do all in hopes of earning enough money to eat.

In eastern California, I saw a Navajo family selling simple silver jewelry at a rest stop; they were on the lookout in case a park ranger came. If one did, they hid their wares in a blanket. Tourist shops in Grand Canyon National Park and large stores sell souvenirs made by

Indians. None are sold by Indians; it seems they cannot even get a permit to sell in the parks as they do in Argentina, so even that small claim cannot be made on their native land. Indigenous people all over the American continents are losing more and more power to keep and own homes on their ancestral lands.

While the selling of souvenirs may seem petty, the fact remains that many tribes in the United States still suffer from great injustices. Many among the Navajo and Hopi are still living without water and electricity, while the Peabody Corporation runs polluting coalmines on Navajo territory to send electricity to Nevada and California. In one of the most prosperous nations in the world, indigenous people live in third-world conditions, exploited by large corporations that take precious resources from them.

In Arizona, mining corporations hire Native Americans to work in plutonium processing without adequate protection or regulations; they are destroying their bodies and their lands. These corporations are using scarce water resources and endangering the health of the people.

Passive aggression and genocide continues in America, where many Indians die of starvation or ailments like diabetes, tuberculosis, and heart disease because they lack food, sanitary housing, and medical care on their reservations.

During the course of the conquest, another group of people was born: the mestizos, offspring of the conquerors and the conquered. When the Spaniards invaded what is now the southwestern United States, they brought indigenous people and mestizos to work on the missions and farms they established. These people really belonged to the lower ranks of the very poor in Mexico. While some were able to settle and get land, the real leaders were the Spaniards, who came to establish their rule. The one thing the Spaniards, the mestizos, and the local indigenous people eventually had in common was religion and language. The indigenous and mestizos did not come as settlers but as laborers for the Spanish conquerors and missionaries; that is why most mestizos never had land in the southwest. It was not common for most of them to own property, since they were the peons, servants, carpenters, and farm hands. Nevertheless, some Mexicans did obtain land in the Southwest according to the existing laws.

When Mexico gained independence from Spain in 1821, slavery was abolished as an institution. In reality, however, indigenous people and mestizos were still treated as peons, servants, and maids; in other words, they were low-wage slaves. Although the Mexican constitution outlawed slavery in 1810, Jose Antonio Navarro, a Texan of Spanish extraction, plotted to create laws making slavery legitimate again in Texas. Navarro welcomed the invasion of the Anglo Americans, and his position on slavery was possibly to sweeten the pot for the new arrivals, who came from slave-owner societies in the United States South. After Texas's secession from Mexico, Navarro kept his place in the courts, and the new government, which did not want to include Mexicans, accepted him. Navarro did not have to move into the poor Mexican neighborhood.

In Texas, for the most part, Mexicans became tenant workers. Being poor and not having a voice in the courts made them easy targets for exploitation. Taxes levied against Mexican property owners were the cause for confiscation of land and property.

The Texas Republic reintroduced the institution of slavery, bringing African slaves from the southern United States. The treatment of Mexicans was no better than that of black slaves. Mexicans did not have access to education and civil rights. Racism was so intense that Mexicans could not even enter business establishments set aside for Anglo Americans. This was similar to what happened in Boston during colonial times, when Indians could not go into town; some Bostonians found a document stating this in 2004 and were scandalized. All over the United States, European Americans and Europeans segregated Indians, regardless of tribal origin.

In Texas, this meant that if Anglo settlers claimed Mexican-owned farms, the owners had no right to take their cases to court. They had no right to vote or even to do business. They had to attend segregated schools that did not go beyond second or third grade; they attended segregated church masses and services, segregated restaurants, segregated courts, and even segregated cemeteries. Segregated Catholic and Protestant churches existed in Texas well into the 1960s. Up to that date, there were restaurants in the southwest where Mexican Americans could not eat. As a teenager in the 1950s, I did farm work in the cotton-growing community of Littlefield, Texas; I vividly remember reading signs in cafes and restaurants stating, "Mexicans and dogs are not allowed."

Mexican Americans could not study or work in offices or do white-collar jobs. Today, some question why more Mexican Americans do not speak English and why they have not assimilated into European American culture. The answer is that legally, they could not assimilate even if they wanted to do so. They lived in segregated neighborhoods. The school system did not teach them English beyond third grade, and there were no further schooling for children who did not speak English. Maybe Anglo Americans feared that light-skinned Mexican Americans would try to integrate if they attended white schools.

After the so-called independence of Texas, many Mexican families who could not take the abuse and racism of the new European American and European immigrants went to Mexico; others, such as my great grandfather, Marcos Jimenez, stayed, working as ranch hands or farm hands. My great-grandfather cleared land for cattle and for farming. His dream was that someday he too could buy a farm near San Antonio, but with a large family to support, he never had the money to buy the land; his earnings were barely enough to feed his family. His daughter Eduarda grew up in Texas and married a Mexican citizen who left Mexico after his mother's death. Pedro Gonzalez Portillo was extremely disappointed after the local priest bilked the family out of their farm. Pedro's mother had died, and the family decided to hold a Mass in her honor, but they did not have sufficient money to pay for the cost of the Mass. The priest convinced the family that if they put up some collateral, such as their farm's deed, they could pay later when they sold their crops. It is interesting to note that these lands had water, a precious commodity in northern Mexico. After the family reaped and sold their crop, they returned to pay off the debt. The priest told them that the deed to the land was in Rome and that it would be very difficult to retrieve. My grandfather was so outraged that he left Mexico feeling betrayed by the Catholic Church.

Thus, Mexicans experienced exploitation and injustice in Mexico and the United States at the hands of the wealthy, who were usually Spaniards or other Europeans. The poor Mexicans were voiceless and landless.

Today some Mexican Americans have regained portions of farmland in the United States. Those who own farms today are usually wealthy businessmen or farmers and live on lands that were not available to them before the civil rights movement, but those farmers are very few.

Cesar Chavez, the great Mexican American civil rights leader, became a migrant farm worker after his father lost a ranch close to Yuma, Arizona during the Great Depression because he could not afford to pay his farm expenses and support his family. Chavez's family was not affluent; thus, the bad economic times immediately affected them.

This illustrates how poor mestizos and indigenous people on both sides of the border ended up destitute and exploited. My Mexican grandfather and his family became migrant workers in Texas; they worked picking cotton all over the state. It was during this time that he met a Presbyterian missionary and became a lay preacher. He had abandoned the Catholic faith when the priest in Mexico stole the deed to the family farm. Yet he was a pious man needing a spiritual faith. He converted and became a Presbyterian. Later he took over a small church and became a lay preacher. He supported his family by planting beans, corn, and other vegetables in the church backyard. His grown children performed all kinds of manual labor; they worked on ranches, on farms, and in small towns and even worked as musicians at night to supplement their wages. The oldest daughter married a railroad worker; at that time, many Mexican families worked on the railroad built to take cattle from Texas to the stockyards in Chicago. As usual, the women supplemented the men's wages by working as maids. The two-parent working family is not a modern phenomenon in the Mexican American community. My mother used to tell me about working for a family when she was very young; the European American schoolteacher she worked for had to give her a crate to stand on so she could reach the sink and wash the dishes and clothes. She never learned English from that teacher.

My mother recalled one incident about her mother doing laundry by hand in large tubs for a European family. After she was ready for the final rinse, the children of her employer, in a devilish mood, poured dirt into the final tub. Silently, she had to start all over and wash the clothes another time. The woman of the house just looked on, making sure the last speck of dirt was removed. This is the history of Mexican Americans, always omitted from history books. Most of us have heard these stories from our families since birth.

History books talk about how hard the pioneer women worked, but they never mention the women behind the idealized pioneer women—the maids, often Mexican American women, who did all the dirty work in Texas and throughout the southwest. The eastern United States had African American maids; the southwest and the west had Indian and Mexican maids. Unless European Americans were very poor, they could always find someone to do their dirty work. Just like today's undocumented immigrants, they had jobs nobody else wanted. Maid work always meant having someone looking over your shoulder, making sure things were cleaned and polished to the highest of standards. It is always easy to set very high standards in housework when you do not do it yourself.

By the 1920s some Mexican American families had made enough money to buy their own homes. In our family, my uncle and mother were able to set up a grocery store and soda fountain store. Unfortunately, when the depression hit in the thirties, poor Mexicans and Mexican Americans were the first to lose what they had gained.

Whenever the United States faces difficult times, the country turns against the most vulnerable. During the Great Depression, the country turned against Mexican immigrants and, by association, Mexican Americans. They deported thousands of people to Mexico, although some of those "Mexicans" had never been there. Actually, they had been United States citizens for many generations. More recently, after the passing of Proposition 187 in California, many Mexicans, Mexican Americans, and even Native Americans reported abuse and intimidation. They all look indigenous!

Unlike the history of other minorities that have been persecuted and abused, our story has remained hidden and ignored. European Americans still refuse to accept the fact that long before they arrived in Texas, California, and other western and southwestern states, Mexican Americans were already there on the lands that had been settled by Spaniards and Mexicans. Most of the Spanish settlers were able to integrate because they were Europeans, while indigenous people and mestizos remained segregated. Many of our indigenous ancestors had been in these lands long before the Spaniards arrived and long before the rest of the European immigrants arrived. In the book *Who Are We?* Mr. Samuel Huntington accuses Mexican Americans of claiming that this is their turf. Well, it is! He implies that Mexican Americans' claim that they are living on their turf is another sign that they are trying to break down the nation. He implies that they are plotting to set up beachheads to invade the United States. If he is worried about invasions, he should look at China, which is actually invading the United States by commerce and industry and leaving us indebted to them. They are making large profits and making us largely dependent on their imports. China is growing at a fast pace, while the United States closes factories and moves its production overseas in order to make higher profits. Outsourcing, not migrant farm workers, is taking over the high-paying jobs of America. China is the major communist nation today. We do not want South America to go leftist, but we sleep in the same bed with China, the major communist country in the world.

In reality, politicians like to scare European Americans with the term *leftist*, but is used mostly to mean any Latin American country trying to get out of European slavery.

Mexican Americans have always been loyal residents and loyal citizens of the United States. We have built cities and railroads and tended ranches and farms. We patriotically go to war, where a large number of our men and women die in the name of America! We are the secret stepchildren of North America, the silent, faceless American workers and soldiers.

There is an ancient Mexican story about a king named Huemac who was very wealthy and loved sports. His ball team was so powerful and mighty that it won all the games. The rain god Tlaloc and the earth god were so impressed that they approached Huemac and asked if he would engage his ball team in a contest against the gods' team. Huemac demanded a wager. If the gods won, he would be willing to sacrifice whatever the gods desired. If he won, the gods would pay with jade and Quetzal feathers.

The team of mortals prevailed over the gods, and with hubris, the king demanded that they pay their debt. The gods agreed, and soon the prize arrived: baskets of beautiful green stalks of corn, Mexico's main food staple. The king became infuriated and cried out that the prize agreed upon had been precious jade and not corn. The gods replied that they had thought King Huemac was referring to corn, but if the king literally meant he wanted jade and not corn, they were willing to give him jade and take away the corn.

What the king did not realize was that without corn, no matter how strong his empire was, it was doomed! Huemac had taken the humble corn plant for granted. Without corn, even the mightiest empire in Mexico could not survive, no matter how much material wealth the kingdom possessed. All his military power and all his political might were worthless against droughts.

As the famine progressed, Huemac realized that his pride had been his downfall and that he would have to apologize to the gods who had granted him the priceless gift of food. In anger, the people of the kingdom banished the king and sent him to spend his life in penitence until the gods once again granted the people corn. This legend mentions King Huemac, a king killed at a cave they called Cincalco, which means that a king by the name of Huemac might have actually existed.[172]

Today, the moral of this story could be applied to our nation. We take the food we eat for granted; we have never experienced great famines. We worry more about material possessions, big football leagues, basketball teams, and monetary gain. Our greed requires that we demand gems that we consider more precious than food: money, cars, houses, and all kinds of expensive toys. Some people say that whoever dies with the most toys is the winner. Thus, we continue to exploit the farm worker and his family, ignoring that they are living in deplorable conditions without decent wages, housing, insurance, or education. Our greed for material wealth has caused us to create a great injustice. While we take the food we eat for granted, we do not realize that food is a gift from God and that our God is not concerned about national sports but about the way human beings treat and respect each other. One can assume that this was the moral of the legend of the foolish king who preferred jade to corn as a reward. The lowly migrant worker, who plants and constructs, is what makes our country powerful. Without the aid of those lowly workers, America is just another vain, arrogant nation. The actor James Edward Olmos, in a television interview, has said that farm workers are a gift of God because they sacrifice their lives so that we can have food on the table.

In the film *Bread and Roses*, one of the main actors points out that by wearing a worker's uniform they can become invisible. The tragedy of New York of September 11, 2001 illustrates the veracity of that remark. We saw all types of family members seeking out office workers; however, no one in the English-speaking mass media mentioned the workers who did the manual work of cleaning and serving food in those offices. Some of the relatives of those Mexican and Central American workers were afraid to seek compensation, because their loved ones were here as undocumented immigrants. Maybe that was one of the reasons the English-speaking media ignored their suffering. Fortunately, the Spanish-speaking mass media did cover those people who worked and died in the Twin Towers. Thus we were able to witness those who were trying to locate their relatives and the suffering of those who had lost family members. These immigrants are invisible, and their cause is never revealed. They are slaves doing the jobs no one else wants to perform.

Like the king in the old Aztec fable, our nation's wealth and greed makes us blind to the sacrifice of those workers.

Some time ago, a college professor told me that it would have been impossible for ancient Mexicans to cross the Sonora desert. Today many of the poor from Mexico and Central and South America die crossing that desert, but some of them make it. It would have been far easier for ancient Mexicans, who knew how to survive in deserts and who did not have to contend with highways or immigration officers or racist Minutemen.

The fact remains that Mexicans have never been strangers to the United States and have continued to come here for generations. They also came with the Spanish explorers, who brought them as slaves to build missions, tend cattle, or do whatever other job the Spaniards wanted done. After the conquest of the Americas by Spain, indigenous people lost all their possessions and their rights and became slaves, a position many still hold in the Americas. Having lost their lands, their culture, and their language, they had to accept a new language and a new culture and live as indenture workers. They raised cattle, cleared land, and lived in small huts owned by the *hacendero*. Today some of the descendants of those farm hands live in cardboard boxes in California, waiting to harvest the crops they maintain and harvest for America's tables, although their own tables are often bare.

Those Mexican and Central American immigrants are similar to Native Americans: poor, uneducated, and lacking fertile land. They come seeking humble jobs, jobs that provide sustenance, yet are treated as criminals. While they are willing to bear the hardships of the burning desert, their most furious enemy is not the desert; it is the humans that deny them even the right of water. The state of Arizona enacted a law making it a crime to litter public lands with plastic bottles. The target of the law was humanitarian American citizens who leave bottles filled with water in the desert. These kind-hearted people recognize immigrants as human beings who do not deserve to die of thirst and exposure. America has not changed much since the Pilgrims claimed these lands and left Native Americans without rivers and wildlife.

Today not much has changed for those enslaved workers who toil from dawn to dusk dragging baskets of produce, their heads bowed, their backs arched, and their eyes nailed to the ground. Not much has changed for those working by the hour with a crew leader behind them, making sure that every minute is occupied, that nothing distracts from the cotton row or that not a single strawberry is missed. Those workers go home to sleep after spending all day in the sun. There is no time for anything before sleep but to wash the dirty clothes and prepare the only hot meal of the day since sunrise. Many sleep on blankets and cots, others on the bare floor. They are physically exhausted, with no time to think of a way out of slavery and insufficient resources to allow the young children to attend school. Even today small children continue to work in the fields just to get enough money to buy groceries and clothing for the whole family. When one keeps one's vision on the soil, one cannot look up to the skies where dreams are born. Worse, all types of agricultural pesticides and fertilizers physically poison our bodies and our children's brains. It is time for our people to leave the fields; in the future, machines might perform most or all farm work. Therefore, there is clearly no future for our people in doing farm work. We need to abandon the fields. We may suffer in the city, but at least there, our vision will not be confined to the soil. If our people would only abandon the fields, a new day would arise. The whole farming hierarchy would break down, and once farm workers are absent from the fields, a revolution will have to take place in America. The United States will probably manage to find farm workers in other places—perhaps in Chile, the Philippines, or some other faraway place with cheap labor. But in those places, there will be no way to guarantee the quality of our food, because American inspectors will be absent.

There is no question that the corporations that own large farms have been happy to have Mexican and Mexican American farm workers. They know those people are bringing millions of dollars into their businesses. At the same time, Mexicans and Mexican Americans are grateful for having a job and a steady salary, but "as they came to realize that the occupations assigned them and the conditions under which they worked were regarded by American urban labor as undesirable and substandard, they began to show signs of restiveness. Not only were they set apart as a caste, [they were] stereotyped, segregated and regarded as an inferior 'race.'"[173]

The Mexican American community has long been aware of the discrimination that the Anglo American community practices against it. In 1883, Juan Gomez promoted the first attempt to form an agricultural union in the Panhandle.[174]

In 1903, over a thousand Mexican and Japanese sugar beet workers went on strike in Ventura, California. In 1922, Mexican field workers tried to establish a union of grape pickers at Fresno. All of those groups failed.[175]

The first organization of farm workers was established in 1927. It was named the *Confederación de Uniones Obreras Mexicanas*, or CUOM. The first strike in Imperial Valley failed, and many workers were arrested and deported. Two years later, five thousand union workers held a strike and won, but later that year the union was kept from striking when the growers arrested 103 union leaders. The county growers bought guns and tear gas bombs and shells to stop the strike.[176]

Many Mexican American people get very excited about Cesar Chavez. He was born in Yuma, Arizona on his family's ranch. When his father could no longer afford to keep the ranch, the family became farm workers. As a youth, Cesar Chavez volunteered in the Navy during World War II and served his term honorably. Mexican Americans volunteered in large numbers to join the armed forces during that war. When Cesar Chavez returned home, he rejoined his family as a farm worker. He was intelligent and a good organizer. He was able to rally migrant laborers and organized the Farm Workers Union. Chavez got the solidarity of other unions, support from community leaders, and even the support of Attorney General Robert Kennedy.

The farm owners were not impressed by Chavez and claimed unions were not needed. John Gregory Dunne, in his book *Delano: The Story of the California Grape Strike*, records the following quotation from Joseph Brosmer of the Agriculture Labor Bureau in 1966: "These pickers don't want a union. They've got a real fine relationship with the employers. Really personal. A union would destroy it." Dunne claims that the grape growers were completely against unions and prepared to fight them.[177]

According to a recent United Farm Workers newsletter, today the attitude of some growers has not changed a great deal. At Ruby Ridge Dairy, a dairy farm in Washington State, a farmer who is against unions made a similar statement. He said he was "opposed to unionization because a union can create an adversarial relationship between the employer and the employees." This is the same man whose workers claim he has threatened them with a gun and makes them work long hours, not even allowing them time for lunch.

Many in the older generation who worked with or met Cesar Chavez are happy to have shared experiences with him. Both fellow workers and politicians praise him. His struggle to set up the Farm Workers Union and demand fair wages and safe working conditions gave farm workers a voice and a degree of self determination.

Cesar Chavez was very charismatic and idealistic. He heard the stories of farm workers and listened to their issues. One of the complaints he heard was from a worker who had come from Mexico named Demetrio Diaz, a seventeen-year-old man brought over to help break up the strike by Mexican American farm workers. He was really a scab, but he was unaware of the union struggle. Cesar Chavez spoke to the young immigrant and learned that the worker had come from Cuamil, Michoacán. He had traveled through the desert for four days, drinking water from cacti and battling all kinds of spines and thorns. While walking in the desert, he had seen cadavers and skeletal remains of undocumented immigrants who had not survived the journey to the United States. Later, when he arrived in the United States, he was forced to work for long periods of time in the lemon groves with little pay. He was paid thirty cents for each bag of lemons, and if he worked very fast, he earned six dollars a day. He and the other workers were charged $15.00 a week for a small sack of flour, two dozen eggs, and some lard. If it rained, they were not given food. They ended up eating oranges from the groves. They slept in boxes or under trees. They were treated worse than slaves. Mr. Diaz claimed that they were always dirty, because there was no place to wash and they had no clean clothes. If they tried to flee, they were warned U.S Immigration would capture them and treat them as criminals.[178]

What this young man described was a complete lack of human justice. It was tales like his that made Cesar Chavez angry. He organized a march to demand justice for farm workers. His inspiration came from the nonviolent philosophy of Mahatma Gandhi. The protest was supposed to be peaceful. Cesar Chavez's march started out with about 70 percent Mexican Americans, Mexicans, and Filipinos; the rest were Anglo Americans, and there were two or three African Americans. It started in Delano, California and headed toward Sacramento. A declaration called El Plan de Delano, fashioned after Emiliano Zapata's Plan de Ayala, was read aloud during the march.[179] By the end of the journey, the number of marchers had swollen to include thousands of farm workers and supporters. Some of the people had marched so far they had blood on their feet. The United Farm Workers Union had formed.[180]

The first proclamation of the Plan of Delano is as follows: "1. This is the beginning of a social movement in fact and not in pronouncements. We seek our basic, God-given rights as human beings. Because we have suffered—and are not afraid to suffer—in order to survive. We are ready to give up everything, even our lives in our fight for social justice. We shall do it without violence because that is our destiny. To the ranchers, and to all those who oppose us, we say, in the words of Benito Juarez, 'EL RESPETO AL DERECHO AJENO ES LA PAZ.' Respect for others brings peace."[181]

Where they have been able to form unions, conditions for farm workers have improved significantly. Those workers are respected as human beings; they are able to obtain work benefits, such as health insurance and retirement, and their children often become professionals or skilled workers. However, these gains are often threatened by politicians who ally with agricultural corporations who want access to cheap labor.

For the rest of the rural laborers, the question today is, Do farm workers require a union? The answer is a very simple and unequivocal yes! For many, conditions have not changed since Cesar Chavez began his marches and strikes.

Last year, we heard about a young woman who had worked all morning in the California sun without water. The field manager failed to get water for the workers early in the day, and by the time they received water, the girl had fainted and died. When there are no regulations to control farm operations, workers depend on the mercy and goodwill of the growers.

Benito Cenobio, a Mixtec Indian from Oaxaca, Mexico, related the following story. He came to the United States because he was jobless and had no food or work. He said he came without documents and feared the *migra* (U.S. Immigration). He spoke very little English. Those two facts made it possible for the growers to exploit him and other workers. For the poor who come seeking work, the growers often do not even provide drinking water or overtime pay. Benito Cenobio is now a United Farm Worker member.[182]

On the other hand, many among the younger generations have never heard of Cesar Chavez. When I mentored at a San Antonio elementary school, I gave a nine-year-old girl a children's book about the life of Cesar Chavez. After she read it, she became very excited and said, "I never knew we had Mexican American heroes too." The idea that a child can say, "We are Americans and we too have fought for a better society," is very powerful. We have American heroes.

Cesar Chavez is an American hero; he represents justice and dignity for our people. We also have other heroes in our community, silent heroes who fight for justice and equality every day—farm workers, factory workers, college professors, doctors, teachers, the poor who continue the struggle Chavez started in his life time; they exist all over the United States and are always fighting for equality.

When Cesar Chavez saw the injustices that were taking place against the poor farm workers, he decided to speak out in their favor. He saw how pesticides rained on the fields over farm workers, poisoning them and their families, causing babies to be born with birth defects. He protested the use of pesticides on fruits and vegetables and denounced their use over people. Because of his stand against pesticides, we have organic food today.

He spent his life dedicated to the farm workers' struggle and spoke up for the Mexican American community. He organized a union so that workers could have a voice, health insurance, and pension plans. He gained a reputation for his fight for justice in the fields. He faced the growers and demanded fair wages and adequate housing. He went before courts and argued for social justice. He was a poor but honorable man who always sought to better the lives of his community and carried the flag of peace following the example of Gandhi. He remained poor but strong among the people in his community and the nation.

We are living at a time when our children need a role model who has experienced the pain and suffering they are suffering, a time when our Mexican American community needs to know that we played an important part in building this nation and its democracy. We need someone to look up to, someone who demonstrates what it means to be an American and believe in the democracy of America, someone who believes that all people are created equal. We have the right to equal treatment in our courts. We have many inalienable rights, such as the right to dignity and equality in our higher institutes of learning. We have a right to fair wages (Mexican American women earn only 57 cents to every dollar a male Anglo American makes going the same job). We need medical care and housing rights. That is why we need more people like Cesar Chavez to help guide and lead our communities and to fight for justice in the workforce, in education, and in health care. These rights belong to all people in the United States, regardless of their ethnicity or nationality.

None of our current rights to health care, fair wages, or other improved working conditions would have come about without unions. The 1960s were the time of the civil rights movement; many of our youth went to Vietnam, and many who stayed behind protested. They protested against the war and social injustices. Many of the protests were by young high school students in California.

Today we are experiencing similar wartime events and the return of neglect in the civil rights arena. Therefore, we must look at the role heroes like Cesar Chavez played in history and follow their examples of leadership. We must also organize more of our youth to lead the country. Cesar Chavez passed away in 1993. The movement he started is not dead; it is now being lead by his son in-law, Arturo S. Rodriguez. Others who participated in the movement have remained true to the cause, including his sister in-law Dolores Huerta, his brother Richard Chavez, his sons and daughters, and many other people. We cannot remain in the past; the struggle continues, and the fight in the fields is not over. We must move forward and emulate Cesar Chavez to meet our future struggles with courage and determination.

In the 1930s Mexican Americans and African Americans were kept out of unions by Anglo Americans who did not want to share skilled positions with them. Those jobs paid better wages and had better benefits. Mexican Americans understood the benefits of unionizing, and some were even successful in establishing unions. In those trades that hired Mexican Americans, only a few unions admitted them as members. Two of the largest ones were Hod Carriers and the Common Laborers Union.[183]

In the 1940s, things changed. With the coming of World War II, labor shortages made it necessary for the business industry to hire Mexican Americans to take the place of Anglo Americans who were going to war.[184] But during that period, many Mexican American men also went to war. These new job opportunities made it easier for Mexican Americans to obtain higher paying jobs, but it did not make it easier for them socially, since the Anglo Americans continued to discriminate against Mexican Americans.

The war years did not improve relations between Mexican Americans and Anglo Americans. The discrimination increased, and there were raids in the barrios. In rural areas, racism remained unaffected by the war against fascists who believed in a superior race. The situation was so dire that Texas was blacklisted from obtaining *braceros,* or Mexican agricultural workers.[185]

In 1973, a riot broke up in Kern County, California, when a group of union organizers protested against the closing down of the union. The farmers did not want a union because of the demands it made on them. That day, a group of police officers descended from a helicopter and attacked the protesters. When they started beating a seventeen-year-old girl, a former mayor of Hollister—Frank Valenzuela—tried to defend her. The deputies attacked him with mace and beat him with batons. That day many other farm workers were also brutally beaten.[186]

A few years ago, Mexican strawberries caused several cases of food contamination in the United States. There is no doubt that in Mexico, strawberry workers labor under as dire conditions as those on this side of the border; in some cases the exploiters are the same. Large corporations from California often own agribusinesses in many countries. To make their operations "efficient", those companies offer deficient working environments and meager salaries. Under those conditions, workers often live in cardboard houses or in overcrowded quarters, such as several families in one small house. Sanitation on the fields is very deficient or missing in some cases; naturally, this leads to improper health conditions and expose workers to all kinds of illnesses. This oppression of human beings is the worst kind of racism; it dehumanizes and tortures people just because they are mestizos and poor illegal immigrants. The United Farm Workers of America, AFL-CIO, filmed and printed a short film that illustrates the poor working conditions of those families. The name of the film is *Strawberries, the Fruit of Injustice*, and it is narrated by Martin Sheen.

In the past, American farmers did not have to contribute to their workers' Social Security funds; they simply paid them in cash and left no record of how much they earned. Most Mexican American workers were glad to get work and never questioned the manner in which they were paid. Therefore, today they have no proof that they worked and should receive Social Security benefits for those years. They did not realize that as they got older they would not be able to get Social Security or medical care. Today, those people often depend on public assistance, giving the impression they are dead beats who never worked when in reality they spent all their productive lives working in the fields. The reason farmers did not deduct Social Security from their employees was that they did not want to spend money, and the government exempted them from paying Social Security. I spent my teen years as a farm worker, and the Social Security Administration does not consider those years when calculating my benefits. My mother never questioned why we did not pay Social Security; as a house cleaner, she did not pay either. She did not even understand the meaning of Social Security until the seventies, when laws were enacted to insure most people contributed to Social Security funds.

It was not until Cesar Chavez fought to unionize farm workers that farm worker retirement plans were established for those who joined the union.

If Social Security laws are weakened, the people who are probably going to suffer the most are the farm workers. They have the lowest wages in our country, so they will not have sufficient funds to pay for health insurance or retirement plans; the struggle will continue for them. The struggle of farm workers has never been documented in the mainstream media apart from a PBS film entitled *A Fight in the Fields* about the movement that Cesar Chavez initiated. Outside of that documentary, no major work has been done to expose the injustice done to the nation's Mexican American farm workers.

There was also the case of the closing down of Kelly Field Air Force Base in San Antonio, Texas. The men who worked at this base devoted their lives to aircraft maintenance and had an outstanding record.

When politicians decided to close down military bases, Kelly was one of the first to go. It employed a large Mexican American work force. The closing of the base was devastating, but even worse was the claim that somehow those skilled workers were academically unqualified even though they had spent many years learning their trade. The truth is that while those men worked at Kelly Air Force base, no major aircraft accidents occurred on planes they maintained. There was a rash of serious military aircraft accidents after the work had been transferred to other cities with new workers. None of those accidents can be attributed to those mestizo workers. The fact is that Kelly was not closed for poor performance. As usual, Mexican Americans are the first to lose their jobs when it the United States of America is faced with a workforce crisis.

San Antonio, Texas is a historic and colorful place. Tourists enjoy the courteous service provided by Mexican Americans and the entertainment they provide—the dances, the music, and the songs lend themselves to a time of frolic and recreation. Meanwhile hotel workers are constantly seeking for better wages and better working conditions. Many of them want to organize unions, but they always fail because many workers get intimidated and fear they will lose their jobs.

Also in San Antonio, union organizers and community members have been seeking to name a street after Cesar Chavez. Politicians have come and gone, and after fourteen years, there is still no Cesar Chavez Street. Anglo American business leaders and some black leaders do not wish to have a street honoring Cesar Chavez. He represents unions, and San Antonio, one of the lowest-paid cities in the country, does not want unions.

If everyone knows about Cesar Chavez, not everyone knows about his sister in law, who has worked with the United Farm Workers Union since its inception. Everyone is now familiar with Barack Obama's campaign slogan "Yes, we can." This slogan resembles the old Farm Workers' cry "Si Se Puede," which is usually attributed to Cesar Chavez. However, people who know the oral history of the farm workers movement assert that it was really started by Dolores Huerta. They claim that every time a goal was set that did not look feasible and the people got discouraged, Dolores would always stand up and say, "Sí se puede!" Yes, we can do it. Dolores Huerta continues to work for the farm workers movement; she attends large meetings and speaking engagements all over the country as well as small community meetings. She has a wonderful personality and continues to fight for the rights of her people. Most people do not realize that she was at the meeting where Robert Kennedy spoke on the day he was assassinated. Cesar Chavez organized voter registration drives to support Kennedy's presidential campaign. Robert Kennedy was a supporter of the farm workers struggle and attended the event when Cesar Chavez ended his famous hunger strike to call attention to the violence that had erupted against union organizers.

Along with Dolores Huerta worked Richard Chavez, Cesar's brother. Richard's most enduring contribution was designing the United Farm Workers' Flag, a red flag with a white center and a stylized black eagle. Traditionally, black and red have been the colors of unions. Richard Chavez was also among the founders of the United Farm Workers.

Many faithful, hardworking union workers made it possible to continue the work of Cesar Chavez. Today, his son-in-law, Arturo Rodriguez, heads the union and continues the struggle of the farm worker.

The very poor and uneducated Mexican American communities that exist in the southwest are among the most silent and invisible in the United States. Of late, northeastern states have seen the influx of many Mexican and Central American immigrants, who come looking for work and often settle in Mexican American barrios.

Poverty among Mexican Americans has existed since the United States annexed Mexican territories after the Treaty of Guadalupe Hidalgo; segregation and racism accompanied this marginalization. Treated as perpetual immigrants, Mexican Americans had no voice in history; they worked and lived in the United States for many generations but somehow remained in poverty, voiceless and invisible as citizens. They existed to perform jobs no one else wanted to perform, such as digging wells on ranches, tending herds, slaughtering cattle, farming, building roads, and housekeeping. These were jobs that were dirty, jobs performed in the heat of summer on commercial farms, jobs that require sweat and toil. Because they are seen as immigrants, their social and economic problems have not become an American problem.

When I was twelve years old, my mother decided we needed to work as farm workers in order to survive. Child labor laws did not exist for farm workers, so I did not have trouble getting hired. It was costly to be migrant workers, because summer jobs did not leave us enough money to survive the winter. I went to work in the summer in Texas; we got up at five in the morning and worked until sundown. We worked long hours with hoe in hand in dry fields, cutting weeds around cotton plants. There were no trees for shade and no place to rest and no time for breaks. We ate in the fields, rested under trucks, and drank water out of communal water buckets open to all kinds of diseases. But the main danger was the insecticides sprayed from crop dusters over our heads. The insecticides covered us from head to toe, moist and sticky. We slept in run-down old housing, often without stoves or running water. It seemed we were always dirty, even when we washed and cleaned our bodies and our clothes when we returned home from work. I remember a woman who had a young teenage son; if we had electricity, she would always press his working clothes. He always started his day with clean, pressed clothes, but by the end of the day, we were all "dirty Mexicans."

In Fredericksburg, Texas, there was a poultry processing plant where workers plucked and cleaned chickens for the market. This job required a person to stand for long hours preparing the poultry for shipment to grocery stores. This type of job also requires such equipment as gloves and rubber boots for protection of the hands and feet. Several years ago, Mexican American workers at this plant protested the lack of equipment and tried to form a union, but the owners did not want them to unionize and make formal demands to management. After the workers resisted pressure and voted to approve the union, the plant mysteriously burned down; it seems that management preferred to close the plant rather than give concessions to the workers. How the factory burned down has never been determined.

In San Antonio, Texas, carpenters in a cabinet factory protested poor working conditions to no avail. Some were dismissed, poor working conditions persisted, and the workers continued earning low wages. Most workers remained in the factory for fear of losing their jobs, which they needed to support their families. When one of those workers suffered injuries on the job, the company took no responsibility; it just fired the injured worker.

In San Antonio, Texas, workers in the hotel industry also found that dismissals were the answer when they tried to negotiate better working conditions. Food workers complained that middle management collected their tip money and they received only a very small portion or nothing. Management policy in all these cases is to fire the leaders of the organizing effort and intimidate the remaining workers with the threat of losing their jobs. Workers dismissed for union organizing have a hard time finding another job, because they are considered troublemakers.

Even in church universities in San Antonio, Mexican American maids have been intimidated into doing hazardous labor, such as climbing on sills to clean windows without safe equipment or cleaning bathrooms without proper sanitary gear. Perhaps because it became not only a labor issue but also a moral issue for the church, these conditions no longer exist.

Workers in a steel foundry in San Antonio labored in the heat without proper safety gear. They breathed in fine particles of iron dust, which spreads everywhere, even covering the cafeteria tables where they eat. They lacked sanitary toilets; the facilities were filthy. They were worse than dogs in a dog pound, but their cries for justice went unheard.

Jaime P. Martinez, labor leader and founder of the Cesar Chavez March for Justice in San Antonio, has heard hundreds of stories about abuse in south Texas, but the organization lacks lawyers to defend the workers; it does not have the political or financial support it needs to protest and make demands for the community. In San Antonio, Texas, Cesar Chavez is not welcome; he represents better living conditions for workers. He is still too radical for many in the community.

Mexican and Mexican American workers continue to be invisible and voiceless in America!

Affirmative Action
and Education

Affirmative Action is a law that proclaimed, among other things, that excluded minorities have a right to get into schools if they qualify. Our nation's higher educational institutions excluded Native Americans, Mexican Americans, and African Americans for many years. They attended segregated, inferior educational institutions. During the decades of the 1960s and 1970s, there was a conscious effort to remedy the evils of the past.

Affirmative Action attempted to remedy those inequities, which started even before our nation began. Blacks experienced oppression during slavery and segregation, Native Americans during their holocaust of the last five hundred years, and Mexican Americans after the Anglo American conquest of their territories. It was not until the civil rights period in the 1960s that these minorities started to demand the right to attend colleges.

Reacting to those advances, the enemies of equality created the biggest myth about affirmative action: that in order to fill quotas, poor minority students get into college because they are given preference over Anglo American students. The implication here is that Anglo American students are brighter and more qualified than minority students. Thus the end of Affirmative Action came to Texas in 1996.

President Clinton stated that as long as students were qualified, they had a right to attend college. He wrote the following statement: "So a middle ground was developed that would change an inequitable status quo gradually but firmly by building the pool of qualified applicants for college, for contracts, for jobs, and giving more people the chance to learn, work, and earn."[187]

It is not a question of who is intelligent and who is naturally mentally inferior. It is a question of what kinds of schools minorities attend and the quality of education those schools offer. Schools that do not meet adequate educational standards will not produce students who are qualified for college. Students who graduate from those schools, unless they are exceptional, will have a difficult time entering college and keeping up with college study requirements. What makes young people qualified for Ivy League schools and other high-ranking colleges are the elementary, middle, and high schools they attended. If those schools provide the proper education in language, mathematics, and science, the students taking college entrance exams usually do well.

Schools that lack training in physics, chemistry, calculus, or creative writing will not prepare students for colleges like Harvard, Stanford, or Yale. Those poorly trained high school students are usually prepared to attend nurse's aide schools and mechanic schools—expensive private schools, slave schools that train people to serve as nurse's aides or car mechanics, all dirty jobs.

In Texas, independent districts administer public schools; each district funds its operations by raising property taxes within its jurisdiction. The result is that wealthy school districts can afford higher paid teachers, better school labs, and smaller classrooms. Students in the poor districts go to what we could call "separate but equal" schools, which is synonymous with inferior schools. Those who still oppose equal access to education fiercely fight any effort to equalize school funding. A few years ago, an effort to channel funds from richer districts to poorer ones originated in the Edgewood district in San Antonio. It was dubbed the Robin Hood plan, robbing from the rich to give to the poor. The wealthy people in town opposed this plan. Today they want to close schools, claiming there is insufficient money to keep the schools open. The fact remains that the old schools are still overcrowded and in poor condition. The current independent district funding system also creates an unfair situation: poorer districts use higher rates in order to compensate for the lower incomes of their taxpayers. In Bexar County, which includes the city of San Antonio, there are twelve or thirteen school districts originally divided along racial lines. Most Anglo American children are still separated from most Mexican American children and from most African American children. In San Antonio, Mexican Americans have been fighting the doctrine of separate but equal for many years. What has been accomplished is that the schools are no longer called Mexican schools, but de facto segregation is still a reality.

Minority students at these schools try to enter college with lower SAT or ACT test scores because they generally attend schools that lack educational materials and have poorly trained teachers. This disparity arises from the inequity in funding; wealthier schools have a higher pay scale for teachers, so naturally they attract people with teaching degrees from better colleges and universities. Poor schools depend mostly on teachers who were not fortunate enough to attend the more advanced schools and have a lower level of training or just do not meet the highest scholastic criteria. Occasionally, excellent teachers appear, such as Jaime Escalante, the Bolivian-born schoolteacher in Los Angeles, who proved that poor Mexican American high school students could master calculus and higher mathematics. More students would excel if we could find more teachers like Escalante and assign them to those poor schools. Unfortunately, many poor minority schools in large cities are understaffed and lack qualified teachers. The fact that those schools do not have sufficient materials and staff to teach advanced mathematics, chemistry, or physics means that students are encouraged to learn trades that will not qualify them for college or for higher paying jobs. They usually receive training to become mechanics or cooks or to do other types of manual work.

Although many Mexican Americans work very hard to educate their children, in poor families both parents often work outside the home, and in many instances, children come from one-parent households. In either case, students do not get the attention they need from their parents, who often do not have the time or the knowledge to support their children's school work.

Here the pedagogical system of teaching Mexican Americans fails. Those children are often bright students, but the environments they live in do not provide a good atmosphere for learning. There are even more difficulties as these children get older; they often work outside the home to help support their younger siblings. At other times, they care for their younger siblings while both their parents work. As young people, they may have to live in dangerous atmospheres with drugs and gangs, atmospheres that often disrupt their studies. Their home environments can also be disruptive when their parents have their own psychological problems, such as alcohol and drug addiction, problems that cause aggression and violence in the home and are not conducive to education. There is no question that those parents also need to grow out of their sociological bad habits. Here Mexican Americans need stronger community support.

Poverty can have a great effect on education. Lack of adequate nutrition, proper housing, and health care contributes to a child's educational outcome; poor children who eat breakfast at school do better in class. Housing is important, and often children move frequently, never finishing a school year in the same home or in the same school. Thus, often a whole school may end up with a very poor rating among its students because the faculty is limited in what it can teach and because of many other negative social factors.

Schools in wealthier neighborhoods have better-equipped science labs, better computers, and larger libraries. The families of the wealthy are usually better educated and can aid their children in their homework. When Mexican Americans from educated families often excel and go on to college without difficulty regardless of the quality of their high Schools, they are usually well prepared to attend most colleges and universities.

Usually, children coming from disadvantaged neighborhoods have two strikes against them. If they have to work part time or do migrant work, they often are not able to keep up with their school peers; thus, the cycle of poverty continues to draw those students down. They could be brilliant students and excel in their high schools, but when they take their SAT or ACT to attend college, their scores are usually lower than those students who attended the wealthy schools.

Affirmative action was a remedy to aid people who came from historically disadvantaged minorities. In the case of Mexican Americans, we see that at times wealthy and middle-class immigrants also compete for the Hispanic college slots. The poor have to compete with those immigrants. Those well-educated immigrants are usually the children of doctors, businesspeople, and professors who emigrate to increase their wealth or to escape the political or drug chaos that is taking place in their countries; they too have the Hispanic label. They come into our country on E-1 and E-2 visas, entry documents granted to professors, entrepreneurs, and venture capitalists. They compete for the same affirmative action programs designed for historically disadvantaged minorities. Thus, we see that sometimes Affirmative Action is still out of reach for the poor; therefore, they have to compete with students who have better educational backgrounds for admission to institutions like

Yale or Harvard. It is generally a myth that the Mexican American poor are taking the place of white students. Very often, those new Hispanic immigrants are also of European extraction. In San Antonio, Texas, this is very common, because many wealthy Mexican immigrants move to the United States and conduct their business from Mexico.

Today, Hispanics include a large number of nationalities and ethnicities: Argentineans, Colombians, Dominicans, Cubans, Puerto Ricans, and many other Spanish-speaking groups in addition to Mexican Americans. This means that when a student of Mexican descent applies for entrance into college, he is not only competing with students in his ethnic group but with students in a diverse group. Those families come from the Caribbean and Central and South America. The ones who attend college often come from upper-class families, such as the Cuban families that came after the Cuban Revolution. When it comes time for wealthy Hispanics to attend college, they also apply under the affirmative action quota, which is meant to help underprivileged minority students. The results is that the students who come from those wealthy families and who are educated in wealthy schools end up with much higher SAT scores. When scholarships and college entrance exams are given, the minority students who attended inferior schools are often not at the same level as the educated foreigners, and consequently they are denied entry into colleges.

I feel that for poor minorities, different criteria should apply. When Mexican American migrant workers compete with the upper-class Hispanic students, they often have lower SAT scores. They are well below the scores of the better-educated upper-class students who come from other countries. This means that if a poor Hispanic student gets into a school like Harvard, Yale, or Stanford, it is because he or she is really gifted and talented.

When they have to make a decision between accepting a poor student with a high SAT score and a wealthy student with a high SAT score, those Ivy League schools are going to take the wealthy student who can afford to pay tuition. If they can find a wealthy Hispanic with a high SAT score, the wealthy school will have fulfilled two of its goals—filling a minority slot and acquiring a paying student. Therefore, when European Americans blame affirmative action for being left out, the truth is that if those minority students were not attending those particular schools, the European American students in question would probably still be left out. Only a few token poor Mexican American students actually attend the best schools; most of them settle for junior colleges and state schools.

Thus, the cycle of poor education continues all their lives. If we have outstanding minority students, it is because of their own intelligence, creativity, and determination and not because they were given special privileges. Many of those students succeeded in spite of poor educational opportunities in grammar and high school. However, the number continues to be very low. Minority students are not keeping Anglo students out of Ivy League Schools. During the civil rights period, many Mexican Americans protested against the schools and colleges in California, New Mexico, and Texas, but today many young people seem to be under the illusion that discrimination does not exist in institutions of higher learning. Thus, they often drown out the voices of those who protest.

This also explains why many Mexican Americans have not assimilated into the so-called American culture. They live and die in the same poor barrios. They never cross their neighborhood boundaries; they are kept there and used as cities need worker bees.

Harry P. Pachon writes that there are also national factors that keep Mexican Americans out of the Affirmative Action dialogue. He claims that the discourse has usually taken place between African Americans and Whites. Pachon feels that since the Affirmative Action discussion usually takes place in New York and Washington DC and most Mexican Americans live in Texas and California, they are not adequately represented.[188]

Mr. Pachon claims that Mexican Americans were not included in the Affirmative Action debate since they were not considered black. He states that Mexicans have a race issue; they are neither white or black and are therefore invisible.[189]

Mr. Pachon claims that "when we are invisible we are not seen in a good light." He goes on to mention how Republican presidential candidate Pat Buchanan stated that Hispanics were not affected by the racial discrimination that took place in the United States. Using the term Hispanics, he failed to recall the racial discrimination that took place in America after the United States invaded Mexico in the 1840s and took territory in Texas, New Mexico, California, Arizona, and parts of Colorado and Utah. Mr. Buchanan also failed to mention the large number of Mexican Americans who have fought in American wars since the Civil War, especially the large number who fought in World War II and Vietnam. By using the term Hispanics, he kept Mexican Americans out of American history books.[190] As a candidate for president, Mr. Buchanan also stood at the border of Mexico with a rifle and demanded that Mexicans stay out of the United States; I guess he forgot that Mexican Americans could also vote, and most of them did not vote for him.

Today, angry Anglo Americans claim that there are people who do not even know how to spell the word *vote* in English who want to vote. I hope they are not referring to Mexican Americans, since *vote* in English is spelled exactly the same in Spanish!

Today there has been no Affirmative Action in businesses such as television, commercial advertising or films. The racism against Mexican Americans is so strong that most television stations in the United States do not hire any Mexican American actors. One television program that actually does is *George Lopez*, and while the main actor is Mexican American, his wife and children are not. His stage daughter is not of Mexican American descent and portrays the life of an ethnicity she has never experienced. If she was portraying just an American girl, she could be from any background, but why can't a Mexican American girl portray a Mexican American girl? In another show, Ugly Betty, the main actress who portrays a Mexican American girl is not Mexican American. This could be acceptable if there were already many Mexican American actresses employed, but the truth is that there are not. Probably there many Mexican Americans who would like to be actresses, but Hollywood won't hire them because they do not fit the stereotype of speaking English with an accent, or are not plain enough to play the part of maids. When real Mexican Americans girls are hired, they will probably play prostitutes who are unable to speak English and have a drug habit—real role models for our youth!

The stage wife in *George Lopez* is supposed to be Cuban, the father-in-law educated, wealthy, and the ideal father. George Lopez's mother is Mexican American and thus a drunk, uncouth, evil old woman. George Lopez is the stereotype, a Mexican American who cannot read well even when he is supposed to be a plant manager. His father, also Mexican American, abandoned them years ago and never supported or cared for the family. Thus, we see George Lopez struggling to read, we see his mother as an evil drunk, and we see his father as an irresponsible deadbeat. Having a very dysfunctional Mexican American family is supposed to be funny!

I am sure there are families among Mexican Americans that fit this stereotype, just like there are dysfunctional families of every other ethnicity. However, they are the exception, not the rule. So why is the only Mexican American family on television a dysfunctional family?

The show *Ugly Betty* is supposed to be based on a program in South America television called *La Fea más Bella* (the most beautiful ugly girl), a romantic comedy. However, in the American version, it is not really about romance but about a Mexican immigrant family that conforms to all the racist stereotypes. But here again, the girl who plays the main character is not Mexican American. Could they not find a Mexican American who could pretend to be Mexican American? They could have just been honest and made the family come from the country the girl is actually from and left Mexico out of their storyline. Instead, the storyline was made to reinforce old stereotypes. Perhaps the title of the show, *Ugly Betty*, is to remind us that Mexicans are ugly people, since we do not see other Spanish dramas from Spanish speaking-countries coming to America. One cannot but wonder if this sitcom is not a new version of *Bronco Billy and the Greaser* from the early 1910s. This old film was produced to stereotype Mexicans as evil villains. *Ugly Betty* just serves to portray Mexicans as illegal, ugly, and stupid.

Hollywood made several films using the role of the greaser, films that helped the nation suspect Mexican Americans as violent, dirty, and devious. These films helped to create hate in the minds of other Americans against Mexican Americans and to reinforce the "evil greaser" image of Mexican Americans. *Bronco Billy and the Greaser* promoted the myth that Mexicans and American Indians were plotting to destroy white settlers. It provoked anger against American natives and Mexicans. It created images that still exist in the minds of many whites, who continue to attack and kill Mexicans in Pennsylvania, New York, and other parts of America.

Aggression against Mexicans is not new. Between 1848 and 1928, more lynching incidents occurred against Mexicans and Mexican Americans than against any other ethnic group. There is a document called *The lynching of persons of Mexican origin or descent in the United*

States, 1848 to 1928, that gives details of the history. William D. Carrigan wrote the article in 2003 in the *Journal of Social Science.*

In modern films, we do not see other ethnicities portrayed in only negative roles. The reason is that those ethnic groups would rightfully protest if there were only negative images of their people. Mexican Americans fail to protest. Maybe we need some of those abusive women shown on television to come out and use their aggressive attitudes toward Hollywood and the television networks. When Mexican American comedians perform, they usually express some very negative ideas about their mothers and friends, and they often go beyond good taste. I believe the reason they are on English-speaking television is that they can say things whites would not dare say; coming out of their mouths, they would be too racist.

Comedians who would otherwise be afraid of making racist comments still feel that they can insult Mexicans and Mexican Americans without consequences. For instance, on Comedy Channel, in an episode of the program *Tosh.0,* the protagonist made a short film in which a small three- or four-year-old Mexican American or Mexican child was playing with a toy car in his yard. The child was poor, and the ground around his backyard was bare. The first joke was that the child's father did not bring his work home with him, implying that his father was a gardener. The second joke was that the child kept cocaine in his toy car. The third joke was that the child, who fell off the car, had not reached the United States. Thus in a few seconds we heard about Mexicans being poor, being drug addicts, and living in America illegally. All the audience laughed; they felt no shame about the comedian's aggressive, racist behavior against Mexicans and Mexican Americans. Unless our community begins to protest and not buy products advertised on those shows, we will continue to be the only ethnic group without respect in our own country.

While Mexican Americans make up two thirds of all Latinos in the United States, they are under-represented among Hispanic actors, who typically tend to have Caucasian looks, the main criteria for acting in Hollywood. Whiteness is a key factor in becoming a movie star; most Mexican Americans have indigenous features. There are also Hispanics of African descent; we rarely see them either. Advertisements, which should include Mexican Americans, usually omit them. Since we do not see any mestizo faces, we take it for granted that they are not including people from other Central or South American countries either.

Why do Mexican Americans spend so much time and money watching an industry that does not hire or promote them as ordinary Americans? The Hollywood industry discriminates against Mexican Americans and usually portrays them as criminals or as ignorant people who do not speak English. Mexican Americans should say, "Include us as hardworking, honest people who have the same patriotic aspirations as other red-blooded Americans. We will not buy your products as long as you portray us as second-class Americans." Just stop watching television and going to movies. Television needs Mexican Americans to buy the products they advertise, from automobiles to soap. Hollywood also needs Mexicans and Mexican Americans to buy movie tickets. Mexican Americans should demand Mexican American actors who play positive roles. We are tired of Hollywood hiring other nationalities to play our roles.

Comedian Paul Rodriguez used to say, "If a Mexican is hit by a car, the television crew will replace him with another nationality before they show him on television." This might seem like a comedic exaggeration, but it is very close to reality. Unfortunately, Paul Rodriguez failed us when he tried to make a film about Mexicans; he too used all the stereotypes of Mexicans as fat and ignorant. The movie was a failure, because Mexican Americans did not accept his portrayals. He has not produced another movie. On the other hand, Robert Rodriguez makes films about common subjects, and while he often uses Mexican American actors, he does not make an issue about their ethnicity. We need more Mexican American filmmakers and actors who see themselves as Americans, and Hollywood needs to hire them.

For the most part, the mass media in the United States does not cover news dealing with Mexican Americans, Mexico, or Latin America. Sometimes, exceptions occur when they report natural disasters, such as hurricanes, floods, or earthquakes. The mass media rarely or never makes us aware of political and social issues, such as civil rights, education, health, or labor issues. Very often, the media shows other international news of countries in Asia or the Middle East.

Why are we not represented or consulted on labor and health issues like the rest of white and black America? I have seen whites and blacks on television talking about education without a single Mexican

American or other Spanish-speaking representative. Why are we always treated as immigrants? A very large number of our people have been here since before this country was part of the United States. Much of our Mexican American population did not come over the border yesterday; they were here before the United States was totally established, before the Treaty of Guadalupe Hidalgo. On February 2, 1848, Mexico lost 45 percent of its territory—916,945 square miles that included the immense riches of Texas oil and California gold as well as more than 100,000 people.[191]

Just as many European immigrants have entered this country over the years, Mexican immigrants have also come to the United States. It is not a new phenomenon; it has existed for as long as immigration to the United States from Europe. Some immigrants came here legally, others illegally, just like the Europeans. And like many of the European immigrants, many Mexican immigrants have become Americans citizens.

The only difference between Mexican immigrants and immigrants from other countries is that Mexican immigrants can and should claim that they are the sons and daughters of American natives, descended from Mayas, Aztecs, and other groups that inhabited Mexico. Mexican Americans are descendants of Mexican Indians who came with the Spaniards during their conquest as well as of the American Indians who inhabited the southwest. The Spaniards took Indian women and often passed them to the Mexican Indians. That is why many Mexican Americans can claim to have Apache or other American Indian heritage.

Ancient Mexican culture extended from the southwestern Unites States to Mexico and most of Central America. Mexicans traveled from their original sites in Mexico to other destinations in the Americas. The evidence is in the way their discovery and development of corn traveled across Mexico and all of the territory in what is now the United States. Nations in North, Central, and South America kept in touch. Religion is a very good example of the close relationships between the Americas. The jaguar played an important role in religion from South America to Mexico; at various times, this feline played an important role in worship, and priests probably took the jaguar into temples in South and Central America. Today those ancient symbols exist in many ruins. It is hard to determine who first arrived at new ideas in agriculture and religion, but the fact is that they were shared; there were no borders in America. In the United States, many tribes were nomads who traveled from region to region according to the climate, following the herds of buffalo, which were their main food staple. Other tribes, such as the ones in Mexico, became sedentary and built cities. In what is now the United States, the Pueblo and other tribes also began to settle down and build cities. All the tribes had cultures and social structures; they might have been different from each other in some respects, but all of them provided their tribes with civilized order and unity. They were not savages!

As a small child, I attended many American films, I know that I attended films like *The Wizard of Oz* and *Alice in Wonderland* at least three times a week. It cost me nine cents, and it got me out of my mother's hair when she was working to keep the family alive. All I had to do was get a ticket and make sure I sat on the proper side of the theater; the left side was reserved for "Mexicans" and the right side for whites. As long as we sat on the left side, we encountered no problems, and none of us dared to sit on the wrong side of the aisle, so it was always peaceful. Today we finally have a handful of actors, and we are no longer segregated by race in the theater. Still, we are not part of American society in films or the media.

In television commercials, the story is different. Sometimes new immigrants from places like India promote merchandise as normal Americans, but we rarely see Mexican Americans in English-speaking television advisements.

When the silver screen used mainly white actors, African Americans protested. They knew filmmaking is a profitable enterprise. Thus, Hollywood began hiring African Americans. On the other hand, very few Mexican Americans are hired to act in Hollywood, although they spend a great deal of money attending movies. Today the only thing that has changed is that Mexican Americans can sit wherever they please, but the silver screen remains void of Mexican Americans. Today we have a few so-called Latino actors, but none that we can call Mexican Americans. We have no Mexican American comedians outside of George Lopez. There are not any singers or directors, with the exception of a few Hollywood directors, such as Roberto Rodriguez, and a few actresses, such as Jessica Alba. The most famous Latino film director in the United States is actually a person from Mexico:

Guillermo del Toro. He is very good, and he has directed great films, so why can Mexican Americans not produce more Mexican American directors besides Roberto Rodriguez of San Antonio, Texas? Why is it that Hollywood has not been able to produce more Mexican American directors and actors? It cannot be their accents or their talent; it must be their looks and the stereotypes about them.

The assumption seems to be that Mexican Americans only watch Spanish television. In reality, most Mexican Americans today mostly watch English-speaking stations, because they either do not speak Spanish or feel more comfortable using the English language. Spanish-speaking television stations usually appeal to very old Mexican Americans or to new Latino immigrants. Spanish-speaking television programs show Mexican or Mexican American characters in their commercials, but we do not see those advisements on English-speaking stations; there, we see mostly commercials with Anglo or African American people. This gives the impression that Mexican Americans do not exist in the Unites States.

This also true of films. A movie can take place in Los Angeles, California without showing a single Mexican American except for servants. Some Anglo Americans complain that there are too many "Mexicans" in Los Angeles, so it is amazing how film directors can make films that take place there without including Mexican Americans. From the silver screen, one could conclude that there must be travel restrictions for Mexican Americans in Los Angeles that determine where they can live, shop, and travel. In the movies, even airports and department stores are void of Mexican Americans.

An important part of this argument is that Mexican Americans are not employed as actors. The movie industry is one of the largest enterprises in America, but it fully discriminates against Mexican Americans. Hollywood often hires other nationalities to play Mexicans. It seems as if there is a plot to keep Mexican Americans from major Hollywood roles in order to keep them from climbing the socio-economic ladder. Nevertheless, Mexican Americans have always spent a great deal of their money attending films. As Mexican Americans, we should make sure our dollars go to enrich our communities. We should demand that our people get positive roles in films so our children can have positive role models.

We should demand Mexican American actors not just to play

gangsters and criminals on television or on the silver screen. Our children never see a Mexican American doctor on television, although in real life, there is a brilliant Mexican national who illegally crossed the border and decided to become a brain surgeon. In San Antonio, I happen to know a brain surgeon, a university president, and multi-millionaire car dealer who are all Mexican American. In a Mexican American city, it is not unusual to have professionals who are Mexican American. Many people in our communities are aware of their Mexican American professionals, but many other Americans are not. I have heard out-of-town people commenting about San Antonio having its first Mexican American mayor when in reality we have had three Mexican American mayors in the past forty years. Unfortunately, we remain lowly workers or criminals in films. Young people never see Mexican Americans who are doctors or professors who can serve as role models.

Advertising in English excludes the Mexican American community! Mexican Americans usually do not appear in English speaking commercials. When they do, it is usually in the background, not as main characters. Why we should worry that advertising is not using our people? We should worry because advertising is big business, and it discriminates against and segregates Mexican Americans as employees. Advertising is one of the largest businesses in the United States; it makes billions and billions of dollars each year. Every time Mexican Americans buy an item, they help pay for those commercials. A certain amount of the money they pay for bread, aspirin, candy, or cars goes toward commercials. In other words, every time they buy a product advertised on television, they pay for commercials. A percentage of the money pays for the commercials. Mexican Americans help support the advertising economy. They pay for commercials in Wall Street, but advertising agents do not hire Mexican Americans. They economically discriminate against Mexican Americans. Rarely do we see commercials with Mexican Americans who are integrated with European Americans. The message that is conveyed is that white Americans do not interact socially with Mexican Americans! They live in their "proper" barrio environment. They work in gardens but do not attend college or drive new cars. Medical corporations do not use Mexican Americans in advertising, although millions of Mexican Americans and other Latinos spend a large amount of money on medication. Here again we pay for advertising we do not benefit from. Most commercials using Mexican Americans or Mexicans appear on Spanish-speaking stations. However, many Spanish ads are dubbed from English commercials, often using poor Spanish translations.

Today a large number of Mexican American young people do not speak Spanish, so they do not watch Spanish-speaking television, but English-speaking stations do not have programs with which they can identify as Americans. Many of the people in Spanish-speaking communities who watch Spanish stations are from less affluent immigrant families who are just beginning to learn English. Meanwhile, younger generations of Mexican Americans do not even watch Spanish stations, because they no longer speak Spanish. Therefore, advertising companies may be losing money by not using advertising agencies that appeal to Mexican Americans. Nevertheless, the same standards for measuring who can appear on television and in films remain in place. The standards call for European features and not mestizo features. The Spanish accent, which many of our youth have lost, is no longer an excuse. Their looks still do not measure up to European American standards. It is time to enter the field of advertising instead of being discriminated against by mass media companies.

The only time one sees commercials that use Mexican Americans or other Latinos is in advertisements that try to get our young people into the military. Are Mexican Americans not being used in commercials to keep them out of American society? It does appear that way.

In military commercials, the youth are promised great careers, but when they leave the Army or the Marines, they have rarely been promoted beyond the rank of corporal. They promise them an education, a career, and a world of travel. They never tell them that they might lose a leg or even their lives. They never mention that at most they will be allowed to advance to the rank of sergeant if they stay in the military for life and become recruiters.

Mexican Americans are supposed to live in their barrios, ghettos where they go to school with their own kind and thus have friends who are of their own kind; in other words, Mexican Americans are supposed to be segregated. Commercials are so racist that when a garbage bag commercial was developed for English-speaking television, it not only showed a Mexican American garbage truck driver but actually gave his Spanish name to make sure he would not be confused with another

American. The driver claimed that his father had also been a garbage collector and that he had loved being a garbage collector since childhood, when his father took him to school in the garbage truck. Another ad about spending too much on telephone bills also showed a Mexican American garbage collector, as if that is the only occupation we are fit to perform. On the other hand, when they make commercials about expensive cars or computers, they never place Mexican Americans in those spots. In reality, I have spent most of my life in San Antonio and have never witnessed a Mexican American driving his kids to school in a garbage truck. I complained about that ad, and maybe other people did too; they eventually stopped running that commercial!

Other businesses that use Mexican Americans in ads include beer companies; they make sure that alcohol continues to distort and harm the minds of our community. Young Mexican Americans become so addicted that they will commit crimes, such as breaking into businesses that sell alcohol, and even fire shots at the employees to get beer. No one in the Mexican American community has ever spoken publicly about the issue of alcohol abuse and its effects on our people. Mexican Americans have never protested the promoting of alcoholic drinks as being immoral, so the youth continue to drink and commit crimes based on beer.

Today, we see more Mexican Americans in commercials, but they are still few. ABC puts Mexican American actors in lead rolls, but NBC and CBS are still lagging behind. NBC and CBS have a tendency to use Mexican Americans and other Latino actors as criminals. Here again it is Mexican American dollars that pay for a great deal of television programming, including programs that reinforce the paranoia about Hispanic criminals. However, you never see companies like Wrigley chewing gum use Mexican Americans in their advertising, even when chewing gum originated in Mexico. This absence is in spite of the fact that Wrigley got the formula for its original gum from a small Mexican factory.

The question is, When will the Mexican American community start complaining that they are sick and tired of segregation in the television world of illusions? It is all smoke and mirrors, but it is still prejudiced against Mexican Americans. How much longer must we remain invisible and voiceless in America?

Before World War II, schooling for Mexican Americans was not a priority. In fact, the European American community discouraged education. They believed that if our people learned English, they would demand to have a voice in politics and government and compete for jobs with the rest of the English speakers. Preventing them from speaking English was a way of keeping them outside of the American mainstream. The myth that they refused to speak English is one the biggest lies of American folklore. Those European Americans were right; during World War II, the young men who went off to fight had to be given a quick course in English, and for the first time, European Americans seriously spent time and effort to teach those soldiers English. Those soldiers found that if they were to survive the war, they needed to speak English. Therefore, one can say that the only benefit that World War II brought the Mexican American community was the ability to speak English. As the old European Americans had predicted, the Mexican American community began to make demands. They had proven that they were Americans by risking their lives. They proved their patriotism by winning a disproportionately high number of Medals of Honor. They proved that they loved and took pride in their country. Yet they also realized that this was their chance to speak out about their inequality as citizens. They had learned to use the English language to survive in time of war; now they were going to use it to battle against the injustices they faced when they returned home. For that reason, the first Mexican American groups that spoke out against segregation in the schools and in job opportunities were organizations like the American GI Forum and other veterans organizations. The League of United Latin American Citizens (LULAC), another activist group, also grew as a visible Mexican American activist group. Among their demands were schools that would allow children to go beyond grammar school into high school.

Mexican American high schools existed before World War II, but only in the larger cities, such as Los Angeles and San Antonio; in the agricultural communities, some children did not even attend school. Migrant workers' children often stayed in the fields during World II. They kept the United States fed while others went to war. The Anglo American community that did not go to war went to work in the factories or in offices. The Mexican Americans kept the food harvested so that there was never a food shortage like there was in Europe. Yes, European Americans owned the farms, but Mexican Americans planted the crops, picked the beets in Michigan, harvested the oranges in California, and dug up the potatoes in Idaho. It was this ragged troop of harvesters who contributed to the war effort by silently working the fields and keeping food on the table for those fighting overseas and those at home. After the war was over, European Americans returned to their middle- and upper-class homes and continued to prosper. However, nothing changed for the Mexican American community except that we went from being Mexican American to being Latinos, a terrible term that still segregated us. We are not Italian, and we do not speak Latin or even live in Italy. The term is a misnomer; it means merely that we speak Spanish, a Romance language.

We are from the United States of America, but as long as we are of a different shade than those who come from Europe, we will continue to need a prefix on our identity. Today we are Hispanics; Mexican Americans are not Spanish, but we at least speak Spanish. Many Mexican American youth only speak English. Should Mexican Americans who only speak English be called Anglo Americans?

Helter-Skelter

In the early days of the republic, colonists were under constant threat
of wars by Englishmen, Frenchmen, and Indians. Bears and wolves also
threatened those who lived in the wilderness. They used guns to fight
their enemies and ferocious wild beasts, they also used firearms to hunt
for wild animals, such as deer, elk, buffalo, and wild fowl; guns meant
protection as well as sustenance.

Not much later, the Indians learned that if they obtained guns,
they could use the guns for the same purposes as the Europeans, and
an arms race soon began. If the Indians were fighting the British, they
could get the guns from the French, who were often also fighting the
British. If Indians were fighting other Indian tribes, they could always
buy guns from the white man. Weapons sellers in America have a long,
profitable history.

Today we live in a very different world; our only domestic
enemies are the mentally deranged and criminals. The mentally ill
who sometimes kill people in public places are hard to detect before
they commit hideous crimes. Often we hear about teenagers who are
unhappy in school and kill fellow students or disgruntled employees
who kill fellow workers.

The other type of criminals strike at their victims when it is least
expected; criminals usually obtain guns from other criminals or under
false names and identities. Those guns kill enemies when people
are angry and friends when they are drunk. They allow people to
commit murders, assault small groceries stores in the barrio, and rob

banks. Teenage gang members who wish to show their power in their communities carry guns. These senseless crimes only serve to bring more tragedy to the families in those poor slums and ghettos.

For Mexican Americans, the availability of guns means having the youth incarcerated for long periods. This causes the lives of those young men to be wasted, and it cost billions of dollars to keep the youth locked up.

These gun-toting people usually have one thing in common: large arsenals of weapons in their homes. There are many ways to obtain weapons without waiting for identification clearance. Guns exchange hands in the communities outside of gun shops, but more often the guns are Saturday night specials or are obtained at gun shows.

Three of the latest major domestic gun massacres occurred within the last four years. One of these was at Virginia Polytechnic Institute and State University on April 16, 2007; when student Seung-Hui Cho, in two separate attacks opened fire on other students and killed 32 people and wounded many others, later he committed suicide.

Another gun massacre occurred at Fort Hood, a large military base in Texas, on November 5, 2009. Major Nidal Malik Hasan killed thirteen people and wounded many others. He was born in the United States, son of immigrants from the West Bank in Palestine. He was a psychiatrist who studied at the Uniformed Service University of Health Science, worked at Walter Reed Army Medical Center, and was later assigned to Fort Hood prior to his commission to the war in Afghanistan. He was very upset about the fighting in Iraq and Afghanistan, as a Muslim he claimed he could not fight against other Muslims. He purchased a FN Herstal 5.7 millimeter pistol at a gun shop in Killeen, just outside the base. He knew he could destroy many lives with that weapon. He will go to trial for his actions, but gun businesses will continue to sell weapons to any of the neighboring military personnel. For those soldiers coming back from war suffering from combat trauma, sometimes emotionally disturbed, owning weapons could lead to similar massacres.

The third tragedy occurred in Tucson, Arizona, on January 8, 2011. Jared L. Loughner, a disturbed criminal slaughtered six people and left fourteen injured at a political event by congresswoman Gabrielle Giffords outside a supermarket. The representative ended up with a bullet through her head but survived; among the dead were John

M. Roll, a federal judge and Christina Green, a nine year old. All those people suffered the violence of a semi-automatic Glock 19, a weapon carrying a magazine with a capacity of thirty-three bullets. Mr. Loughner purchased the weapon and the extended magazines legally, without much background checking on his mental stability or previous police record.

In spite of these bloody examples of gun abuse, the National Rifle Association continues to buy off and control Congress. Not even living inside a military base offers protection. Guns are not America's answer to crime. Why then are guns so sacred to Americans?

A person can buy an unlimited number of weapons despite the fact that one weapon should be enough to defend oneself. Why do some people feel the need to stockpile high-caliber weapons? It is our obsession with guns that keeps weapons clear of any regulation. Anyone can buy as many guns as he or she wishes—semiautomatics, machine guns, and all types of rifles. American sportsmen claim they need weapons to hunt, but many of the weapons on sale without any regulation or controls are not for hunting; they are war weapons meant to hurt large numbers of people. We get checked at airports for weapons and even undergo full body searches. Yet guns are not controlled, and no serious records are in place to see who is dealing guns.

The NRA is a wealthy, powerful lobbying group in Washington DC that demands that the government not place any restrictions on gun sales. They leave the gun control advocates helpless.

We must view Mexico in this context to understand the terrible carnage that is happening there on a daily basis at the hands of drug lords. People are dying daily in all parts of the country: hundreds of police officers, soldiers, newspaper reporters, and private citizens have been killed. Mexico estimates sixty thousand citizens have died by guns. Ninety percent of the weapons confiscated from criminals have entered Mexico from the United States. As the drug lords get stronger, they get more brazen, and they come closer to our borders. Our government claims we are ready to confront them, but it does little to stop the American gun smuggling taking place through Texas, Arizona, California, and New Mexico. It is our own businesses that are providing the Mexican drug cartels with all sorts of powerful weapons, including semiautomatic guns and grenades—enough firepower to commit over sixty thousand murders. Drug dealers are also obtaining small aircraft from the United States to help in their drug smuggling.

Laura Ling, a courageous reporter who works for Current television and was once a prisoner in North Korea, presented an excellent television documentary on the drug wars in Mexico. In 2008, she went to Mexico and recorded the massacres that occurred in the streets of many towns and cities. She traveled to Sinaloa—a state that has become the center of drug dealing—to describe how rival gangs assassinate each other on nearly a daily basis. She also interviewed people in the streets, where many confessed that the poor often accept the drug dealers and join drug gangs in order to have jobs.[192]

Unemployed Mexicans, in desperation, will swell the ranks of drug gangs. If the drug dealers become very powerful, they may start entering the United States and continuing their battles in our country. They will be able to do that because we have no control over guns, and gun dealers are making large profits. As long as the NRA keeps manipulating Congress to let gun dealers sell weapons without regulations, both are endangering the United States, a country they profess to love. In the United States, Mexican and Mexican American citizens, who are already stereotyped, will see increased racism directed at them. Many poor Mexican Americans will also have the potential to become involved in drug gangs in their barrios. Self-appointed Anglo American vigilantes will add fuel to their hate campaign against Mexicans.

This has already happened: Jason Eugene Bush, Shawna Forde, and Albert Robert Gaxiola, members of the Minutemen American Defense group, attacked a Mexican family in southern Arizona. Their organization was short on funds, so they decided to rob a Mexican family known to be drug dealers. Dressed as police officers, they invaded the home, stole the money, and tried to kill all the members of the family to eliminate any potential witnesses. They killed the husband and the nine-year-old daughter; however, when they shot at the wife, she fired back and wounded one of the attackers in the leg. The home invaders fled, but the police found them and arrested them. The Minutemen American Defense members claimed they were shot while patrolling the border, but the police did not believe them since they had a witnesses to their crime; they are now being charged with two counts each of first-degree murder.[193]

This type of gun violence can continue to spread, and law-enforcement could lose control as is happening in Mexico, where drug dealers have impersonated soldiers to commit crimes. If Americans impersonate police officers and American soldiers, the lines will blur, and the authorities will not know whom they are fighting. The answer seems easy: stop the flow of guns into Mexico. Or has Pandora's Box already spilled its contents?

As drug-related violence continues to spread in Mexico and innocent people continue to die, Americans continue to fear the border and its violence while doing nothing to curtail the sale of drugs and guns in the United States. The problem of drug dealing will stop when Americans stop buying drugs and selling weapons to Mexico. Selling weapons to Mexico will only stop when Congress stops taking money from the NRA lobbyists who control the sale of weapons in the United States. The United States, with the Merida Initiative, is arming Mexico for an all-out war on drug trafficking. The United States is spending $400 million on aircraft, military equipment, and training of Mexican police and military personnel. This presents a danger to the United States. If drug dealers infiltrate the Mexican police and military, it could start a war that would spill into the United States. This would be tragic for the Mexican American community, which will be suspected of being on the side of the enemy.

Who is buying huge quantities of drugs in the United States? Why do we only see the arrest of minor drug traffickers and not the arrest of the multimillionaires? Who is making the largest profits from illegal drugs in the United States? Could some so-called respectable men in banks and other businesses be laundering money for the criminals who are profiting from drugs? We never hear about prominent, wealthy men arrested for drug dealing. Only the very wealthy can afford the price of the large shipments of drugs that come into the United States. However, all we hear about is the arrest of mules that carry the supplies. Where are the wholesale drug buyers? We never see the arrest of those men. We do not know who the multimillionaire drug dealers are in the United States.

Today we know our government is sending more military forces to the borders to fight against drug dealers from Mexico. The question is, Who is in charge of capturing the very wealthy drug lords in the United States? Why are these men still distributing drugs all over the United States? We need to capture the drug lords who are living in the

United States. Who are those extremely wealthy drug lords? Where do they live? Who is protecting them?

Sending the military to the borders armed with weapons is a very dangerous endeavor that could accidentally lead to a real military confrontation between Mexico and the United States. Setting up military forces to fight drugs across the border can lead to tension between our soldiers and the Mexican soldiers who do not always trust Americans. We need to do a clean sweep of American drug dealers of all races in the United States.

We need to spend money on the treatment of drug users and educate our youth on the danger and affliction of drugs. If Americans would stop the demand for drugs, dealers would not have any customers. Drug dealers would not have enough demand for all the drugs they sell. We need to learn why our children fall into the trap of drugs. Many children fall prey at the hands of drug dealers while they attend college. We need to involve parents, schoolteachers, police officers, college deans, and our children's peer groups. Simply advertising on television might be profitable for advertising firms, but it is not enough for our children. We need to invest more money and use professionals to fight drug problems. Without the demand for drugs, Mexico would not have to support drug lords, and the United States would not have to spend money on the war on drugs. America is draining a large portion of the nation's money into drug prevention in Colombia and Mexico without any major results. The United States has been fighting drugs in Colombia for many years with military power, and now it wants to do the same on the Mexican border. This is dangerous, because it could cause a major conflict between Mexico's army and the United States. The tension that could arise could be disastrous. The people of Mexico no longer feel they can trust the United States since it built a fence of distrust across its borders. As racial and economic tensions increase in the United States, so does the tension in Mexico, and it will take more than a handshake to heal the wounds of hatred and distrust.

When I say that America has no respect for Mexicans and Mexican Americans, we only have to look at Arizona Maricopa County prison and see how it treats the people there, starving them and punishing them for smuggling minor articles like sugar and cigarettes while incarcerated. Prisoners live in tents and eat very cheap food; the sheriff claims to pay 15 cents per meal. Joe Arpaio is very proud of his prison, where inmates are humiliated by forcing them to wear pink underwear. This treatment does not help rehabilitate prisoners or make them learn a trade. He seems to have an obsession with cruelty.

Many of those prisoners are Mexicans and Central Americans whose only crime is coming to look for a job in the United States. The tent prison is hot in the Arizona summer and cold in the winter. No one protests this prison, because its population consists mainly of Mexican Americans, Mexicans, and Central Americans, people who are too poor to hire lawyers. This is another version of American racism toward mestizos.

Secretary of Homeland Security Napolitano has now terminated the agreement with Sheriff Joe Arpaio, the racist sheriff of Maricopa County who calls himself the toughest sheriff in America. Mexican Americans have protested against him without results. As long as we do not have support in Washington, we remain voiceless and invisible in America. We must change this abuse!

Working in Filth
for a Fistful of Dollars

The key to America's economy is not Mexican immigrants from Mexico. Poor workers who come seeking work in America doing jobs that no one else wants to do have nothing to do with our economy, because those are jobs Americans have no desire to perform. Those jobs are degrading and dangerous to the workers' health, jobs like working in the heat of Arizona's desert, jobs where people become ill due to sun exposure.

Mexican and Central American immigrants worked in Louisiana cleaning up the deplorable filth left by the tragic hurricane Katrina. Those people were exposed to mold and other hazardous items. They encountered thieves who felt they could get away with their crimes without being reported to the police because the victims were illegal immigrants. Mexican and Central American immigrants even went over to Iraq to defend our nation. These immigrants perform jobs that former President Bush claimed no one else wanted to do. They are America's untouchable underclass, always doing dirty jobs, always poor, always treated as inferior because of their race and poverty.

Who are the people who are actually taking jobs from the United States of America? Corporations are outsourcing those jobs all over the world. Those big industries have sold out the nation. Big American capitalists have gone all over the world, outsourcing jobs to China, India, and other countries. All those workers are invisible on the streets of the United States but are actually doing the jobs Americans used to perform. Big corporations are moving to China. We have seen the outsourcing of manufacturing to China to save money. Clothing factories, pottery factories, shoe factories, and toy factories are all gone from America. Even cookies, candy, and food products are manufactured outside of the United States, where they are not subject to our health regulations! Big businesses, chain stores, and merchandising stores are profiting at the expense of the American consumer. Communication companies are moving to India. American companies go wherever labor is cheaper and they can exploit the workers. They have no loyalty to our nation or its citizens; they have no allegiance to the United States. They are motivated by greed. American industries go where the hours are long, where working conditions are miserable, where labor laws are nonexistent or ignored. They leave our nation without labor opportunities and the economy worsens. Our mass media, which are also allied to or owned by those big corporations, distract us by pointing fingers at the "illegal immigration problem." Opportunistic politicians and the mass media promote the myth that Mexicans are taking jobs from the United States.

It is those invisible workers overseas that American businessmen hire in other countries who are leaving America jobless. Those workers do not even step on American soil. The wealthy corporations are destroying our economy. They are leaving this nation without factories, without our once-mighty industries, without a source of income. Where is the American factory worker? Today even many of the American office workers are gone, and those who are fortunate enough to have jobs in offices are required to work like slaves. Gone are their forty-hour weeks; now they are required to work as long on Saturday and Sunday, because as staffs have been reduced. At the same time, we see big computer companies sitting in the lap of China, where they send the computer manufacturing jobs. We depend on communist China for the plates we eat on, for the clothes we wear, for the plastic children's toys we buy, and now for our cars. We sell our worst enemy our souls for a toilet seat. Now we literally owe our souls to China, which holds our biggest debts, so they in turn buy our companies for pennies on the dollar.

The United States even buys piñatas from China, along with the poisoned toys and the poisoned drywall we use to build houses (which now we must tear down).

Our businesspeople's greed is what is destroying our economy, but instead we point to the poor Mexican and Central American immigrant workers who sweep our streets, cook our food, and build our homes. Yes, America is full of new immigrants; they come from all four corners of the world. But we only see the poor, Spanish-speaking immigrants who clean our streets, feed us, and build our homes. For generations we had the luxury of having workers to do the jobs that no one else would, because it was economically wise. Now we want to blame those same workers for all our financial woes.

This is unjust; the problem is not Spanish-speaking workers. The problem is wealthy American manufacturers who are outsourcing our jobs. Let us point the finger at companies like a large lumber company that bought thousands of electric fans in China because they were cheap. Let us blame megastores for buying from Asian countries and not American companies that still employ Americans.

Let us blame communications companies who hire and buy outside of the United States and leave Americans jobless. Outsourcing, not Hispanic immigrants, is the real threat to American workers. We want our industry back, we want our manufacturing back, and we want wages that can support American families and keep them from losing their homes. Americans want wages that will pay for health insurance and build schools for our children regardless of if they are Americans or the children of new immigrants. If we work, we want just compensation. Stop the globalization that exploits our planet and its people and makes a few wealthy while the poor of the world die of lack of food and water. Our environment is sacred; humanity belongs to God and not those who exploit the poor.

Recently, terrorism has come from countries that were once American allies in the Middle East. Once again, the United States keeps arming its borders with Mexico, although Mexican citizens have never attacked America. Yet one does not hear a great deal about arming the Canadian border, which is wide and isolated. The truth is that Canadians actually are of European descent. That is why Americans have never discouraged Canadian immigration, even when many of them come illegally.

Because in recent times Canadians have been more racially tolerant, many Central and South Americans have actually found it easier to travel to Canada and enter the United States via Canada, because there is not any one seriously guarding the northern border. On the Canadian border, I met two young Mexican girls from Durango who were going to Niagara Falls; they each had three full suitcases of clothes and confided to me that they planned to get jobs in New York. I warned them about unscrupulous men who often hire pretty girls as prostitutes, but they claimed they had good connections in New York. They were very attractive and young and naïve about what can happen to immigrant girls in a large city. They both came from small towns in remote parts of Mexico.

Nevertheless, because of the poverty in Mexico, people find ways to immigrate, although they have to travel farther and farther away from home. Yet in spite of all the guarding we do at the border, the true terrorists are not poor illegal immigrants; so far, terrorists from the Middle East have come here with money and visas. In California, people from Saudi Arabia and other parts of the Middle East have bought mansions and established themselves in their own secret worlds for years, but no one has questioned them because they have money. Maybe we should be hiring more investigators who can check on legal visas, since they have failed to keep our borders secure. Nevertheless, our country never learns; now they want to grant full citizenship to families who denounce terrorists who live among them. That means that immigrants can now invent terrorist threats among their own families in order to remain in the United States. If people are willing to blow themselves up, why should we expect them to remain loyal to their families? We are creating a nation of suspects in which anyone bearing a grudge against someone will be able to get revenge by accusing them of terrorism and going to a secret court. Our own government destroys our nation's democracy with legislation like the Patriot Act. Do we need to kill democracy in order to save it? September 11, 2001, is making us as savage as the terrorists who attacked us. However, outside of having our sons go to the front lines to be killed, we are never consulted on how to run the nation. Today we are arming our borders in the south, but the border with Canada remains unsecured even when terrorists can use that route.

Mexicans Need
a New Revolution

Mexicans have dreamed for too long that the United States is their salvation; coming to the United States is considered to be like dying and going to heaven. Their dreams of America were and are still just that—dreams. They are beautiful dreams, but when they arrive—if they do arrive—those dreams soon turn into nightmares. Some drown crossing the Rio Grande; some die in the deserts of heat exertion. Some are lucky and enter the United States safely but often are caught by immigration, imprisoned for two years, and then deported. Other people who try crossing the wall have fallen and suffered severe spinal trauma; they will never be able to walk again.

In the United States, no one is standing up and crying out, "United States, tear down this wall." It seems that while it was terrible for the communists to have a wall in Berlin, it's okay for the United States to have a wall on the Mexican border. This just shows the hypocrisy among American politicians. Some people in Mexico are not making any commentary about the fence; they are just quietly tearing it down and selling it as scrap metal.

Once in the United States, the nightmare becomes worse, as Mexicans work from dawn to twilight. They toil in the fields in the hot deserts of Arizona picking lettuce. In California, they often sleep in cardboard boxes and spend the day stooping to pick up strawberries.

They do all this daily work just so they can survive. Besides the Farm Workers Union, who complains about the harsh treatment of the workers? Nobody—not the justice system, not the Catholic Church, not the Protestant churches. None of them protest the inhuman treatment of farm workers, who are invisible and voiceless in America.

Today some Mexican and Central American immigrants go to New York, where they live in horrible living conditions, often crowding themselves into small underground apartments, which are unhealthy and bad for their families. They work from sunup to sundown cleaning offices, cleaning windows, cooking, and doing janitorial work. They do not earn enough money to pay for health benefits or for their families' groceries. Sometimes, they progress sufficiently to earn enough to rent a home. In some places, neighbors who distrust them and have racial prejudices toward them attack them. The main reason they do not fit in is that they are racially different from European immigrants. European immigrants, who often come here without an education or money, find other European Americans who are sympathetic toward them. People like Schwarzenegger, who came as a poor Austrian immigrant with his physique and attractive looks but not very much formal education, became a commodity for sale to the highest bidder, who happened to be a Kennedy. His good looks and connections to the rich enabled him to become governor of California. The people of California, who have such a strong anti-immigrant mentality, quickly endorsed Schwarzenegger, an Austrian immigrant.

Poor Mexican Indians do not have such luck; they are simply too racially different from white people. Indians have been slaves for too long in Mexico. They do not succeed there, because the native people do not run Mexico. It is usually old Spanish and other European families who live in fortresses who run Mexico along with the United States. Those people keep Indians and mestizos as low wage earners and as their modern day slaves. As long as Mexicans remain uneducated and poor, they will continue to be victims of the wealthy and the Mexican drug dealers. Many poor young Mexicans are tempted into joining drug lords as the soldiers who violently murder and intimidate citizens. These young men often become the victims of rival gangs, who murder them and desecrate their bodies so that now Mexico is engaged in a bloody and horrific war, a war fueled by the United States' hunger for drugs and the greed of gun dealers who sell weapons to Mexico. The NRA will continue to demand fewer gun laws, and no one will protest; thus Mexico will continue to bleed and suffer.

Acclaimed Mexican author Carlos Fuentes tells us about what it means to become rich in Mexico. In his novel *The Crystal Frontier*, Juan Zamora is a fictional student who experiences pain and shame regarding his behavior toward Mexico. Carlos Fuentes explains that in the period between 1970 and 1980, Mexico experienced a surge of wealth due to the demand for Mexican oil. At the same time, Mexicans experienced a sense of shame and pain. He claims Mexico "celebrated the boom like a bunch of nouveaux riches. Pain because the wealth was badly used. Shame because the President said our problem now was to administer our wealth. Pain because the poor kept on getting poorer. Shame because we became frivolous spendthrifts, slaves of vulgar whims and our comic macho posturing."[194]

My grandmother used to say it was possible her father could have bought land in Texas if he had not always spent his money on big fiestas. Maybe it is true that Mexicans love big fiestas, but now it is time to stop that. It is time for them to stop coming to the United States and Europe to buy "rich rags." Mexico needs to start producing for its people, not taking from them. This would not only help the lower classes but also increase the upper class's wealth.

For too long, the wealthy have run to Mexico seeking more wealth; Spaniards, other Europeans, and Anglo Americans have gone to Mexico to seek profits. Mexico needs to liberate itself from those tyrants. For too many generations, its elites have known that they can release the pressure valve of social discontent by allowing poor Mexicans to immigrate to the United States. This has kept Mexico from another revolution. The United States, which needs workers to do jobs no one else wants to do, such as picking fruit or sewing in sweatshops, allows those immigrants into the country. Today, when the United States has exported all the jobs to other nations, Americans are jobless and blame Mexican immigrant workers.

In Pottsville, Pennsylvania, two white youths are on trial for the killing of a young Mexican. Today Mexicans are no longer needed, so they are now treated as criminals. The young Mexican was told to leave the United States because he did not belong in their nation. They fatally injured him when they attacked him. He died two days later in the hospital. The young men who killed him were two European Americans. They attacked him and told him to go back to Mexico; it was a hate crime. The young man, Luis Ramirez, tried to defend himself from the aggression, but the group of football players that attacked him was too powerful. Now Frederick Finely and Brandon Piekaski's lawyer is saying the fight was started after an innocent comment. He raises the question of why it has been labeled a hate crime. Six white football players making derogatory comments and attacking a single

Mexican man not a hate crime? Where is America's sense of justice and dignity?[195]

In Suffolk County, dozens of attacks have taken place against Latinos. Not long ago, immigration agents raided a poultry processing plant in Carthage, Missouri, and arrested a woman from Guatemala working there. Encarnación Bael Romero was charged with the crime of entering the country illegally. She was arrested and put in prison. However, she did not come to the United States alone; she came with her infant. The child has been taken away from her and awarded to another family. Mrs. Romero will not be able to have her son returned to her; she will be held prisoner, and then she will return home to Guatemala without her baby. Judge David C. Daily of the Circuit Court of Jasper claims Mrs. Romero has little to offer her son, since she is in jail for daring to commit the crime of coming to work in the United States. This means this mother has lost her son and will never see him again unless she repeats her illegal entry into the United States. Her only crime was working to support her family, and it led to her greatest loss, her son. Ms. Bael Romero was not fully aware of how the American court system works, and she did not have access to a lawyer. She is only one of thousands of Central American and Mexican victims in the United States prison system. Mrs. Romero sits invisible and silent in jail without a judge or a court to defend her and her son.[196]

According to a doctor, an acquaintance of mine, in Tucson, Arizona, illegal aliens occupy hospital beds, injured with broken legs, broken arms, damaged spines, or damaged internal organs from jumping the border fence. Some will return to face time in jail after they leave the hospitals; others will remain crippled, unable to move. Their crime is having crossed the American border. The price is steep for those invisible and voiceless Mexicans. They come for work only to meet tragedy and lie helpless in a hospital while prison guards stand at their doors. The case is clear: Americans do not want Mexicans in the United States.

So what are Mexicans to do? They need a new revolution. They need to demand that their Mexican government stop spending money in the United States and provide more money for the Mexican economy. Mexico has a lot of sun; the ancestors of the current residents worshipped Huitzilopochtli, the sun god. They need to turn back to the sun by investing in solar energy, which can enrich the nation. Mexico needs to invest in sun power. It also needs to revisit the god Olin and build wind mills to provide power for industries. Mexico has natural resources that can enrich the country. It has silver mines; it should not give them away to another country. It has land; it should be used to grow and to benefit the nation as it has in the past, when food for the Mexicans was plentiful. Food grown in Mexico shouldn't be given away to the United States. Today, many crops of vegetables are exported while the people starve; they cannot even afford their own corn. It is time for Mexico to build an agricultural industry to benefit its people and not other nations. The power is in the people's hands. Finally, Mexico has to educate its children and keep them out of the drug lords' hands. The drug lords are destroying Mexico. Mexico has some of the least educated people in North America.

Mexicans need to remain in Mexico. Yes, comparatively speaking, Mexico is geographically small, but so are Japan and many other prosperous nations in the world. Regarding education, Charles Miller, who was chair of the University of Texas System Board of Regents from 2003 to 2004, claims that the Texas-Mexico border divides the most educated nation and the worst educated nation. He feels the United States should help Mexico educate its citizens.

The reality is that Mexico has enough wealthy citizens to educate its children. Mexicans need to stop investing their wealth in the United States and Europe. They need to go home and invest in Mexico. They have been hiding in their haciendas for too long. They need to open their doors to the Mexican citizens that need better homes, better health care, and better education. Mexico needs to return to the vast wealth of knowledge it had when the Spaniards arrived. Educated Mexicans can become scientists, engineers, doctors, and the other types of specialists a nation needs. They must insist that the government educate their children and get sufficient political power to oust those wealthy politicians who prefer to keep the nation uneducated for their own prosperity. They have to break the chain of ignorance. They need to be self-sufficient and start their own industries, build wind power and solar power infrastructure to clean the air. They need to become leaders in clean fuels. They need factories where they can produce their own shoes, make their own tools, and make their own futures. As long as they remain the slaves of the United States, they will not prosper. They need to abandon the *maquilladoras*, which are sweatshops. Dignity and pride can only come when Mexico is no longer dependent on another country; it must let go of the American tits. No one is going to come and defend Mexicans. All foreign nations come to the Americas to exploit. China and Russia are foreign invaders, not liberators. Only Mexicans can accomplish this job with their own hard work and with a new order. Mexico's greatest wealth is its youth. Breaking away from the powerful United States would be casting off the chains of slavery. That is the hardest chain to break, but it is still a chain, and it can be broken.

Take the example of Brazil, where everything is Brazilian. From soccer shirts to dishes, everything reads "made in Brazil." For too many years, Mexicans have lived in poverty, and Mexicans in the upper echelons of Mexican society are tempted to continue the exploitation of their own people. Ideally, however, bringing down the slave society could be the answer to Mexico's problems. On Mexican television, I saw a program in which Mexicans rounded off their pesos in grocery stores and department stores so that the money could go to educating children. Something more still needs to be done. Mexico cannot continue to sell its labor cheaply. It must open Mexican markets to its citizens and must educate its citizens so that they can hold jobs that pay enough money to support their families. Mexico must develop jobs that will prevent Mexicans from migrating to the United States as modern slaves. Mexicans must demand that their government open the door of progress to them.

When Do We
Become Americans?

Republican and Democratic administrations have ignored the Mexican American community; politicians have absolutely no concern for us except when it comes to getting our vote during elections. Candidates from both parties feel it is easy to pander to Mexican Americans when campaigning by uttering a few words in Spanish. Today that is no longer necessary; the majority of Mexican American citizens speak English. Those who do not understand English often are not American citizens, and they cannot vote anyway. Politicians must remember that they are not speaking to immigrants but to English-speaking US citizens; they could avoid the trouble and embarrassment of stumbling over a few phrases of broken Spanish and instead focus on the real political issues facing all Americans. We do not want to hear about fiestas or tamales; Mexican Americans want to hear about jobs, education, health care, and decent, affordable housing, American issues that most politicians cannot speak about in Spanish.

Language is no longer a barrier; Mexican Americans want to hear about issues like social security, taxes, military service, and war, topics that are important to their communities. Those are issues that Mexican Americans learn about from newspapers, magazines, and television, and they require in-depth analysis and not just a few trivial, irrelevant words in Spanish. Mexican American issues differ very little from the issues of other Americans. However, one serious problem is that we are never consulted in the American dialogue. According to census figures, we are the largest minority, yet we are minimally represented or not at all.

Our issues must be addressed and discussed not only during elections but also all year long. Yet during discussions of education, housing, jobs, health care, and civil rights, Mexican American representation is usually absent. We have one of the lowest representations in Washington, with only a few congressional representatives elected by Mexican American communities and very few in major positions appointed by presidents. During the 2008 presidential election, I watched on television a bipartisan discussion panel about education. The program mentioned Mexican Americans, but none were present; the discussion took place mostly between European Americans and African Americans.

This is wrong! Mexican Americans must demand to be present when discussions about economic and educational issues take place. Politicians from both parties use Mexican Americans as background decoration during elections; they like to place a few children or adults behind them while they are speaking. This is supposed to show inclusion! After delivering the speeches, after clearing the confetti and the balloons, after electing the politicians, Mexican American education remains mediocre, salaries remain low, unemployment remains high, and health care remains poor. Statistics may claim Latinos are now one of the largest minorities in the United States, but they still have very little political power.

In Texas, during George W. Bush's presidency, Republicans gerrymandered the state to dilute Mexican American political power; over two thirds of Mexican Americans are traditionally Democratic. There is no question that Mexican Americans are not respected or loved as Americans despite all the service they have given this nation.

Democrats believe that by speaking to us in broken Spanish during elections they can gain our votes. They take us for granted year after year. They pretend to listen but eventually ignore our major concerns. Since many electoral campaigns take place in the north or the east, in Texas, Mexican Americans are lucky if they get a president's wife to visit. During Bill Clinton's administration, Democrats joined forces with Republicans and enacted laws that negatively affected our community. As a result, the government sent troops and militarized our border with Mexico. Politicians never speak about militarizing the border with Canada; they do not seem to mind immigration from Canada, even if some of it might be illegal. Some in the United States may assume immigrants from Canada are all white, although today that is not true anymore. Many of those immigrants are from Asia, the Middle East, Europe, and Central America.

In the past, the border with Mexico was different: the United States guarded against immigrants coming to work as migrant workers in the fields. President George W. Bush expressed the core of the racist idea behind his new policies when he said that Mexicans could come to the United States for three years as guest workers "to do jobs that no Americans want to do because they are below their standards." Television often shows the people who want those workers—farmers who need someone to pick crops, restaurant and hotel owners who feel they need cheap labor to clean and do manual work. All of those employers are looking for slave labor. Mexico must stop exporting slave labor to the United States.

Today, the real danger on the border is drug trafficking. Mexican police have not been able to control drug traffic. As long as the United States' demand for illicit drugs persists and as long as Mexican drug cartels' demand for guns from the United States continues, the carnage will increase and blood will go on flowing in Mexico. Today drugs are a persistent threat to the United States as well as to Mexico.

While this is happening, business and academic communities claim that they have to go to Europe and Asia to get qualified professionals, but the reality is that American business leaders just want to pay lower wages. Yet when college graduates are out of a job, they often blame Mexican workers, who only go into offices to clean them. The truth is that racism is alive and well in this country. The loophole that allows discrimination is that you need only hire a few token Mexican American professionals to comply with equal opportunity laws. Today some Mexican Americans are under the illusion that discrimination does not exist against them. Unfortunately, some of those who refuse to acknowledge that discrimination exists may lose their jobs in the future because European Americans will want those jobs for their people. In San Antonio, Texas, the closing of the Kelly Air Force Base in the 1990s was an example of Mexican Americans losing their jobs in large numbers. Many of them had worked at the base since the end of the Korean war.

The issue for Mexican Americans today is not just jobs but civil rights. As politicians continue to debate about illegal immigrants, Mexican Americans are often viewed as non-American. Soon we will need to show papers to prove we are Americans.

The terrorists who committed the 9/11 attacks came to the United States from the Middle East, entered the country legally, and received training in our own flight schools. Yet the Department of Homeland

Security has spent millions of dollars persecuting Mexican and Central American immigrants while letting terrorists from other continents come into the United States. Extremists like Lou Dobbs make many false claims to support their propaganda. He proclaimed that Mexicans were a real threat to America and would destroy our nation. Many politicians like to promote this idea in their communities. The militarization and closing of the Mexican border started in 1996, long before the tragedy of 9/11 occurred.

Some towns in the state of New York protest the coming of Mexican and Central American workers into their communities. Crime has always been a high concern in New York, but some people are now blaming crime rates on the immigrants who have to work in construction jobs, as janitors, or as kitchen workers.

This treatment is part of a campaign that keeps reminding everyone that Latinos are now the largest non-European population in the United States. Oppression of Mexican Americans is intended to keep us as a slave society; they know that numbers mean nothing if the people that make up those numbers are slaves. We are being crafted into a powerless ethnic group that is controlled by simply being forced into an economically and politically deprived society. We must not become America's untouchable society, willing to perform jobs no one else wants to do.

Many Mexican Americans are under the mistaken illusion that once they become a majority in the United States, they will be able to participate in the development of this nation. This is not necessarily true; numbers are not the solution for the Mexican American community. The European Americans will continue to control this nation regardless of population size, because the issue is not the number of people in each group but the amount of economic power held by the elite, who are educated and own the land and means of production. A small number of people can exploit an entire nation. Such was the case when wealthy companies like the United Fruit Company had more power in the so-called banana republics than the people of those countries. Population size is insignificant in nations where a small number of people exploit the rest of the population for the benefit of those in power.

A small number of politicians and businesspeople can manipulate a nation. Nowhere was this more evident than in South Africa during the time of apartheid. For years, a strong European African military and a few powerful European African landowners kept that nation in slavery. This is also true of countries in Central and South America where a few European Latin Americans and Europeans are in charge of the economy and dictate the political and economic policy that controls the masses of mestizos and indigenous people.

In the United States, the enslavement of farm workers and unskilled labor will continue to bring in massive profits for those who exploit the poor. Successive administrations continue to ignore our desire for equal education; by inaction, they have allowed the end of Affirmative Action, which gave our children a level playing field to compete in business and the professional world. Ending affirmative action means that universities and colleges will be able to refuse admittance to bright and talented students without having to justify their decisions. During the 1990s, Governor Pete Wilson of California promoted the myth that minority students were less qualified than white students.

A high profile case of civil rights abuse occurred when President Clinton and his administration refused to acknowledge that there had been civil rights violations committed against our people. The most outrageous violation was the death of Ezekiel Hernandez, a young American high school student. Marines shot him dead on our southern border while he was tending his goats on his father's land on United States soil. This case left many questions unanswered. Did the camouflaged Marines ever identify themselves? Did young Hernandez ever fire his rifle as claimed by the Marines? We will never find the answers, because the case was never tried in public. Neither Bill Clinton nor any of the Democrats in office ever apologized to our community for this great tragedy. It was as if our youth were somehow less valuable. In a different case, the FBI apologized for the attack on a right-wing radical militant group at Ruby Ridge that was plotting against the American government. Yet Ezekiel, who had a Marine poster in his room because he wanted to become one, did not get justice in our American courts. The family settled in court and got reparations, but the real issue was not money; it was justice. We feel that we did not have the Democratic Party as our allies in this crucial crisis although we are always expected to vote Democrat. We usually vote for the lesser evil when we should be voting for justice.

For years, Mexicans and Mexican Americans have received most of the blame for drug traffic; the military is spending millions of dollars on the southern border while drugs are also pouring in from other countries in Asia and Europe. This negative stereotyping will lead to more tragic deaths of American citizens who are of Mexican descent. This happened recently in the case of a teenage girl in San Antonio, Texas, who was killed during FBI surveillance. Her father was the alleged drug dealer, but the agents shot her when she went outside to her driveway. The girl was killed, and the community remained silent over her death. Dealing in drugs is a terrible crime, and offenders should be arrested, but children should not be attacked.

It is a known fact that illegal drugs enter this nation by way of Florida, New York, San Francisco, the Canadian border, and other means. However, the idea of sending the military to those areas has never come up. The militarization of the Mexican border is based on race. Now they claim the border is also a terrorist breeding ground, although no terrorist has been found coming through Mexico's borders. The only terrorists present in the area are powerful drug dealers who have enough weapons to fight a war. Mexican drug dealers obtain most of their weapons from the United States, yet no one has taken any serious steps to stop the arms traffic. The NRA does not want laws restricting the sale of arms, thus its lobbyists in Washington become the drug lords' best friends by allowing gun dealers to sell thousands of weapons to criminals. NRA lobbyists are very powerful in Washington DC and can buy politicians.

We should insist that the Democratic and Republican parties open dialogue with our Mexican American community and appoint Mexican American judges. Judges who are not from our communities try the majority of legal cases concerning jobs (Kelly military base), concerning affirmative action (University of Texas), and concerning justice (Ezekiel Hernandez). We also need representation in the Supreme Court, where many of the cases concerning our rights as United States citizens are reviewed. The Supreme Court has representatives from all the major groups—Catholics, Jews, Protestants, African Americans, and women—but while we are part of a large segment of the citizenry of the United States, we have no representation in our Supreme Court. As American citizens who vote and pay taxes, we feel that we are experiencing taxation without representation in the American judicial system. If the Democratic Party is serious about our vote, it should give us a voice on the Supreme Court. It should give us a voice that actually represents our community, not an outsider. We do not want a token judge; we want one that understands and will defend us when our rights are being trampled. At the present time, the Supreme Court has all its doors closed to our community.

The Mexican American poor will continue to be powerless as long as they do not have wealth to promote their cause. Those who are rich control the poor; in the United States, the European Americans are the ones who have money. They will continue to exploit the poor as long as they have power in Washington. Money equals power, and power means having control over those who are poor. This was evident in the year 2009 during the debate to set up health insurance legislation. Although a majority of Americans wanted a public option, the wealthy health insurance cartel controls Democrats and Republicans using financial influence. The resulting health care legislation was much less than promised.

Our way out hangs on gaining political power, and it also requires that all Mexican Americans demand equal education, civil rights, and higher paying jobs for workers in offices and in agricultural work. Today, Mexican American wages lag behind the wages of most other ethnic groups; at the bottom of the scale are farm workers, whose meager earnings do not even allow them to get enough food or proper medical care.

We need to organize; we need to vote and use our votes as our voice. We need to get educated so we can have a voice in politics. After we get equal representation in Washington, we must lobby for changes to education, health care, and citizenship policy. We must speak up and, if need be, sleep at the doors of Congress. We must learn who our governors and state officials are and where they stand on the environment, on housing issues, and on civil rights issues. Whether we agree or disagree with them, we must contact them and let them know what we think of the issues. We want to elect politicians and make them work for us. We pay their salaries with our taxes. How do we contact them? We can write them, we can telephone them, we can e-mail them, or we can even twitter them. If you do not know how to use a computer, ask an adult family member or even a grandchild to help. If you do not have a computer, use the library or family center computer.

We need to go to Washington and state capitals. Get together with friends and carpool or get a bus but make sure the community is aware of what you are doing. Insist that the mass media does not ignore you. In October 2009, a very large number of Latinos went to Washington DC to demonstrate for immigration reform. The mass media, which controls politics in the United States, did not cover the event. That same day, the White House hosted a Latino feast, and we could see President Obama on television dancing with the participants around the room while the demonstrators stood outside voiceless and invisible. We do not need a president who can dance salsa; we need a president who promotes justice for even those who many Americans consider insignificant—immigrants who have come to America seeking refuge and dignity.

For years, I have argued that we need to educate our children. We need to have more lawyers, and we need to have a voice in the human rights department. But I am not the only one concerned about having more lawyers. The Anglo American establishment is also aware that having more minority lawyers will make it more difficult for them to exploit American minorities. Professor Conrad Johnson oversees admissions at the Digital Age Clinic at Columbia University. Professor Johnson observes that while entering blacks and Mexican American students have improved their college grade point averages over the years, they now have fewer students entering law schools than before. According to his findings, from 2003 to 2008, law schools denied acceptance to 61 percent of African American and 46 percent of Mexican American applicants. During the same period, the figure for Caucasian applicants was 34 percent.[197]

Anglo Americans know that degrees in law can increase the power of minority communities by giving them the means to demand more civil rights. Therefore, they try to keep certain minorities out while allowing other minorities who may not be as interested in civil rights to enter law schools. This demonstrates the importance of maintaining our Mexican American identity so we can gauge to what extent colleges allow our young people to attend their institutions; the Hispanic and Latino labels obscure our existence.

We must encourage every Mexican American to attend college, and we must dedicate part of our earnings to pay for those children's college. In other words, we should set up scholarships. Most importantly, we must monitor our schools and make sure that our children are properly educated from kindergarten to high school. If our grammar schools and our high schools are not adequate, our children's education will not be adequate for college.

Population size does not count; power comes through wealth and political leverage, and wealth comes through education. People who run corporations are educated; lawyers, doctors, and engineers all require a diploma. Mexican Americans often feel they are so deep in poverty that they cannot afford to educate their children. This is where we need to demand fair wages so our children can be educated. For American citizens of Mexican descent, the issue is not simply increasing the population of Mexican Americans; that is not the solution to any of our economic or social woes. As long as we are the poorest citizens, as long as we have the weakest political role and the least educated youth, numbers are meaningless.

In San Antonio, Texas, a Mexican American family sent its twins sons to Harvard. Today one is a state representative and the other is the mayor of the city. To become leaders in a community, we need to be educated. There is no question that Mexican Americans can be leaders, but it becomes much harder for those leaders if they lack an education. We need doctors to care for illnesses such as diabetes. We need young women and young men to become astronauts and explore the solar system. Mexican Americans are bright and can perform many skills, but they must first be educated, and it is the duty of parents to sacrifice so that their children can become educated. Parents must understand that education is the only answer to poverty in the barrios. They must learn that education has to come first, and then everything will fall into place. Mexican Americans are not here as visitors; they are here for the long haul, so they had better be educated or they will become the untouchables who are used to do jobs that are dirty and pay meager wages. They will never afford their own homes or medical care.

Most Mexican American communities are poor, but since there are many of us in the United States, we could raise funds to gain power. A few dollars each could multiply into millions. Poor people like Cesar Chavez were able to organize and set up funds for migrant workers. There are a number of honest Mexican American men and women who can help the community organize and raise funds. We can set up radio stations to keep people informed about schools, medical treatment, classes for adults, and other services they need. People must have funds to travel to Washington to demand civil rights. We also need to raise money to help Mexican American candidates go and serve as congressional representatives and senators in their states and in the federal government. Money runs the national machine, and we need to set up a powerful machine that says no to jobs no one else wants to do. We are also aware that there are a number of educated, wealthy Mexican American people who know how to organize and can provide funds. This must be a joint effort of poor and wealthy Mexican Americans. Future generations depend upon our united efforts all over the United States. We need to assume power, have more self-confidence, and not wait on an outside hero to deliver us from evil. We need to organize and educate our people to become leaders.

The answer to the migrant worker's plight is to walk out of the fields and leave the farm labor to others; after all, they too have to eat. Other people who immigrate to this nation rarely work in the fields; they come seeking jobs in the cities, where they can operate businesses or do professional work and send their children to school. Our indigenous people have a long tradition of agriculture. They love the land, and they were the people who from ancient times cultivated a large number of the food staples that the world now takes for granted. Nevertheless, they also worked as artists, architects, scientists, and teachers. Today, we lack artists, musicians, poets, civic leaders, and scientists.

I have seen a Mexican American migrant worker go to college and get a degree. Later, as a mother, she sent her child to college, and I saw that child graduate from MIT and Stanford and become an aerospace physicist. This can only occur now because this nation went through a time of civil rights struggle and gains for minorities. Sadly, we will lose those gains if we refuse to walk off the fields. The living conditions and abuse can be no worse off the fields than they are on them. The only thing that may differ is that other segments of society will have to work in the fields.

Technology might create a future in which farm hands are no longer necessary, so why not get ready for the time when the migrant worker will be obsolete by coming into the technological arena and demanding jobs with a future. We need to demand schools and medical care so that our children do not grow up poisoned by agricultural chemicals that make them sickly and may poison their brain cells permanently. Now that the United States is cutting off illegal immigration, we need to tell our brothers and sisters in Mexico that it is not worth trading health for eternal slavery. Tell them that here in this nation, there is no future for them, and the same people who exploit them in Spanish-speaking countries will exploit them here; the only difference is that they will exploit them in English. Ask them to tell the Mexican elite to return their country to them so they can reap the benefits of the nation. Tell them to stop raising food for the United States and to start feeding the Mexican population.

One of the greatest criticisms of migrants is that they rarely succeed in life; most of them are doomed to repeat the poverty cycle as if they lack the intelligence to leave the fields. European Americans accuse them of lacking ambition and drive. The truth is that when human beings are subject to constant hard labor under adverse conditions, they lose hope. Their defeatist attitudes drive them to negative activities, such as drug addiction, drunkenness, and the abandonment of family and family values. They often vent their frustration against society on their own families.

Changing the mindset of society will not be easy in Mexico or in the United States, but unless this change takes place, Mexicans and Mexican Americans will be doomed regardless of their societal status. Mexico must stop depending on the United States to deal with the overflow of poor Mexicans. Mexico must stop spending its wealth in the United States and in Europe. The wealthy in Mexico have enough wealth to invest in infrastructure, jobs, and the construction of roads to move vegetables and other products, and they have human resources, a young, dynamic work force. They just need to educate their youth to produce scientists and engineers, businesspeople, and doctors. A healthy, educated, well-nourished population will enrich all of the Mexican community, including those who are already wealthy.

In the United States, the challenge is different; Mexican Americans must use their voices to demand equal civil rights. They must demand better wages if there is discrimination in wages. They must not be afraid to enter careers in science and medicine; they must demand jobs in those fields. Women can be doctors and lawyers and must not be afraid to enter those professions. Mexican Americans must not live under the illusion that there is no longer racism in America just because some Mexican Americans have crossed the discrimination barrier; we must speak up for our brothers and sisters who are lost in the fields and "jobs no one else wants to do."

We must also demand that society recognize us as mainstream American citizens and not just criminals in television programs and films. We must demand jobs in advertising; we all pay for those commercials when we buy products. We have to contact those companies and let them know that if they do not hire Mexican Americans, we will not buy their products. We can also contact television and film companies to let them know we will boycott their films if they do not hire Mexican Americans and portray them in positive roles.

As a child migrant worker, I remember reading signs that said "No Mexicans or dogs allowed" on the fronts of restaurants in Littlefield, Texas, a stone's throw from Lubbock. This was an area where Mexican Americans went to work. The racism in this region of Texas was well known. There still seems to be a great deal of animosity against Mexicans and Mexican Americans in that part of the state.

So it was no surprise when I read in the New York Times that a fourth-generation American citizen, Monica Castro, had her daughter—also an American citizen—kidnapped by the border patrol and deported to Mexico with her Mexican father. The police sought Mr. Gallardo, the undocumented father, because he witnessed a murder. The police assured the mother that they would return her daughter if she turned in her estranged husband to immigration officials. She turned him in, but the police did not return her daughter. Instead, the baby went with her father to Mexico, because immigration officers claimed the mother did not process a court order on time. On the day of the arrest, the Immigration and Naturalization Services office gave her half a day to produce the required documents. A lawyer unsuccessfully sought an extension on her behalf. The child was taken away, and it was three years before the mother got her back. Fortunately for the child, she stayed with her paternal grandmother and received proper care. Mr. Gregory Kurupas, an immigration agent, stated that the reason for not giving Ms. Castro more time to file the proper court papers was that it would have been too expensive for them to hold Mr.Gallardo. When asked how expensive, he replied over two hundred dollars. This news item came out years after the child was rescued by the mother; today this child is seven years old, and the mother is still seeking justice in the courts.[198]

It seems a Mexican American's right to care for her own child is not worth two hundred dollars! This is an outrageous scandal, yet this injustice did not circulate in the Texas newspapers or get national attention. This story, which occurred in 2003, is reminiscent of what happened in the 1930s, when the United States deported Mexican Americans by the thousands. This story shows that it can happen again to any Mexican American if we do not expose the injustice these cases can bring. In Texas, many Mexican families are imprisoned with their children; one cannot know how many of those children might actually be American citizens.

One of our most important goals must be equality under the law. As Americans, we must receive justice. When our civil rights are violated and we complain, we are often ignored. Mexican Americans must cry out for justice.

So yes, if you are a Mexican American citizen, you are still a stepchild of America, and it is up to you to guard and demand you rights as a citizen as racism keeps creeping back into our nation.

We all can do our part as long as we do not remain silent. We must stop being invisible and voiceless in America.

Endnotes

1. David Montejano, *Anglos and Mexicans in the Making of Texas, 1836–1986,* 6th ed. (Austin: University of Texas Press, 1997), 113.

2. Southern Poverty Law Center, *Intelligence Report: The Puppeteer* (Montgomery, Alabama, Summer 2002, issue 106).

3. Lewis Hanke, *Aristotle and the American Indians: A Study in Race Prejudice in the Modern World* (Chicago: Henry Regnery Company, 1959), 3.

4. Sarah Vowell, *The Wordy Shipmates* (New York: Riverhead Books, 2008), 2.

5. Bartolome de Las Casas, *Brevisima relación de la Destrucción de las Indias,* ed. Andre Saint-Lu, 5th ed. (Madrid: Catedra, Letras Hispanicas, 1991), 87.

6. Bartolome de Las Casas, *Historia de Las Indias,* vol. 1, ed. Agustin Millares Carlo (Mexico: Fondo de Cultura Economica, 1986), 405.

7. Jill Lepore, *The Name of War: King Philip's War and the Origins of American Identity* (New York: Vintage Books, 1999), 30.

8. Jill Lepore, *Encounters in the New World: A History in Documents* (New York, Oxford: Oxford University Press, 2000), 33.

9. Alejandro Lipschutz, *El problems racial en la conquista de America,* 3rd ed. (Mexico: Siglo Veintuno Editores SA, 1975), 83.

10. Lewis Hanke, *Aristotle and the American Indians: A Study in Race Prejudice in the Modern World* (Chicago: Henry Regnery Company, 1959), 13.

11. Stuart J. Fiedel, *Prehistory of the Americas* (Cambridge, Massachusetts: Cambridge University Press, 1989), 342.

12. Lewis Hanke, *Aristotle and the American Indians: A Study in Race Prejudice in the Modern World* (Chicago: Henry Regnery Company, 1959), 13.

13. Lewis Hanke, *Aristotle and the American Indians: A Study in Race Prejudice in the Modern World* (Chicago: Henry Regnery Company, 1959), 18.

14. Paul Tillich, *The Courage to Be* (New Haven and London: Yale University Press, 1962), 182.

15. Benjamin Keen, *Readings in Latin American Civilization, 1492 to the Present* (Cambridge, Massachusetts: Houghton Mifflin Company, the Riverside Press, 1955), 52.

16. Bartolome de Las Casas, *Historia de Las Indias*, vol. 2, ed. Agustin Millares Carlo (Mexico: Fondo de Cultura Economica, 1986), 440–441.

17. Lewis Hanke, *The Spanish Struggle for Justice in the Conquest of America* (Boston and Toronto, Little, Brown and Company, 1965), 20.

18. Bartolome de Las Casas, *Brevisima relación de la Destrucción de las Indias*, ed. Andre Saint-Lu, 5th ed. (Madrid: Catedra, Letras Hispanicas, 1991), 121.

19. John L. Kessell, *Spain in the Southwest: A Narrative History of Colonial New Mexico, Arizona, Texas, and California* (Norman: University of Oklahoma Press, 2002), 14.

20. Bartolome de Las Casas, *Brevisima relación de la Destrucción de las Indias*, ed. Andre Saint-Lu, 5th ed. (Madrid: Catedra, Letras Hispanicas, 1991), 122.

21. Bartolome de Las Casas, *Brevisima relación de la Destrucción de las Indias*, ed. Andre Saint-Lu, 5th ed. (Madrid: Catedra, Letras Hispanicas, 1991), 122.

22. Bartolome de Las Casas, *Brevisima relación de la Destrucción de las Indias*, ed. Andre Saint-Lu, 5th ed. (Madrid: Catedra, Letras Hispanicas, 1991), 162.

23. Bartolome de Las Casas, *Brevisima relación de la Destrucción de las Indias*, ed. Andre Saint-Lu, 5th ed. (Madrid: Catedra, Letras Hispanicas, 1991), 123.

24. Bartolome de Las Casas, *Brevisima relación de la Destrucción de las Indias*, ed. Andre Saint-Lu, 5th ed. (Madrid: Catedra, Letras Hispanicas, 1991), 104.

25. Ian K. Steele, *Warpaths: Invasions of North America* (New York: Oxford University Press, 1994), 4.

26. Jill Lepore, *The Name of War: King Philip's War and the Origins of American Identity* (New York: Vintage Books, 1999), 30.

27. Bernadino de Sahagun, *Historia General de las Cosas de Nueva Espana*, ann. Angel Maria Garibay, K., vol. 4, (Mexico: Editorial Porrua SA, 1956), 47.

28. Sophie D. Coe and Michael D. Coe, *The True History of Chocolate* (New York: Thames and Hudson, 1996), 103.

29. Salvador Rueda Smithers, *La Essencia de Mexico* (Corpus Christy, Texas: Grunwald Printing Co., 2000), 109.

30. Salvador Rueda Smithers, *La Essencia de Mexico* (Corpus Christy, Texas: Grunwald Printing Co., 2000), 109.

31. Fray Diego Durán, *The History of the Indies of New Spain*, trans. and ann. Doris Heyden, (Norman and London: University of Oklahoma Press, 1994), 561.

32. Fray Diego Durán, *The History of the Indies of New Spain*, trans. and ann. Doris Heyden, (Norman and London: University of Oklahoma Press, 1994), 561.

33. Bartolome de Las Casas, *Brevisima relación de la Destrucción de las Indias*, ed. Andre Saint-Lu, 5th ed. (Madrid: Catedra, Letras Hispanicas, 1991), 121.

34. Bartolome de Las Casas, *Brevisima relación de la Destrucción de las Indias*, ed. Andre Saint-Lu, 5th ed. (Madrid: Catedra, Letras Hispanicas, 1991), 108.

35. Fray Diego Durán, *The History of the Indies of New Spain*, trans. and ann. Doris Heyden, (Norman and London: University of Oklahoma Press, 1994), 538.

36. Fray Diego Durán, *The History of the Indies of New Spain*, trans. and ann. Doris Heyden, (Norman and London: University of Oklahoma Press, 1994), 555.

37. John L. Kessell, *Spain in the Southwest: A Narrative History of Colonial New Mexico, Arizona, Texas, and California* (Norman: University of Oklahoma Press, 2002), 41.

38. John L. Kessell, *Spain in the Southwest: A Narrative History of Colonial New Mexico, Arizona, Texas, and California* (Norman: University of Oklahoma Press, 2002), 40.

39. Bartolome de Las Casas, *Brevisima relación de la Destrucción de las Indias*, ed. Andre Saint-Lu, 5th ed. (Madrid: Catedra, Letras Hispanicas, 1991), 162.

40. John L. Kessell, *Spain in the Southwest: A Narrative History of Colonial New Mexico, Arizona, Texas, and California* (Norman: University of Oklahoma Press, 2002), 8.

41. Lewis Hanke, *The Spanish Struggle for Justice in the Conquest of America* (Little, Brown and Company, 1965), 93.

42. Lewis Hanke, *The Spanish Struggle for Justice in the Conquest of America* (Little, Brown and Company, 1965), 93.

43. Dee Brown, *Bury My Heart at Wounded Knee: An Indian History of the American West* (New York: Bantam Books, 1972), 144.

44. Jill Lepore, *The Name of War: King Philip's War and the Origins of American Identity* (New York: Vintage Books, 1999), 30.

45. Jill Lepore, *The Name of War: King Philip's War and the Origins of American Identity* (New York: Vintage Books, 1999), 205.

46. Colin G. Calloway, *New Worlds for All: Indians, Europeans, and the Remaking of Early America* (Baltimore and London: Johns Hopkins University Press, 1998), 98.

47. Colin G. Calloway, *New Worlds for All: Indians, Europeans, and the Remaking of Early America* (Baltimore and London: Johns Hopkins University Press, 1998), 99.

48. Grant Foreman, *The Five Civilized Tribes: Cherokee, Chickasaw, Choctaw, Creek, Seminole* (Norman: University of Oklahoma Press, 1989), 97.

49. Jill Lepore, *The Name of War: King Philip's War and the Origins of American Identity* (New York: Vintage Books, 1999), 11.

50. Jill Lepore, *The Name of War: King Philip's War and the Origins of American Identity* (New York: Vintage Books, 1999), 108.

51. Grant Foreman, *The Five Civilized Tribes: Cherokee, Chickasaw, Choctaw, Creek, Seminole* (Norman: University of Oklahoma Press, 1989), 75.

52. David Colin Crass, Steven D. Smith, Martha A. Zierden and Richard D. Brooks; ed. , *The Southern Colonial Backcountry: Interdisciplinary Perspectives on Frontier Communities*, (Knoxville, University of Tennessee Press, 1998), 193.

53. R. B. Bernstein, ed., *The Constitution of the United States with the Declaration of Independence and the Articles of Confederation*, (New York: Barnes & Noble, 2002), 29.

54. R. B. Bernstein, ed., *The Constitution of the United States with the Declaration of Independence and the Articles of Confederation*, (New York: Barnes & Noble, 2002), 29.

55. Lewis Hanke, *Aristotle and the American Indians: A Study in Race Prejudice in the Modern World* (Chicago: Henry Regnery Company, 1959), 30.

56. Lewis Hanke, *Aristotle and the American Indians: A Study in Race Prejudice in the Modern World* (Chicago: Henry Regnery Company, 1959), 16.

57. Lewis Hanke, *Aristotle and the American Indians: A Study in Race Prejudice in the Modern World* (Chicago: Henry Regnery Company, 1959), 35.

58. Benjamin Keen, *Readings in Latin American Civilization, 1492 to the Present* (Cambridge, Massachusetts: Houghton Mifflin Company, the Riverside Press, 1955), 91.

59. Grant Foreman, *The Five Civilized Tribes: Cherokee, Chickasaw, Choctaw, Creek, Seminole* (Norman: University of Oklahoma Press, 1989), 17.

60. Gilberto López y Rivas, *Los Chicanos, Una Minoría Nacional Explotada*, 2nd ed., (Editorial Nuestro Tiempo SA, 1973), 24.

61. Gilberto López y Rivas, *Los Chicanos, Una Minoría Nacional Explotada*, 2nd ed., (Editorial Nuestro Tiempo SA, 1973), 23.

62. David Montejano, *Anglos and Mexicans in the Making of Texas, 1836–1986*, 6th ed. (Austin: University of Texas Press, 1997), 24.

63. Rudolph O. de la Garza, Z. Anthony Kruszewski, and Tomas A. Arciniega, *Chicanos and Native Americans: the Territorial Minorities* (Englewood Cliffs, New Jersey: Prentice-Hall, Inc., 1973), 7.

64. James C. McKinley Jr., "An Arizona Morgue Grows Crowded," *New York Times*, July 29, 2010.

65. Richard E. W. Adams, *Prehistoric Mesoamerica*, 3rd ed. (Norman: University of Oklahoma Press, 2005), 28.

66. Jose Fuentes Mares, *Cortes El Hombre*, 5th ed., (Mexico: Editorial Grijalbo, SA, 1981), 52.

67. Miguel Leon-Portilla, *The Broken Spears: The Aztec Account of the Conquest of Mexico* (Boston: Beacon Press, 1992), 168.

68. Benjamin Keen, *Readings in Latin American Civilization, 1492 to the Present* (Cambridge, Massachusetts: Houghton Mifflin Company, the Riverside Press, 1955), 52.

69. Benjamin Keen, *Readings in Latin American Civilization, 1492 to the Present* (Cambridge, Massachusetts: Houghton Mifflin Company, the Riverside Press, 1955), 53.

70. Agence France-Presse, "Brazil: Tribe Dwindles to 5 People," *The New York Times,* October 20, 2009).

71. Sophie D. Coe and Michael D. Coe, *The True History of Chocolate* (New York: Thames and Hudson, 1996), 73.

72. Sophie D. Coe and Michael D. Coe, *The True History of Chocolate* (New York: Thames and Hudson, 1996), 72.

73. Miguel Leon-Portilla, *La Filosofia Nahuatl: Estudiadas en sus Fuentes,* (Mexico: Universidad National Autonoma de Mexico, Instituto de Investigaciones Historicas, 1979), 153.

74. Miguel Leon-Portilla, *La Filosofia Nahuatl: Estudiadas en sus Fuentes,* (Mexico: Universidad National Autonoma de Mexico, Instituto de Investigaciones Historicas, 1979), 152.

75. Sophie D. Coe and Michael D. Coe, *The True History of Chocolate* (New York: Thames and Hudson, 1996), 69.

76. Sophie D. Coe and Michael D. Coe, *The True History of Chocolate* (New York: Thames and Hudson, 1996), 69.

77. Fray Diego Durán, *The History of the Indies of New Spain,* trans. and ann. Doris Heyden, (Norman and London: University of Oklahoma Press, 1994), 21.

78. Hernan Cortes, *Cartas de relacion de la conquista de Mexico,* 5th ed. (Madrid: Coleccion Austral, Espasa Calpe, SA, 1970), 70.

79. Fray Diego Durán, *The History of the Indies of New Spain,* trans. and ann. Doris Heyden, (Norman and London: University of Oklahoma Press, 1994), 563.

80. Sarah Vowell, *The Wordy Shipmates* (New York: Riverhead Books, 2008), 31.

81. Jill Lepore, *The Name of War: King Philip's War and the Origins of American Identity* (New York: Vintage Books, 1999), 12.

82. Jill Lepore, *The Name of War: King Philip's War and the Origins of American Identity* (New York: Vintage Books, 1999), 17.

83. Rudolph O. de la Garza, Z. Anthony Kruszewski, and Tomas A. Arciniega, *Chicanos and Native Americans: the Territorial Minorities* (Englewood Cliffs, New Jersey: Prentice-Hall, Inc., 1973), 61.

84. Fray Diego Durán, *The History of the Indies of New Spain*, trans. and ann. Doris Heyden, (Norman and London: University of Oklahoma Press, 1994), 537.

85. Sarah Vowell, *The Wordy Shipmates* (New York: Riverhead Books, 2008), 193.

86. Sarah Vowell, *The Wordy Shipmates* (New York: Riverhead Books, 2008), 193.

87. Colin G. Calloway, *New Worlds for All: Indians, Europeans, and the Remaking of Early America* (Baltimore and London: Johns Hopkins University Press, 1998), 98.

88. Colin G. Calloway, *New Worlds for All: Indians, Europeans, and the Remaking of Early America* (Baltimore and London: Johns Hopkins University Press, 1998), 98.

89. Colin G. Calloway, *New Worlds for All: Indians, Europeans, and the Remaking of Early America* (Baltimore and London: Johns Hopkins University Press, 1998), 98.

90. Sarah Vowell, *The Wordy Shipmates* (New York: Riverhead Books, 2008), 196.

91. Sarah Vowell, *The Wordy Shipmates* (New York: Riverhead Books, 2008), 194.

92. Carey McWilliams, *North From Mexico: The Spanish Speaking People of the United States*, ed. Matt S. Meier, paperback ed. (Westport, Connecticutt: Praeger Press, 1990), 122.

93. Sophie D. Coe and Michael D. Coe, *The True History of Chocolate* (New York: Thames and Hudson, 1996), 67-68.

94. Eduard Seler, *Comentarios al Codice Borgia*, 2nd reprint, vol. 1, (Mexico: Fondo de Cultura Económica, 1988), 154 (figure 386).

95. Muriel Porter Weaver, *The Aztecs, Maya, and Their Predecessors: Archaeology of Mesoamerica*, 2nd ed. (Orlando, Florida: Academic Press, Harcourt Brace Jovanovich, 1981), 128.

96. Popol Vuh, *Las Antiguas Historias del Quiche*, 7th ed., trans. Adrian Recinos (San Salvador, El Salvador: UCA Editores, 1987), 15.

97. Richard E. W. Adams, *Prehistoric Mesoamerica*, 3rd ed. (Norman: University of Oklahoma Press, 2005), 53.

98. Muriel Porter Weaver, *The Aztecs, Maya, and Their Predecessors: Archaeology of Mesoamerica*, 2nd ed. (Orlando, Florida: Academic Press, Harcourt Brace Jovanovich, 1981), 66.

99. Muriel Porter Weaver, *The Aztecs, Maya, and Their Predecessors: Archaeology of Mesoamerica*, 2nd ed. (Orlando, Florida: Academic Press, Harcourt Brace Jovanovich, 1981), 78.

100. Muriel Porter Weaver, *The Aztecs, Maya, and Their Predecessors: Archaeology of Mesoamerica*, 2nd ed. (Orlando, Florida: Academic Press, Harcourt Brace Jovanovich, 1981), 78.

101. Fray Diego Durán, *The History of the Indies of New Spain*, trans. and ann. Doris Heyden, (Norman and London: University of Oklahoma Press, 1994), 204–207.

102. Fray Diego Durán, *The History of the Indies of New Spain*, trans. and ann. Doris Heyden, (Norman and London: University of Oklahoma Press, 1994), 206.

103. Miguel Leon-Portilla, *Los Antiguos Mexicanos a Traves de sus Cronicas y Cantares*, 4th reprint (Mexico: Fondo de Cultura Económica, 1974), 37–38.

104. Richard E. W. Adams, *Prehistoric Mesoamerica*, 3rd ed. (Norman: University of Oklahoma Press, 2005), 408.

105. Bob Libal, "Detention Update," *Sojourn: Newsletter from the American Friends Service Committee* Volume 22, Number 2. 1, 3.

106. Gregory Rodriguez, *Mongrels, Bastards, Orphans, and Vagabonds: Mexican Immigration and the Future of Race in America* (New York: Pantheon Books, 2007), 123.

107. Carey McWilliams, *North From Mexico: The Spanish Speaking People of the United States*, ed. Matt S. Meier, paperback ed. (Westport, Connecticutt: Praeger Press, 1990), 156.

108. David Montejano, *Anglos and Mexicans in the Making of Texas, 1836–1986*, 6th ed. (Austin: University of Texas Press, 1997), 192.

109. David Montejano, *Anglos and Mexicans in the Making of Texas, 1836–1986*, 6th ed. (Austin: University of Texas Press, 1997), 193.

110. Richard H. Immerman, *The CIA in Guatemala: The Foreign Policy of Intervention*, (Austin: University of Texas Press, 1982), 25.

111. Jill Lepore, *The Name of War: King Philip's War and the Origins of American Identity* (New York: Vintage Books, 1999), 109.

112. Jill Lepore, *The Name of War: King Philip's War and the Origins of American Identity* (New York: Vintage Books, 1999), 109–110.

113. Lewis Hanke, *Aristotle and the American Indians: A Study in Race Prejudice in the Modern World* (Chicago: Henry Regnery Company, 1959), 89.

114. Ralph Ketcham, ed., *The Anti-Federalist Papers and the Constitutional Convention Debates: The Clashes and the Compromises that gave Birth to our Form of Government* (New York: Signet Classics, 2003), 161.

115. Ralph Ketcham, ed., *The Anti-Federalist Papers and the Constitutional Convention Debates: The Clashes and the Compromises that gave Birth to our Form of Government* (New York: Signet Classics, 2003), 161.

116. David Montejano, *Anglos and Mexicans in the Making of Texas, 1836–1986*, 6th ed. (Austin: University of Texas Press, 1997), 146–147.

117. Ralph Ketcham, ed., *The Anti-Federalist Papers and the Constitutional Convention Debates: The Clashes and the Compromises that gave Birth to our Form of Government* (New York: Signet Classics, 2003), 162.

118. Ralph Ketcham, ed., *The Anti-Federalist Papers and the Constitutional Convention Debates: The Clashes and the Compromises that gave Birth to our Form of Government* (New York: Signet Classics, 2003), 163.

119. Ralph Ketcham, ed., *The Anti-Federalist Papers and the Constitutional Convention Debates: The Clashes and the Compromises that gave Birth to our Form of Government* (New York: Signet Classics, 2003), 165.

120. Bartolome de Las Casas, *Historia de Las Indias*, vol. 3, ed. Agustin Millares Carlo (Mexico: Fondo de Cultura Economica, 1986), 7.

121. David Montejano, *Anglos and Mexicans in the Making of Texas, 1836–1986*, 6th ed. (Austin: University of Texas Press, 1997), 180.

122. Richard H. Immerman, *The CIA in Guatemala: The Foreign Policy of Intervention*, (Austin: University of Texas Press, 1982), 68–69.

123. Richard H. Immerman, *The CIA in Guatemala: The Foreign Policy of Intervention*, (Austin: University of Texas Press, 1982), 70.

124. Richard H. Immerman, *The CIA in Guatemala: The Foreign Policy of Intervention*, (Austin: University of Texas Press, 1982), 71.

125. Richard H. Immerman, *The CIA in Guatemala: The Foreign Policy of Intervention*, (Austin: University of Texas Press, 1982), 122–123.

126. Richard H. Immerman, *The CIA in Guatemala: The Foreign Policy of Intervention*, (Austin: University of Texas Press, 1982), 124.

127. Richard H. Immerman, *The CIA in Guatemala: The Foreign Policy of Intervention*, (Austin: University of Texas Press, 1982), 143.

128. Dee Brown, *Bury My Heart at Wounded Knee: An Indian History of the American West* (New York: Bantam Books, 1972), 144.

129. David Montejano, *Anglos and Mexicans in the Making of Texas, 1836–1986*, 6th ed. (Austin: University of Texas Press, 1997), 117.

130. Gilberto López y Rivas, *Los Chicanos, Una Minoría Nacional Explotada*, 2nd ed., (Editorial Nuestro Tiempo SA, 1973), 31.

131. Gilberto López y Rivas, *Los Chicanos, Una Minoría Nacional Explotada*, 2nd ed., (Editorial Nuestro Tiempo SA, 1973), 31.

132. Carey McWilliams, *North From Mexico: The Spanish Speaking People of the United States*, ed. Matt S. Meier, paperback ed. (Westport, Connecticutt: Praeger Press, 1990), 126.

133. Carey McWilliams, *North From Mexico: The Spanish Speaking People of the United States*, ed. Matt S. Meier, paperback ed. (Westport, Connecticutt: Praeger Press, 1990), 101.

134. Carey McWilliams, *North From Mexico: The Spanish Speaking People of the United States*, ed. Matt S. Meier,

paperback ed. (Westport, Connecticutt: Praeger Press, 1990), 101.

135. Carey McWilliams, *North From Mexico: The Spanish Speaking People of the United States*, ed. Matt S. Meier, paperback ed. (Westport, Connecticutt: Praeger Press, 1990), 101.

136. Carey McWilliams, *North From Mexico: The Spanish Speaking People of the United States*, ed. Matt S. Meier, paperback ed. (Westport, Connecticutt: Praeger Press, 1990), 122.

137. Carey McWilliams, *North From Mexico: The Spanish Speaking People of the United States*, ed. Matt S. Meier, paperback ed. (Westport, Connecticutt: Praeger Press, 1990), 122.

138. Carey McWilliams, *North From Mexico: The Spanish Speaking People of the United States*, ed. Matt S. Meier, paperback ed. (Westport, Connecticutt: Praeger Press, 1990), 122.

139. Carey McWilliams, *North From Mexico: The Spanish Speaking People of the United States*, ed. Matt S. Meier, paperback ed. (Westport, Connecticutt: Praeger Press, 1990), 122–123.

140. John L. Kessell, *Spain in the Southwest: A Narrative History of Colonial New Mexico, Arizona, Texas, and California* (Norman: University of Oklahoma Press, 2002), 32.

141. David Montejano, *Anglos and Mexicans in the Making of Texas, 1836–1986*, 6th ed. (Austin: University of Texas Press, 1997), 52.

142. Grant Foreman, *The Five Civilized Tribes: Cherokee, Chickasaw, Choctaw, Creek, Seminole* (Norman: University of Oklahoma Press, 1989), 99.

143. John L. Kessell, *Spain in the Southwest: A Narrative History of Colonial New Mexico, Arizona, Texas, and California* (Norman: University of Oklahoma Press, 2002), 32.

144. David Montejano, *Anglos and Mexicans in the Making of Texas, 1836–1986*, 6th ed. (Austin: University of Texas Press, 1997), 27.

145. David Montejano, *Anglos and Mexicans in the Making of Texas, 1836–1986*, 6th ed. (Austin: University of Texas Press, 1997), 230.

146. David Montejano, *Anglos and Mexicans in the Making of Texas, 1836–1986*, 6th ed. (Austin: University of Texas Press, 1997), 231.

147. David Montejano, *Anglos and Mexicans in the Making of Texas, 1836–1986*, 6th ed. (Austin: University of Texas Press, 1997), 231.

148. David Montejano, *Anglos and Mexicans in the Making of Texas, 1836–1986*, 6th ed. (Austin: University of Texas Press, 1997), 231.

149. David Montejano, *Anglos and Mexicans in the Making of Texas, 1836–1986*, 6th ed. (Austin: University of Texas Press, 1997), 83.

150. David Montejano, *Anglos and Mexicans in the Making of Texas, 1836–1986*, 6th ed. (Austin: University of Texas Press, 1997), 29.

151. David Montejano, *Anglos and Mexicans in the Making of Texas, 1836–1986*, 6th ed. (Austin: University of Texas Press, 1997), 165.

152. Sam Dolnick, "Immigrants Suing a Connecticut Police Dept.," *The New York Times,* October 26, 2010.

153. Geoffrey Fox, *Hispanic Nation: Culture, Politics, and the Constructing of Identity* (Secaucus, N.J.: Carol Publishing Group, 1996), 9.

154. Geoffrey Fox, *Hispanic Nation: Culture, Politics, and the Constructing of Identity* (Secaucus, N.J.: Carol Publishing Group, 1996), 14.

155. Nathan Thornburgh, "Postcard from Sells, Ariz," *TIME,* November 1, 2010.

156. Carey McWilliams, *North From Mexico: The Spanish Speaking People of the United States*, ed. Matt S. Meier, paperback ed. (Westport, Connecticutt: Praeger Press, 1990), 109.

157. David Montejano, *Anglos and Mexicans in the Making of Texas, 1836–1986*, 6th ed. (Austin: University of Texas Press, 1997), 268.

158. Fray Diego Durán, *The History of the Indies of New Spain*, trans. and ann. Doris Heyden, (Norman and London: University of Oklahoma Press, 1994), 21.

159. Carey McWilliams, *North From Mexico: The Spanish Speaking People of the United States*, ed. Matt S. Meier, paperback ed. (Westport, Connecticutt: Praeger Press, 1990), 112.

160. Geoffrey Fox, *Hispanic Nation: Culture, Politics, and the Constructing of Identity* (Secaucus, N.J.: Carol Publishing Group, 1996), 177–178.

161. David Montejano, *Anglos and Mexicans in the Making of Texas, 1836–1986*, 6th ed. (Austin: University of Texas Press, 1997), 315.

162. Ignacio M. Garcia, *Hector P. Garcia: In Relentless Pursuit of Justice*, (Houston, Texas: Arte Publico Press, 2002), 118.

163. Ignacio M. Garcia, *Hector P. Garcia: In Relentless Pursuit of Justice*, (Houston, Texas: Arte Publico Press, 2002), 152.

164. Michael D. Coe and Rex Koontz, *Mexico from the Olmecs to the Aztecs*, 6th ed. (Singapore: Thames and Hudson, 2008), 62.

165. Richard E. W. Adams, *Prehistoric Mesoamerica*, 3rd ed. (Norman: University of Oklahoma Press, 2005), 39.

166. Sean B. Carroll, "Tracking the Ancestry of Corn Back 9000 Years," *New York Times*, May 25, 2010.

167. Richard E. W. Adams, *Prehistoric Mesoamerica*, 3rd ed. (Norman: University of Oklahoma Press, 2005), 28.

168. Richard E. W. Adams, *Prehistoric Mesoamerica*, 3rd ed. (Norman: University of Oklahoma Press, 2005), 392.

169. Sophie D. Coe and Michael D. Coe, *The True History of Chocolate* (New York: Thames and Hudson, 1996), 73.

170. Sophie D. Coe and Michael D. Coe, *The True History of Chocolate* (New York: Thames and Hudson, 1996), 72–73.

171. Barbara Ganson, *The Guarani Under Spanish Rule in the Rio de la Plata* (Stanford University Press, 2003), xii.

172. Nigel Davies, *The Toltecs Until the Fall of Tula* (Norman: University of Oklahoma Press, 1987), 394.

173. Carey McWilliams, *North From Mexico: The Spanish Speaking People of the United States*, ed. Matt S. Meier, paperback ed. (Westport, Connecticutt: Praeger Press, 1990), 174.

174. Carey McWilliams, *North From Mexico: The Spanish Speaking People of the United States*, ed. Matt S. Meier, paperback ed. (Westport, Connecticutt: Praeger Press, 1990), 174.

175. Carey McWilliams, *North From Mexico: The Spanish Speaking People of the United States*, ed. Matt S. Meier, paperback ed. (Westport, Connecticutt: Praeger Press, 1990), 174.

176. Carey McWilliams, *North From Mexico: The Spanish Speaking People of the United States*, ed. Matt S. Meier, paperback ed. (Westport, Connecticutt: Praeger Press, 1990), 174-175.

177. John Gregory Dunne, *Delano: The Story of the California Grape Strike*, (New Yok: Farrar, Straus, and Giroux, 1969), 100.

178. Susan Ferriss and Ricardo Sandoval, *The Fight in the Fields: Cesar Chavez and the Farm Workers Movement*,

ed. Diana Hembree (New York: Hartcourt, Brace & Co., 1997), 118.

179.Susan Ferriss and Ricardo Sandoval, *The Fight in the Fields: Cesar Chavez and the Farm Workers Movement*, ed. Diana Hembree (New York: Hartcourt, Brace & Co., 1997), 119.

180. Susan Ferriss and Ricardo Sandoval, *The Fight in the Fields: Cesar Chavez and the Farm Workers Movement*, ed. Diana Hembree (New York: Hartcourt, Brace & Co., 1997), 122.

181.Cesar Chavez, *An Organizer's Tale: Speeches*, ed. Ilan Stavans (New York: Penguin Books, 2008), 13.

182. Arturo Rodriguez, United Farm Workers Letter, June 2009.

183. David Montejano, *Anglos and Mexicans in the Making of Texas, 1836–1986*, 6th ed. (Austin: University of Texas Press, 1997), 268.

184. David Montejano, *Anglos and Mexicans in the Making of Texas, 1836–1986*, 6th ed. (Austin: University of Texas Press, 1997), 268.

185. David Montejano, *Anglos and Mexicans in the Making of Texas, 1836–1986*, 6th ed. (Austin: University of Texas Press, 1997), 268.

186. Susan Ferriss and Ricardo Sandoval, *The Fight in the Fields: Cesar Chavez and the Farm Workers Movement*, ed. Diana Hembree (New York: Hartcourt, Brace & Co., 1997), 185.

187.George E. Curry, ed., *The Affirmative Action Debate._* (Reading, Massachusetts: Perseus Books, 1996), 264.

188. George E. Curry, ed., *The Affirmative Action Debate._* (Reading, Massachusetts: Perseus Books, 1996), 186.

189. George E. Curry, ed., *The Affirmative Action Debate._* (Reading, Massachusetts: Perseus Books, 1996), 186.

190. George E. Curry, ed., *The Affirmative Action Debate.* (Reading, Massachusetts: Perseus Books, 1996), 187.

191. Gilberto López y Rivas, *Los Chicanos, Una Minoría Nacional Explotada*, 2nd ed., (Editorial Nuestro Tiempo SA, 1973), 34.

192. Laura Ling, "The Narco War Next Door," *Vanguard,* Current Television, aired February 25, 2009.

193. "Home Invasion Suspects Tied to Border Group," News 4, Tucson, Arizona, aired June 15, 2009.

194. Carlos Fuentes, *The Crystal Frontier* (New York: Farrar, Straus, and Giroux, 1997), 30.

195. Sean Hamill, "2 White Youths on Trial in Killing of a Mexican," *New York Times,* April 28, 2009.

196. Ginger Thompson, "After Loosing Freedom, Some Immigrants Face Loss of Custody of Their Children," *New York Times,* April 23, 2009.

197. Tamar Lewin, "Law Schools Admissions Lag Among Minorities," *New York Times,* January 7, 2010.

198. Adam Liptak, "A Family Fight, a Federal Raid, a Baby Deported," *New York Times,* September 21, 2010.